REAL POWER
Stages of Personal Power
in Organizations
Revised Edition

Janet O. Hagberg

To Caryl
More power to you –
Janet Hagberg

Sheffield Publishing Company

Salem, Wisconsin

For information about this book, write or call:

> Sheffield Publishing Company
> P.O. Box 359
> Salem, Wisconsin 53168
> (414) 843-2281

"Tales the Silent Watchers Tell" appeared in the June–July 1977 issue of *Sunrise*, Theosophical University Press, Pasadena, CA. Reprinted with permission.

ISBN 1-879215-17-9

Printed in the United States of America

7   6   5   4   3   2   1

I dedicate this book to my late father,
who is my favorite stage four person,
and to Bill,
whose love transcends power.

Where love rules, there is no will to power;
and where power predominates, there love is lacking.
Carl Jung

Contents

Preface to the Revised Edition

It is difficult for me to venture into the second edition of a book that captured so much of my soul in the first writing. Yet as I approached this work, new ideas of power and leadership beckoned me to explore them further, mine their riches, and discover new depths. Feedback from many readers, as well as my own research, have resulted in several changes; a new introduction, a new chapter called "Beyond Ego and Gender: Leading from Your Soul," a revised power survey, and an instrument for readers to measure their own stages of personal power.

I believe individuals and organizations are more receptive than ever to the ideas in *Real Power* and to true leadership. The pace of change and the pressure on organizations to find ways to innovate are stronger, and it will take leaders of immense courage, who operate beyond the cultural norms to move us into the twenty-first century.

I could not have written this edition until now. I could not take this work to a deeper level until I had experienced deeper levels within myself. As I journeyed through my own transformation, I learned a great deal more about inner power. I experienced my own core, that dark, painful place of intense light, in which compassion and connectedness reveal themselves. This experience gave me the courage to draft this new edition. My soul is in this book, and I hope it reaches out and touches your soul. I hope you are ready to experience your own inner power and the journey that will transform your life.

Janet Hagberg, June 1993

Preface

Let me tell you a story. Several years ago I had a friend who, I am quite convinced, was powerful and successful. She was almost totally in control of her life and able to plan systematically for her future. As far as I was concerned, she had it made. She traveled the world over with her clients and friends, always priding herself on doing things first class. She was making money and writing a book, was professionally respected, and could afford to be confident—even a little cocky. Her consulting clients were of the Fortune 500 and her friends were some of the "movers and shakers of the community." She also had the knack of turning every experience into a plus for herself and spoke of her future as a series of new challenges to be met. She was a successful woman in a man's world, loving it and relishing her achievements. Her dreams had come true. I admit to being greatly intimidated by her at times because she seemed to be so clear in her direction, so sure of herself, so strong and not easily bemused. Her run of successes seemed to be endless.

Then her dreams turned into nightmares. The bottom dropped out of this carefully designed life. Her husband, the love of her life and her symbol of emotional stability, left her for another life. She was set adrift on a sea of anger, confusion, and self-doubt. She was crushed. Never before had she failed at anything. And this situation seemed to be out of her control, something she could do little about. But she also felt a strange sense of exhilaration at times. She wanted to leap out of her emotional cocoon and start a new life. That was on the good days. Most of the time confusion reigned. Illness and death in her family added to the shock; more doubts and questions surfaced; and the confusion left her feeling totally alone in her tumultuous sea. I almost lost her there for awhile, as she dove deep inside to sort out her sense of life, hope, and meaning. It was a long, slow process she experienced in starting to redefine herself, in struggling with the questions of what life means, what success is, and what it is all worth.

Gradually, oh so slowly, she started to return from the depths. But she was re-emerging with some different features—ones that were not so sharp at the edges but more rounded and smooth. She was warmer than before, not so cold to the touch. She was deeper and wiser, calmer and sadder, not as devoted to the goals she had previously held so dear but feeling success in a different way. It took us a long time to sort out what was happening to our friendship, too, because the rules and roles seemed to be changing. A part of me mourned the old friend because she was so familiar. But another part of me was curious and a little fearful of the new friend. Our experience was uncharted territory to us both. It was an uncertain time.

Eventually, I stopped thinking of this "friend" as someone outside of me, separate and distinct. I began to understand the deep changing and reshaping that was occurring in us both. Gradually, I came to admit that both of us were actually me. This acceptance was perhaps the most painful and healing step in my life's journey. I came to know this person as complex yet terribly simple, wise and at the same time childlike, strong at the center and wobbly at the edges, always curious, sometimes afraid, eager to experience life yet overly sensitive to it, wanting peace and needing love. This turning point in my life led me on a long, meandering path to a deeper understanding of personal power. This is the impetus and the story behind this book.

Now, why would you want to read this book? Well, I wrote it for a variety of special groups: for individuals who aspire to power, who long to understand what power really is; for leaders, to provoke their thinking about what true leadership is; for organizations, as a practical tool for developing people and vision for the future. I see power occurring in stages. And in the following chapters I describe six distinct stages of power. They are arranged in this developmental order: Stage One: Powerlessness; Stage Two: Power by Association; Stage Three: Power by Symbols; Stage Four: Power by Reflection; Stage Five: Power by Purpose; and Stage Six: Power by Gestalt.

In my experience in speaking about the stages of power, I find that the concept appeals to a wide variety of audiences because the idea can be applied to almost any work or life situation. Let's examine some specific motivations that may appeal to you as a reader of *Real Power*.

For Leaders:

As a leader or potential leader, you will see a vision of organizational leadership for the future. As the world becomes more of a global village, we will have to expand our concept of what power and leadership mean and how they are acted out. We will learn to go beyond our own egos.

In organizations many people see power as finite. In their view, power can be represented by a box of individually wrapped gold coins. Let's say I have twelve coins in a box, and they are mine. If you take two from me, I now have only ten, and therefore, you have taken power from me. There is only so much, and in order to pass it around it must be taken from one and given to another.

Now suppose power can be imagined differently: I have a bed containing eight tulip bulbs and I give you half of each bulb. Because I believe power multiplies when I give it away, now instead of eight tulips my bed has grown to sixteen.

I am suggesting that true leadership does not begin until the later stages, in which power can be seen as infinite and valuable insofar as it is given away. Michael Maccoby's latest book, *The Leader*, describes some leaders who would accept this concept of power. Chapters Four through Seven (in *Real Power*) address these issues.

For Managers:

As a manager, you will learn how to effectively manage people at various stages of power who want and need different things from you, from their work, and from the organization. The way you would develop each type of person might be quite different. For instance, persons at the first stage will not be interested in intangibles like being invited to lunch with a client but will be much affected by your willingness to teach them concrete skills and knowledge. The old phrase "different strokes for different folks" applies here. You may also better understand the behavior of some people that was perplexing to you before. Perhaps you will also understand your own behavior and why you are more effective at managing some people than others. Chapters One through Six and Eight address these issues.

For Women and Men:

As a woman or a man, you can learn about ways in which women and men are alike and ways in which they're different. Two of the stages seem to be more feminine and two others are more masculine, yet both sexes can move through all the stages. Some men avoid the feminine stages because they frighten these men by reminding them of the feminine side of themselves. Some women grasp onto the masculine stages because such women seek to downplay their feminine side in a masculine world. What will convince us that our differences are not so bad and that one style or the other is not better just because it's feminine or masculine? How do women keep from becoming "honorary men," as Carolyn Heilbrun so aptly puts it in her book *Reinventing Womanhood*? When men feel discontented, how do they move beyond the stereotypical roles and view of success that they learned in their youth? How do women fulfill leadership roles while maintaining a healthy balance of feminine and masculine qualities? How do we all learn about the masculine and the feminine within us? Chapters One through Six, and Nine through Eleven address these issues.

For Thinkers and Problem Solvers:

As a thinker and problem solver, you can use the stage model as a practical tool for understanding organizational and personal situations that may transcend conventional logic or rational explanation. The model is based on fifteen years of organization field research, including observation, discussions, interviews, and the meeting of hundreds of minds. After discussing the model for a time, one woman manager exclaimed, "At last I can put into words what's been happening to me for the past eight years!" Chapters One through Eight address these issues.

For Powerless People:

If you are powerless, you can use the model to think of ways to move into power and avoid being overcome by the victim mentality especially prevalent in organizations. There are no easy solutions to the problems of powerlessness, but there are ways to think and act so as not to be powerless forever. An entire book has been dedicated to that topic— Elizabeth Janeway's *Powers of the Weak*. Chapter One (in *Real Power*) addresses these issues.

For Researchers:

As a researcher or student of power, you will find in the model a wealth of opportunity for further study and research. I welcome others to further refine the model so it can become more understandable and useful. I value comments and suggestions on the model from anyone and look forward to reading the results of the power questionnaire in the back of the book.

What would I like this book to achieve? I enjoy trying to make abstract ideas and concepts understandable and practical. I hope I have accomplished that in this book. I hope I have made it clear how strongly I feel that a general reawakening is necessary in our country if we are to survive and maintain our health and vitality in the future. I would like this book to influence leaders to lead with more vision and less ego. I would like women to believe that there is indeed life beyond the masculine stages. I would like men to accept themselves and *be* themselves—not who they think they ought to be. I would like members of minorities to help us consider what implications the various stages of this model have for those who are not part of the prevailing socio-economic system. I would like powerless people to learn about themselves and the system and to gain some self-worth in the process. I would like organizations to be more tolerant of visionaries and truly wise persons. I would like people to talk more openly to each other about the taboo topic of power and see that it may not be what they think it is. I would like people in organizations to see more choices for themselves as the years progress rather than fewer choices every day. I would like to see more and more healthy, innovative managers. I would like people to understand power and beyond. . . .

Henry David Thoreau sums up for me one of the underlying issues of this book when he asks why we should be in such desperate haste to succeed, and in such desperate enterprises? If we do not keep pace with our companions, perhaps it is because we hear a different drummer. Let us step to the music that we hear, however measured or far away (paraphrase, *Walden*).

Acknowledgments

Although my application of stage theory to the specific concept of power is a new application, stage theory itself has been around for a long time. And while this book is the product of many years of thinking, reading, observing, learning, interviewing, and speaking, it is not the product of one mind alone.

I owe a deep debt of gratitude to the theoretical pioneers whose ideas over the years have been planted as ripe seeds in my mind. These theoreticians and teachers greatly influenced me in the final germination of the stage model applied to the concept of personal power. First is Dr. Margery Brown at the University of Minnesota, who imprinted cognitive stage theory *a la* Harvey, Hunt, and Schroeder on my formative mind. How I struggled in those early years to find my own developmental level and to analyze my behavior, hoping I was more developed than I feared I was! Second, my social work professors and peers taught me much about the range of complex human behavior and the motivations that drive us. Third, Dr. Howard Williams introduced me to the theories of Kohlberg, Loevinger, and Perry as well as Levinson, Gould, and Valliant. These writers opened my mind further to ways of thinking about development and life, some of which evolved into the basis for my stage model. Last, I would like to thank all those individuals whom I observed, questioned, and interviewed. I then quoted, summarized, or consolidated their responses into the case examples in each chapter. The book would be less instructive without these rich illustrations from real people.

I would like to thank several other people for being supportive and lovingly critical as I proceeded through the early drafts of *Real Power.* They listened, read, made suggestions, and encouraged me on the long journey toward publication. I deeply appreciate William Svrluga, who critiqued the book and also coauthored the chapter on men, and Barry and Bradley, my stepsons, who lovingly questioned what I was up to with this "power stuff." I am grateful to other dedicated early draft readers such as Bob Bro, Knox Coit, Karen Desnick, Bob MacLennan, Ken Melrose, Miriam Meyers, Martha Myers, Susan Sands, Suzanne

Sisson, Bobbie Spradley, and Norm Stanton. Later reviewers were Bob Andringa, Kay Barber, Sue Boehlke, Con Brooks, John Cardozo, Bill George, Marty Hanson, Hugh Harrison, Duane Kullberg, Paul Morrison, Elsa Nad, Betty Olson, Jeff Pope, Al Quie, and Steve Rothschild. My editor, Pat Lassonde, has done a superb job of guiding the process and giving me invaluable feedback. A special thank you to Steve Nelson at Sheffield Publishing for a fine revised edition.

My invitation to you all as readers is to collaborate with me on the next edition of this book. Write me your stories, tell me your tales; share your ideas, disagreements, and questions. Complete the power survey in the Appendix. Let's learn together for a more intriguing next edition.

More (personal) power to you!

Janet Hagberg

Introduction

What Is This Book About?

This book is about power, real power, the kind of inner power you develop after you think you have everything figured out. And it is about true leadership, transformational leadership that allows you to go beyond ego and gender to lead from your soul.

Why did I write this book—yet another book on power and leadership? I believe our culture still misunderstands both concepts. Most books on the topic are written by people in power positions or to describe people in power positions. As Stephen Covey has so aptly pointed out, the trend since World War II is to perceive the personality traits of leaders as the key to leadership instead of looking first at the character ethic we want from our leaders and then finding leaders who exemplify it.

The model of power and leadership I propose here describes six stages of personal power which we accumulate as we develop. They are: 1. power-lessness 2. power by association 3. power by symbols 4. power by reflection 5. power by purpose and 6. power by gestalt.

People with position power are predominantly at stage three, power by symbols. This is the most externally oriented of the stages, the stage where most of our power comes from outside ourselves, from making things happen, and from external recognition. It is the most rewarded stage in our culture, requiring hard work, competence, a strong knowledge of the culture, a mature ego, and political astuteness. Fifteen years of research shows me that stage three is the most common stage in organizations.

But stage three is only part way to full personal power, part way to wholeness. One compelling reason for writing this book is to suggest an organizational agenda for the next era, one that allows leaders to develop as whole people, as true leaders operating at the inner power stages (power by reflection, purpose, and gestalt) and moving creatively into the future.

Why is it necessary for true leaders to operate at the inner power stages? A corporate officer from Herman Miller, Rob Harvey, says it well.

Leadership always comes back to the issue of character, of deep foundational values. In the current reformation this country is experiencing, and the instability we are feeling, you cannot lead by forcing compliance. It simply doesn't work. The rate of change is too high to be managed from the top down. In order to lead, one must engage followers. You will not find followers without caring, connecting and creating. Would you follow someone who did not care about you, connect with you, or did not wish to create a new reality? Mere compliance today is a recipe for disaster. As leaders, or would-be leaders, we must be vulnerable. None of us has arrived. We must recognize our own voyage. We can only lead effectively by enabling others to maximize their contribution. We are all on the journey together, accomplishing things that none of us could accomplish alone.

In the next evolution of American business, it will be necessary to go beyond the ideas that made us great world leaders initially—ideas like rugged individualism, and "the quick technological fix." The whole western world is turning to new ways of operating in order to compete in the global economy.

A corporate officer at General Mills said, "New competition is virtually rewriting overnight the rules of how entire markets function. We are facing a revolutionary shift in consumer attitudes and employee expectations."

To contend with these changes, companies are trying things like integrated work teams, total quality, diversity, innovation, and personal empowerment. They are spending more time and money on developing their people, and they are encouraging involvement, workplace freedom, and trusting environments.

These innovations, although thoughtful, will not work if we continue to operate with a predominantly stage three (power by symbols) mentality behind them. They require people who are more internally developed and do not revert to authoritarian styles when things get tough. Stages four and five represent people who have integrity, can give power away, and are reflective, courageous, collaborative, and spiritual. It is not necessary to leave stage three qualities behind, but we need to add these other qualities in order to move to the next era of leadership in the world.

For people in the nonprofit environment, the world is a different place than it was fifteen years ago. With the splitting of our culture increasingly into haves and have-nots, it will take even more grounded and creative people in social service and religious organizations to work on the problems threatening the soul of the United States today. Violence, abuse, crime, poverty, hunger, homelessness—the list goes on and on. They are symptoms of cultural neglect that are apparent in every large city in our country.

People who work on these immense challenges need to be secure in themselves and spiritually grounded so they are not burned out but transformed by embracing people who face poverty, abuse, or homelessness. It is critical that they are a hopeful presence in the world and operate with peace under stress. They cannot do that if they cannot operate beyond stage three.

These are challenging times. Are you up to the challenge? Let me tell you the story of one person who learned to lead from his soul.

John was a chief executive officer of a large corporation. In his mid-forties, he was excited about the future and the direction in which he was taking the company. He was a hard charger, working long hours and loving his work. His management team was equally high achieving, bringing him the results he needed most of the time even though his new task team approach with the plant managers was floundering. He even had a woman and an African-American man on his team. Life was good. Stock prices were climbing.

Then his life took an abrupt turn. His sixteen-year-old daughter stopped eating. Nothing he or his wife did would make her eat more than half a roll for breakfast and a diet soda and a few leaves of spinach salad for dinner. He tried sweet talk, rewards, prodding. Eventually he started screaming and ordering her to eat. She got thinner every week. Her hollow cheeks began to look like a corpse's.

At that point John got scared. He felt worn thin at work. He resented his family life for infringing on his heavy work schedule. He was used to having everything go his way, even if he had to resort to ordering someone else around. But his own daughter was immovable. Here he had no control.

She ended up in the emergency room of a hospital after a collapse. The doctors told John that unless she was force-fed, which would require a court order, she would die. John thought he was going to die too.

During those long months of her agonizingly slow recovery, John found out that her problem was also *his* problem. He was a controlling personality who always got his own way. Even more devastating was the fact that his own self-image was inextricably tied to the health and success of his business and his children. John had a lot of his own work to do. And he did it. He dug into his own family issues and found a driven, rageful father image that he had suppressed for a long time. He dug into his own pain, childhood shame, over achievement, and fear of abandonment. He struggled courageously with his inner monsters and found out a great deal about his masked inadequacies and dependencies. He also found out he was addicted to work, as many executives are.

What did all this have to do with business? Plenty. John realized, despite all his rhetoric to the contrary, that he was a top-down leader at work, just as he was at home. He felt compelled to single-handedly set the company's vision and then make sure everyone else agreed and carried it out. Sure, he involved people, but in the end his ego was always on the line.

The experience with his daughter taught him to let go of control, and now he didn't need it as much. He knew himself better and could trust himself more. Therefore he could be more vulnerable, ask for suggestions, and use them without damaging his own ego. And he could admit mistakes. His people began trusting him more. They began bringing him ideas. He was surprised. They had never spontaneously brought him ideas before. But now he didn't need to be the idea-approver. He could tell them to go back and get people around them interested enough in the idea to make it happen. If it met all the criteria the team had set up for itself, then it was a good idea.

New products and improvements in service began emerging from the very teams that had been floundering before. It wasn't all smooth sailing, but now he handled conflict by listening to people and helping them work things out among themselves rather than setting himself up as the final judge. He had learned at home that control doesn't empower anyone.

The company began operating more like a community than like several communities competing with each other. It did surprisingly well, even in turbulent times. Once, in a particularly bad recession, when the company stock fell, John almost panicked. But he decided not to take the recession personally. Instead he looked at all the factors and counted on his community to come up with suggestions. They came up with a part-time policy instead of a lay-off policy. It worked wonders in the crisis and is now an option for everyone. People were so excited, they even called the office on their days off to make sure everything was working all right.

John did not single-handedly change the workplace. He changed himself.

That had more power than anything else he could have done. He moved from ego leadership to soul leadership. He and his people flourished.

What Is Power?

Power is probably not what you think it is. In fact, it may not even be what others think it is. Power is elusive and confusing. Perhaps that's why it is so powerful. Consider these ideas and descriptions of power from various literary sources:

> To know the pains of power, we must go to those who have it: to know its pleasures, we must go to those who are seeking it: the pains of power are real, its pleasures imaginary.
>
> (C. C. Colton: Lacon)

> Power tends to corrupt and absolute power corrupts absolutely.
>
> (Lord Acton in a letter to Bishop Mandell, Creighton, 1887)

> Self-reverence, self-knowledge, self-control, These three alone lead life to sovereign power.
>
> (Tennyson: "Oenone")

> He who makes another powerful ruins himself, for he makes the other so either by shrewdness or force, and both of these qualities are feared by the one who becomes powerful.
>
> (Machiavelli: The Prince III)

> I am more and more convinced that man is a dangerous creature; and that power, whether vested in many or a few, is ever grasping, and like the grave, cries "Give, give!"
>
> (Abigail Adams in a letter to John Adams, Nov. 27, 1775)

> Then everything includes itself in power,
> Power into will, will into appetite;
> And appetite, an universal wolf,

So doubly seconded with will and power,
Must make perforce an universal prey,
And last eat up himself.

(Shakespeare: *Troilus and Cressida* I, iii)

Is power good, bad, corrupting, polluting, dangerous, controlling, or freeing? Because all of these descriptions are true to some extent, the concept of power becomes all the more complex. Which of these statements are we to believe, and how will we ever be able to understand power?

Real Power is an attempt to set forth a simple model of power as an ever-evolving concept. In this model, power takes on different appearances at each of its six separate stages. Think of the stages as different dances. Each stage's dance has different steps from the basic to the more difficult. After you learn the basic dance, it becomes easier, and you begin to offer your own renditions. Sometimes you are content to do the same dance for a long time, getting better or just having a good time. At other times you feel like learning a new dance, and you start again on the basics of the next step. It's easier though than the first dance you learned because you understand the idea of dancing. So it is with power stages. Some people dance at the same stage forever, while others like to move on to other stages. A few are driven to learn as much and as fast as they can, while others take their learning in time.

I maintain that we all can develop personal power, and that people who aspire to be leaders need to be more personally powerful than they are. Some people may need to expend more effort to develop personal power due to life circumstances that must be overcome. Some people seem, for various reasons, to be born with a head start. At any rate, the way in which we perceive our own and others' power affects our behavior, our leadership, and our relationships with others. Power is absent, obviously, if there are not relationships with others; therefore, it is impossible to be powerful in a vacuum. As in the dance example, we are learning the steps with others, and we are able to learn more and more complex steps as we go along.

The idea of power appearing differently in separate stages may be a new concept for many people who have come to think of power in one or two limited definitions such as control, influence, or the capacity to act.

In fact, most organizations (a functional structure such as a corporation, non-profit group, or political party) suffer from power myopia, the problem of seeing power in too narrow a vision. Not all people are motivated by the same type of power, and not all power is of the Machiavellian type in which the end justifies the means. Most of the books currently available about power are designed to help us get more by intimidating and manipulating others or by learning the games and maneuvering in our jobs to assure winning or at least to avoid losing. These theorists assume that most people in organizations seek position and status for themselves while having ever more control over a greater number of people, money, and sources of information. Although I do not discount this approach, I am suggesting that there is more, much more, beyond the traditional forms of power. *Real Power* is about people becoming more than externally "powerful"; it is about people becoming *personally powerful.*

Personal power is the extent to which one is able to link the outer capacity for action (external power) with the inner capacity for reflection (internal power).

Personal power can be seen on a continuum, from very little personal power at one end to a great deal of personal power at the other end. Personal power at the highest stage *includes* the power derived from external sources represented by organizational and political positions, expertise, titles, degrees, control, material goods, responsibility, and authority *but combines* with the power that can be derived only from within. Inner power develops from introspection, personal struggles, the gradual evolution of the life purpose, and from accepting and valuing yourself. If you have external power but not internal power, you have very little personal power. Therefore, some people in the highest positions in organizations are not very personally powerful. And likewise, the most personally powerful people may not have the most prestigious titles or roles in the organization. Organizational power—the "how-to-get-ahead" type of power—is represented in my model predominantly by the first three externally-oriented stages of power; inner, reflective power is represented by the last three internally-oriented power stages. At any of the stages you can be satisfied, and at any of the stages you can feel stuck.

A Model of Personal Power

Before I go further in applying power concepts to life and work situations, I want to explain more thoroughly the stages of power. The model
of personal power includes six distinct stages, occurring in this order:

Stage One: Powerlessness
Stage Two: Power by Association
Stage Three: Power by Symbols
Stage Four: Power by Reflection
Stage Five: Power by Purpose
Stage Six: Power by Gestalt

Each stage represents a different manifestation of power. In other
words, power can be described differently at each stage. In addition,
each stage has a symbol that describes the key idea at that stage. Since all
the stages relate to the central theme of personal power, they've been
graphically represented on the following page. Read over the stages and
the symbols until you become acquainted with them.

This model is simple and complex at the same time. It reminds me of
the oriental concept of *shibui*. Oriental art—particularly painting and
pottery—looks simple from a distance, but the closer you get to it the
more detail and complexity you see. Usually, if you look closely, more is
revealed, and you are drawn even more deeply into the art. Much of the
detail recedes when you back away and allow distance to create once
again the more simple idea. The power model is similar. You can use or
understand the model on several different levels. The stages themselves
appear to be quite straightforward and simple, yet the more deeply you
look, the more the model may speak to you. In fact, you can use the
simple six-stage model to understand yourself, your relationships, your
organization, your country, or the world from a personal power perspective. Let's begin by understanding the model itself.

We must start with some assumptions, those underlying ideas from
which the model evolved. They answer questions such as: Why do
people get stuck? Can I be at more than one stage at a time? Do men and
women see these differently? If you prefer, you may want to go ahead and
start reading the other chapters rather than digesting each assumption.
However, as questions arise in your mind, they can probably be answered

HAGBERG'S MODEL OF PERSONAL POWER

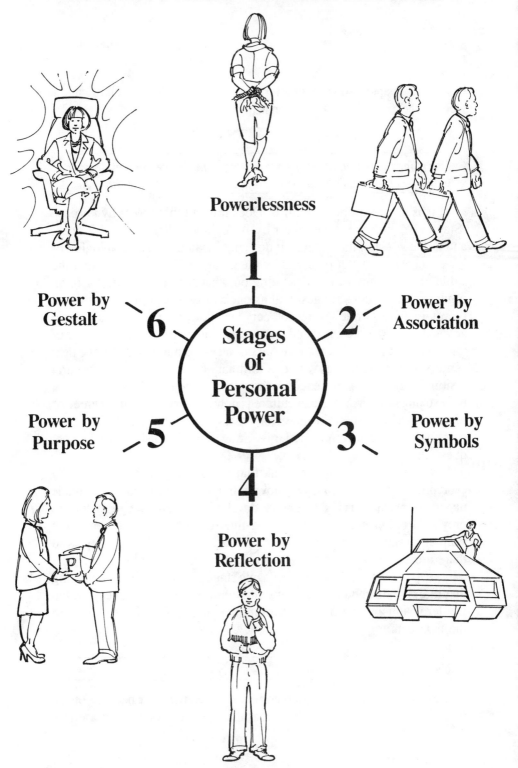

Powerlessness

Power by
Gestalt

Power by
Association

Stages
of
Personal
Power

Power by
Purpose

Power by
Symbols

Power by
Reflection

best in this chapter, so you can return here when you desire reclarification. Here is the first assumption upon which the model is based:

The stages of personal power are arranged in a developmental order with Powerlessness as Stage One and Power by Gestalt as Stage Six.

This is a controversial premise. Does it mean that Power by Purpose (Stage Five) is better than Power by Association (Stage Two)? It does, and it doesn't. Let me explain: It does not mean that people at higher or lower stages are better or worse by the nature of their stage but that the value of the stages varies depending on what they are aiming for in an organization. It does suggest that as one's level of external and internal power increases, one's stage of personal power increases also. I am advocating that more advanced stage people are necessary for the kind of leadership we will need to move our country and our world into the next century and to provide us with extraordinary organizational and cultural vision. Therefore, I am encouraging development to higher stages. I believe most of our American culture is now at Stages Two and Three. At higher stages one can do more for others, see more possibilities, get more of the good accomplished, give away more, and ask more pertinent questions.

I am not naive enough to think that these things will be valued by everyone or that all are ready to move to higher levels. The world is made up of people at varying stages of development, and we need that to provide a balance of interaction and interrelationships. We would not want an organization or a world of all Stage Sixes or Stage Ones. And there are some overwhelming blocks, both internal and external, that may keep people from moving from one stage to another. But I am saying that individuals and organizations at the more-advanced stages develop greater vision and wisdom and thus more potential for us to emerge into the next century as a healthy society.

Each stage is different from all the others.

Stage One cannot readily be compared to Stage Four because of the behaviors and assumptions that accompany each of them. A powerless person may dream of being in charge but would be intimidated by power if the opportunity arose. You do not jump readily from Stage One to Four. You can understand and experience stages preceding your own, but it is more difficult to understand stages beyond yours. For example, Susan is in Stage Three (Power by Symbols), has been in an organization for a while, and has succeeded in achieving titles and responsibility. Suddenly she gets passed over for a promotion and believes her job responsibilities are shrinking. For a period of time she feels as if she has retreated to a former mind set or circumstance, that of being powerless and confused. She experiences her former feelings and behaviors once again but hopes they are only temporary. Soon she regroups, moves to another position, and feels back in balance within herself. Susan may have trouble understanding why another person deliberately turned down a promotion in favor of family relationships and more personal time. She has trouble seeing power as a concept that extends beyond titles and status.

One can move through the stages only in the order in which they are numbered.

A powerless person cannot move into Power by Purpose (Stage Five) until he or she has experienced Stages Two, Three, and Four, if only fleetingly. Each stage, in fact, leads by a natural evolution into the next, although some stages are more comfortable for individuals than other stages. Not all people stay in each stage the same length of time nor move through them in the same way, *but each person moves in the same sequence.* It is possible to regress to a previous stage temporarily, for instance, when you enter a new career. But you would then continue from that point in sequence once again.

You could think of power as a six-act play (our power play!) in which the main character (power) appears in all acts wearing different costumes—perhaps representing different parts of itself. So in each act the "power character" is the same person but looks and acts differently and indeed does change as the play evolves. You can't see act six and understand it fully unless you have seen acts one through five.

Power is described and manifested differently at each stage.

Which of these words best describe power according to your understanding of it as you begin reading this book? Check your two top choices.

_____ integration		_____ strength
_____ responsibility		_____ money
_____ control		_____ capacity to act
_____ service		_____ position/title
_____ femininity		_____ acquisition
_____ competence		_____ self-esteem
_____ purpose		_____ magic
_____ competition		_____ wisdom
_____ access to information		_____ masculinity
_____ knowledge		_____ intellect
_____ influence		_____ manipulation
_____ authority		_____ domination

I believe that people at each stage of personal power would describe power in a different way because at each stage we view power from a different perspective. Think again of the dance analogy: Each new dance requires different steps, a different beat, different movements, and a new synchronization. You are still dancing, but you call the dance by a certain name at each stage. I use six nouns to illustrate how power presents itself at various stages: manipulation, magic, control, influence, vision, and wisdom. As you read the chapters describing the stages, note the descriptive word appearing under the symbol at the beginning of each chapter. Then think about which word fits most closely with the words you chose just now.

Each stage of personal power has positive and negative dimensions as well as developmental struggles within it.

Just because someone is at a more-advanced stage than others does not mean life is easier or better. At the same time, those who have little access to power aren't necessarily in a dismal life situation, nor are they bad people. Each stage has different struggles and different rewards. Students, for example, are usually the least powerful people in the institution (except when they unite), and most students are in school to gain more access to information or knowledge of skills that may, over time, increase their power. They are temporarily powerless, but not necessarily dissatisfied. People at other stages may be struggling to find the purpose in their lives, the meaning of their work. This search is not the same as struggling for one's equality or for recognition, but it is, nevertheless, a deep-seated struggle. Women, minorities, and certainly the poor, on the other hand, may feel more of the chronic powerlessness that can over time be demoralizing unless they take some action on their own behalf.

Each stage invites individuals to indulge in it, to soak in the delights of recognizing their potential for development in that stage. The initial entry into each stage usually is accompanied by high hopes, aspirations, new ideas, willingness, eagerness, anticipation, and fear. These motivations help people look further into the stage for answers to their needs. But as they progress through the stage, its values, costumes, dance steps, and behaviors may cause them to become disillusioned, fearful, or confused. The way in which they react to these feelings will determine whether they continue to move through the stage or get stuck in it. A particular characteristic of the stage may so absorb some people that they overdo that behavior and it becomes a negative trait. Vivid examples in history dramatize the negative sides of power. Take power through symbols, for example: Confident, bright, controlling, strong, charismatic, and seemingly reputable people in history have persuaded whole groups or countries to participate in horrifying activities because of their own intense and disguised hatred of others or a need for ultimate control or ego gratification. They are tyrants, not leaders.

People can be in different stages of power in different areas of their lives, at different times, and with different people. However, each of us has a "home" stage that represents us more truly than the others.

After hearing about each stage in more depth, you might respond as a friend did, "But I feel like I'm at several of those stages somewhere in my life almost every day." That can be true, to a certain extent, because we have so many compartments in our lives. We may influence a decision at one meeting only to feel powerless at the next meeting because of our role with a different set of people. We do not act as if we are at the same stage all the time, at home or at work, but we each have a "home" stage, a stage in which we operate most of the time or in which we feel the most comfortable. We identify with it more closely than with others, and we understand its behaviors, whether we like them or not. Sometimes we feel consistently at one stage in one part of our life and at another in most other areas. Over time this difference can become wearing, especially if the stages are more than two stages apart. Women most frequently report the phenomenon of being in Stages Two (Power by Association) and Five (Power by Purpose) simultaneously. Although their home stage is more likely to be Stage Two at work, they have experienced tremendous inner growth that causes them to identify with the characteristics of Stage Five away from work. The frustration is that the inner power has yet to be integrated into their work, and until that happens the dichotomy will become more difficult to manage. One of the things you may learn from this book is how to translate your most personally powerful self into situations in which you feel less powerful. The more you can integrate the parts of your life into similar stages, the less split apart you will feel. Moving to another stage is difficult, however, without experiencing some pulling and tension.

We can tell what our home stage is in several ways: by reading each stage description and deciding which one seems most familiar, by observing what situations and behaviors make us uncomfortable, or by asking other people what they think our home stage is. For example, Ahmad is not sure what stage he's in, but he's new to his accounting profession. Someone in his professional network asks him to speak at a meeting on a specific accounting concept. Ahmad is scared. He immediately envisions the other accountants at the meeting asking him questions he won't be able to answer. He's sure he'll be embarrassed. He thinks he just cannot do it until he's more experienced. He goes for advice and help to his boss, who assures him he can do it and offers to coach him on the speech. If seeking his boss's help is characteristic behavior for Ahmad, he is probably at Stage Two (Power by Association) in his work. Ahmad is being asked to use a Stage Three behavior, speaking before a group on a topic about which he has a certain expertise. But he thinks he's not experienced enough yet. In fact, in his work, Ahmad may already be approaching Stage Three, but personally he has a hard time accepting it. By giving this speech and having a Stage Three experience, and then repeating the experience again, Ahmad may eventually move his home stage of personal power to Stage Three. And Ahmad's willingness to take this initial risk will have contributed to his development.

Women are more likely to identify with certain stages and men with other stages.

I do not intend this to be a book on women and power, or on men and power. It is, rather, a book on people and power. But I was motivated to describe different power stages when I noticed that some of the stages seemed to appeal more often to men and others more often to women. This situation was complicated by the fact that the more masculine stages seemed to appeal to many women at times and the more feminine stages to many men at times. I chose to explore and explain this by accepting the facts that some masculine and feminine behavior is in all of us and that we may be less comfortable with some stages because of our orientation to either our masculine or our feminine dimensions. This concept of having both the masculine and feminine at our disposal is called androgyny. It will be explained further in Chapter Nine.

I have always felt uncomfortable with "male" versus "female" behavior models because no one fits completely into either model, even though a person may fit one more than the other. For example, I've always known women who fit the "male" model perfectly, and men who fit the "female" model. I have chosen to use the terms "masculine" and "feminine" which allow for more flexibility, since they are not tied only to gender. I do think, however, that because of our socialization, we experience the world in a manner similar to others of our own sex. Other factors though, like position in the family, self-esteem, decade of birth, heredity, etc., also influence our view of the world. Certain personal power stages appear to be more masculine-oriented, and others appear to be more feminine-oriented. They are illustrated on the following page.

You do not necessarily proceed to new stages merely with age or experience, although both are factors.

HAGBERG'S MODEL OF PERSONAL POWER

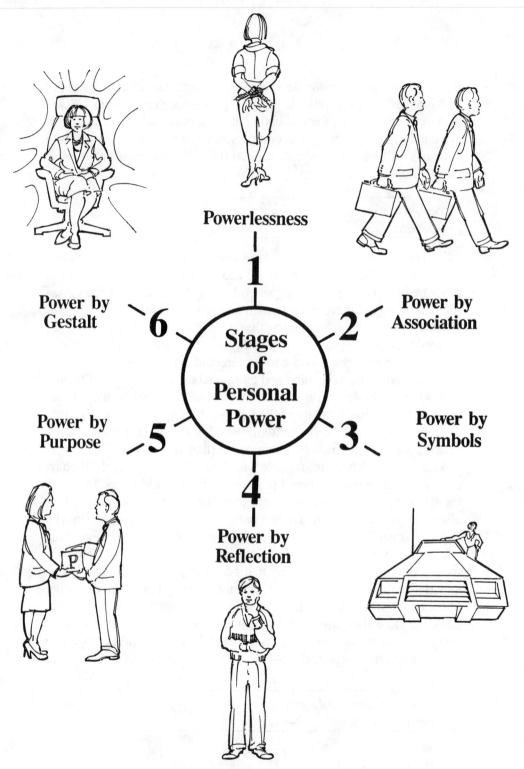

Powerlessness

Power by
Gestalt

Stages
of
Personal
Power

Power by
Association

Power by
Purpose

Power by
Symbols

Power by
Reflection

1 2 3 4 5 6

Stages Two and Five
appear to be more feminine.

Stages Three and Four
appear to be more masculine.

Stages Two, Three, and Four
are most often rewarded in organizations.

Life would be much easier, but not as interesting, if we developed fully just by aging. Although many more older people than very young ones are in the more-advanced stages, an equal number of older people have chosen not to move at all. They believe they cannot move or they have become fixed at earlier stages. Feeling stuck and at the same time unwilling to take a risk to move on makes it hard for these people to comprehend the question, "How does one move to a new stage?" to say nothing of answering it.

So age and experience alone do not a Stage Six make. The key is what we do with our experience, how our experience causes us to see ourselves more accurately, how we think about and learn from age and life events. In the earlier stages we build up our confidence, skill, responsibility, knowledge, and ego. We learn to promote ourselves and to expect our best. Then at some point we are all given opportunities to become more self-accepting, to see ourselves as others see us, to get out of the perfectionist mold we may have created for ourselves. For many of us, that self-acceptance comes painfully at first through some event, crisis, time of reckoning, or rude awakening. And usually this occurs after Stage Three (Power by Symbols) has become familiar. Then as we realize that we are not totally what we had hoped to be, or that we are what we had hoped but discover it isn't satisfying, we also may find that we have the possibility of slowly becoming more than we had expected. The transformation at this point is miraculous. It is clearly apparent in some—dramatic even—and subtle in others. It often calls into question all principles and goals. It makes life appear in retrospect excruciatingly simple. I call it "letting go of trying to be." Knowing who we really are, although difficult at any age, is more powerful than any title or position. I believe the mind of a wise and perceptive person is like that of Virginia Woolf's creative person: "incandescent," "unimpeded," with "no obstacle in it, no foreign matter unconsumed" (*A Room of One's Own*).

There is no one right way to move or change. Some people don't even want to, and for others the timing isn't right. Probably the best thing I can do is to give you several examples of people at various stages, what they think about themselves, and how they've moved to other stages. You may identify with one or several of them and draw some conclusions for yourself.

Some folks need to be pushed and prodded to think about themselves, others need to be left alone to reflect and think. On the other hand, a crisis or external event may provide just the opportunity for a long neglected personal look. One woman told me that people in her life who ask her questions she can't answer help her to think more about herself and motivate her to take more risks. Another person images himself at another stage and writes in a journal as the first step in a new direction. Another person goes to seminars, workshops, and guided retreats to think more clearly about change.

The most externally- and organizationally-oriented power stages (Stages One through Three) show a marked contrast to the internally-oriented power stages (Stages Four through Six).

The first three stages are much more externally-oriented, meaning that the power that is primarily sought and obtained comes from outside the person, from titles, positions, or other symbols of status. These rewards have been accumulated traditionally within the organization. People in Stages One through Three may also be growing and developing on the inside, but the balance is clearly in favor of growth for the sake of external recognition and career movement. That's why it is possible to name some jobs or job families that may be identified with Stages One through Three, although all individuals in these jobs are not necessarily in these stages.

In Stages Four through Six the *inner* journey is more critical, and the balance tips in that direction. It is more difficult to tell by external cues (titles, etc.) what stage the person lives in; therefore, the quality of the person takes on more significance. It is possible, for instance, for one to be stuck in a Stage Two job in the organization, and to decide in the meantime to get more personal power by becoming involved in outside organizations, support groups, or leadership activities. One cannot predict with any accuracy what types of jobs or careers people beyond Stage Three will have. Living out one's life purpose, having integrity, and empowering others—all hallmarks of the higher stages—can be accomplished in a wide variety of settings.

These stages describe the development of individuals who live and work in the United States of America in the last half of the twentieth century.

The observations and interviews upon which this model is based were limited to current American examples and should be interpreted within that context. There may be similarities in the ways people develop across cultures, but it is not the intent of this book to explore that. The stages can certainly be applied to American families, communities, and relationships as I will show by cases and examples. The primary application in this book, however, is to people in organizations.

One warning I have for you is not to pursue the stages of power as if they were a task to be accomplished or a pinnacle to be achieved. There is wisdom in letting a natural process or people or events guide you, and there is wisdom in being open to the next thing life has in store.

Consider the following fable as an example of the folly that you may commit if you are not careful:

The Wise Fox and the Forest
(It may be more blessed to live
than to achieve.)

A wise old fox noticed that young animals in the forest had a difficult time at first knowing where to find fruits and berries. He thought and thought and finally devised a practical path through the forest that would lead young animals to several types of fruit and berries, helping them to identify them for the future. He also provided helpful survival directions in case of emergencies.

The fox was widely praised for his worthwhile contribution, and the animals called his path the Wonderful Way. He was proud of the fact that the animals had learned how to hunt for food.

Word caught on fast about the Wonderful Way, and animals came from miles around to participate. The animals began scurrying along the Way, efficiently collecting their fruit and berries at each strategically placed marker. They worked hard and fast at collecting their berries, trying to get as many as they could and hoarding them for the future.

One day there was a terrible fire in the forest, and the Wonderful Way was burned—berries and all! Because they had always hurried past and had not read the survival signs, the animals could no longer find fruit and berries to eat. Thus, most of them starved.

Moral: In the quest to find the way, it is possible to miss truth and lose life. *OR* Life is more than just a bowl of berries.

If you would like to know which stage of power you identify with most and how that affects you, send for a copy of the Personal Power Profile. It is a self-scoring instrument measuring your six stages of personal power.

Write: Personal Power Products
      1735 Evergreen Lane North
      Plymouth, Minnesota 55441-4102
      612/551-1708

Enclose $4.95 each plus $1.00 postage/handling for each.

Ask yourself these questions about Stage One:

Yes No

___ ___ 1. Do you feel secure because someone else is taking care of you?

___ ___ 2. Do you dream of possible futures (another career, higher salary) with little or no idea of how to get there?

___ ___ 3. Do you frequently question your self-worth?

___ ___ 4. Do you find risk-taking unthinkable?

___ ___ 5. Do you feel you have to ask or coax or cajole others in order to get things you want?

___ ___ 6. Do you know little or nothing about how the organization's decisions are made?

___ ___ 7. Do you feel you are just a number and not seen as an individual in your work?

___ ___ 8. Do you fear physical or emotional abuse in your relationships?

___ ___ 9. Do you think somone else is to blame for your lot in life and that you are a victim?

___ ___ 10. Do you feel overwhelmed and confused when asked to make decisions?

___ ___ 11. Do you ever try to manipulate or coerce others to get things done?

___ ___ 12. Do you feel you have a characteristic that draws discrimination from others?

Yes answers indicate that you identify with this stage.

Chapter 1

Stage One: Powerlessness

Manipulation

What Is Stage One Like?

We all feel powerless at times, so we can all identify at least slightly with the stage of powerlessness. Whole portions of our society feel they are permanently powerless as victims of the powerful "system." Just as the symbol indicates, they feel stuck, tied down with no relief in sight. Examples of people who feel powerless might be secretarial pool members, children, wage employees, high school and college students, floor nurses, public school teachers, clerks, waitresses and waiters, the unemployed, homemakers, taxpayers, abandoned women with few marketable skills, minorities, undocumented workers, welfare recipients, the elderly, handicapped or emotionally disturbed people, clients in the human services, even governments of Third World countries.

You might argue that some of these groups have become quite powerful in the last several years. True, they have, but only because they are no longer individuals but groups working collectively. The irony is that powerless people are usually grouped together for identification, which

1

adds to their sense of alienation. "I'm just a number" or "Give this to the secretarial pool" are examples of the ways in which Stage One people are viewed. However, grouping together is the only way they can gain power for more than one member at a time. The power model suggests that anyone who resides on the lowest rungs of any ladder experiences powerlessness. For example, if you change careers at age thirty-two or forty-five, you may temporarily feel a sense of loss of power because you are not yet familiar with the new environment. You haven't found your niche, nor have you proven yourself in the new organization. You don't know the language or the norms, and your successful prior experiences don't count for much. It takes time and experience in your new arena to gain the confidence and responsibility you once had. It's quite a shock to people who are not expecting it.

The description of power at Stage One is manipulation. This has two meanings. Powerless people feel they are constantly being *manipulated by others,* pushed around, helped, controlled, duped, or taken care of, but they also find they depend upon *manipulating others* to get things done or to acquire things for themselves. They feel they are put in the position of making a case for themselves, pleading, persuading, cajoling, sweet-talking, or seducing to get what they want. They are rarely in the position of having access to resources themselves, whether they be people, information, skills, or money. They need to obtain approval for almost everything they do and usually have a limited area of discretion. This comes out painfully in organizations when a Stage One person has a good idea that is immediately squelched by a boss who claims it is too complicated or cannot be implemented in the budget. If the Stage One person is not assertive (and usually he or she isn't) it is easy to accept the verdict and become discouraged.

Characteristics of Stage One People

Dependent, Getting Things Through Others

Powerless people feel almost totally dependent on other people or organizations. Sometimes this can result in safety and security and is highly valued by some if the other person or organization is trustworthy and if that is what the person wants. Many married women are examples of powerless but happy people, secure and dependent, with their own interests and busy lives. I would agree that this is the case, and that it holds true especially for the period of time in which things seem to be going along smoothly. If, after having been taken care of all their lives, these women then become widowed or divorced in middle age, they find life extremely difficult. They have to start from scratch in areas like finances, decision making, housing, and socializing. They often feel angry that they had depended so much on their spouse. One widow told me that she felt as if her thirty-year-old cocoon had just opened, and she didn't want to leave it.

One of the major ways in which men are seduced into secure and dependent behavior at this stage is through a dependency—chemical, emotional, or physical. Whenever someone or something has more control over you than you have over yourself and can be used to harm you in any way, you may be able to identify with the descriptions of Stage One behavior.

An important struggle at this stage is wanting to overcome dependence but not knowing how to become more independent without risking too much. A great deal of fear and confusion can be associated with Stage One: on the one hand, lacking the knowledge of what exactly to do and fearing the repercussions if one were to break away from dependence, yet on the other hand fearing the consequences of prolonged security. Many people remain in Stage One until it gets impossible to stay there or they are forced out of it by another person or a life event. But as long as they are in Stage One they are held in a powerless state, secure yet dependent on others for basic life needs.

People at Stage One understand from experience that there are two types of people—those who have power (the haves) and those who don't (the have-nots). In fact, we can all identify with this because of our experiences as children. We all chose various ways to get things from our parents: asking them, being good, playing sick, showing them affection, helping them, or threatening them. If one method didn't work, we just moved to the next one. As a child I found out that whether my parents seemed reasonable or not, they still had the resources and I had to do something to get them. They shared, but they were in charge. The resources were not mine to begin with, that is, not until I began to earn my own money and assert my own judgments. With powerless adults, feelings of having fewer resources or less access to resources than another continue to exist. I heard a couple talking recently in the following manner, which illustrates this point: He said, "Well, as long as we're going to spend our vacation with my parents, I think I'll take a long weekend to ski this winter." She replied, "Well, then, I'd like to take a long weekend on the beach while you ski." He looked up and laughed, "Well, where will you get the money?"

People in organizations often feel this same sense of control by other people. If those at the top of the organization are perceived to be making all the decisions, then those on the bottom think of themselves as powerless and subject to changes over which they have no control. They feel like puppets on a string who have to respond directly to any movement of the puppeteer.

Uninformed

One of the reasons powerless people in organizations are so dependent is that they have little access to information. Because they know little about how the organization is run they are forced to rely on those who have that information; as a result, these people tend to participate only in their own world—usually limited to people who sit next to them or who supervise them. They have low-level skills and their positions are generally at the entry level, causing many of them to see their work as "just a job." For some this is acceptable, and they are proud to do a good job at what they do. Some of them shrug off efforts to further themselves because they don't believe their efforts will make any difference. This is due to low self-esteem and sometimes to reality. Some may be waiting for Prince (or Princess) Charming or for the lottery or sweepstakes to rescue them. Since they tend to be unrealistic or unaware of the rules they may have more daydreams of get-rich-quick schemes or lucky breaks. A small survey of prison inmates, for example, showed that making lots of money was a recurring goal.

In organizations some powerless people can be very difficult to deal with. Rosabeth Kantor, author of *Men and Women of the Corporation*, speaks of people who hoard what little bit of territorial control they have to show others that they will not be dominated on their own turf. You may recall examples of times when you've filled out an extraordinarily long bureaucratic form under a deadline, following the instructions explicitly, only to find out too late that the person in charge wanted it another way, and you are now subject to a penalty.

Low in Self-Esteem

People feel generally confused at this stage, not knowing which way to turn and having frequent bouts of low self-esteem coupled with self-doubt. Powerless people do not know who they are as individuals largely because they are afraid to take a close look. Sometimes they don't know how, but generally they're too busy with work, or making ends meet, or escaping from life to care at all or be aware that self-esteem matters. They just take what life dishes out and they don't ask questions. They learn to accept it and hope it doesn't get worse. They say to themselves, "What makes me think I deserve better, anyway?" Low self-esteem seems to feed on itself, too. The paradox about low self-esteem is that people also get some benefits out of that state of mind. They can feel sorry for themselves; they can arouse their anger at others; they can prove to themselves how much they deserve to be in this terrible spot; they can use it as an excuse to stand still. So one of the ways for people to increase their personal self-esteem is to learn to speak honestly to themselves about their worth.

Helpless But Not Hopeless

I think of Stage One as helpless but not hopeless. There are things to do, ways to get out, further steps to take, but not if people endlessly continue to reinforce their own powerless status. Sexism and racism, to be sure, are factors that feed into a powerless position; witness the failure of our country to pass the Equal Rights Amendment and the overproportionate number of minorities in prison. Cultural and attitudinal barriers are almost insurmountable at times. But it is possible to make some progress to other stages. The first step is the will to change, and the second is knowing how to build coalitions to help break out of Stage One. You cannot do it alone, and someone else cannot do it for you. It involves taking responsibility for yourself and taking some initiative on your own or others' behalf. It means not blaming others or the system entirely. It means that you do something to effect change in the system and in yourself.

I do not intend to analyze cultural powerlessness in this book; that is a book all its own. I am describing Stage One as it *is* in our society, not as it *ought* to be. In terms of organizational leadership, which is one of my themes, Stage One people are not effective as organizational leaders. They have little external and no internal power, and they tend to abuse it when they get it. Stage One people as leaders tend to get things done by coercion, which is ineffective in the long run. Examples are the revolutionaries in various countries who, once powerless and abused, turn around and kill their oppressors the first chance they get.

Let's Meet Some People at Stage One

Todd, the Chemically Dependent Executive

(Chemicals can cause a dependence that is every bit as powerful as it is destructive, leaving people debilitated. Chemically dependent people are deluded into thinking they are powerful when, ironically, they are powerless.)

> What a farce I made out of my life. High roller was what I called myself. For fifteen years, my motto was "live hard, work hard, drink hard." And I did. I thought the way to reach the top was to be everything to everybody, to be the friendly guy who everybody liked. I had a lot of energy, good health, lots of contacts. I had the world by the tail and was swinging it around. I traveled seventy-five percent of the time and was always ready for the next challenge.
>
> The only trouble with my life, which I totally denied at the time, was that I was numb most of the time, due to my total dependence on alcohol. Alcohol gave me the feeling I could do all these things or at least allowed me to escape the feeling that I couldn't. I was under the powerful spell of self-delusion. I wanted so desperately to be approved of, to be needed, yet I just could not be vulnerable or

realistic. Now I can see I was feeling guilty and shameful for never measuring up, but my way of coping was not to feel at all—to numb myself. I was so good at the whole charade that I even had my family convinced that my behavior was benefiting them.

Thank God for my wife. After a serious illness of her own, she woke up to the fact that she was helping me toward my own destruction. She left me for a time and got help for herself. I hit bottom after several months of hell and finally agreed, for the sake of the family, to go into chemical dependency treatment. That was the hardest thing I've ever done, but it saved my life.

After a long, hard struggle back to life, I can say I would not be alive emotionally or physically if I had not taken that step. I have had to completely rethink my life and my work. It's been a real awakening. I am more aware now of who I am and what I am capable of doing. I am willing to admit my weaknesses and get help when I need it. Now I just live from day to day, more self-accepting, more honest, and very grateful for life. My motto has become "live more fully, love more fully."

Andy, the High School Student

(Andy is an example of a young, unskilled student who has very little to rely on and some life situations to overcome.)

I just got my first part-time job. I don't know how much I'll like working, but it's better'n sitting around in front of the tube all night. I'm working as a part-time janitor washing floors and cleaning up in offices after supper. Pay's not so hot but it's better'n nothing. Gives me a little extra money to spend on stuff I want. The way I see it, when I hit eighteen, I'll go to where my dad lives, and maybe he can set me up with something better. He's been unemployed mostly since he left us, but there's bound to be something for a guy who don't mind working. If I did better in school, maybe I could get into one of them tech schools, but school and me don't get along so hot. There's too much going on at home with the four little kids around. Makes it tough to study, and I have a hard time seeing where it will all get me anyway. Guess I'll just stick it out until I can leave.

Margaret, the Homemaker

(Margaret illustrates power within powerlessness. Margaret is a happy and dependent homemaker who loves her life and will meet the crises as they come.)

I've been married to the same man for twenty-six years. We've done everything together. We've raised five kids, built a house, traveled across the country, suffered over deaths, taken in foreign students, laughed, fought, and loved. It doesn't seem like there's much we haven't done. I encouraged him, even knocked on doors for him when he decided to run for mayor of our town. And he won. I've lived for him and my family for twenty-six years. He and our five children are my entire life, my full-time job. Oh, I have outside interests like my sewing club, my occasional craft classes at the high school, and my garden, but these things are secondary to my job at home. Everything my husband does needs my support, and I enjoy being there when he needs me. In turn he makes a comfortable living for us all to enjoy and is the strong, decisive father for the family. We discuss all the major family decisions together, but he usually makes the final decision because of his broader perspective.

He is very supportive of me when I want to do things for myself or the children. If I want to take the kids to grandma's for a week in the summer, he always sees to it that we get there. When I want him to go to the children's special events, he usually makes time for them. We have had our troubles, believe me, illness, depression, fights, but on the whole, we've had a very good life. I guess we've learned to accept each other and not try to change each other any more. And our children are all grown up and either going to school or married and into their own lives. Now it's time for us to think about his retirement. I wonder sometimes exactly what we'll do because time has been more heavy on my hands these last few years, but we'll talk it over like we usually do and it'll work out somehow.

Joe, the Junior High School Teacher

(Joe is a victim of teacher burnout and bitterness. He sees few resources and feels trapped by a system that does not appreciate him.)

When I went into teaching I felt great. I was the first one of all my relatives to go to college, and I knew all along I wanted to work with kids. Some of my teachers had been so important in my life that I wanted to be something special for other kids. I was ready to work and to really make a big difference. I wanted to be the most popular teacher around. That was how I felt then. Now I've been teaching math for eight years and, boy, have my eyes been opened! Teaching is a thankless, pressure-packed job. We're never appreciated, always blamed. If I had known all the other things that go with teaching that have nothing to do with the kids I would have become a playground director. We're all alone in our classrooms, and there's little time to really work together as teachers, except on problems. And this year there have been a lot of cutbacks on top of it all. With each cutback we get special resources taken away.

And the kids. Thirty-five kids staring at you or fooling around while they wait for the bell to ring hour after hour, day after day. Some of them are really super kids, but the amount of time you get with them alone or in small groups is so little, you always feel they are sliding past you. And then there's my future to think about. There's nowhere to go from here. I don't want to be an administrator, and teaching for the next twenty years would kill me. Who knows if anything's available to teachers outside the school system? And why should I try to do new or creative things? No one notices (the principal especially), only a few of the kids seem to care, and it takes me all evening to prepare. Most of the other teachers seem to be as burned out as I am, so all we do is complain. And it seems like all my friends are teachers too. Maybe the best thing for me would be to get laid off so I would be forced out of this mess.

Joan, the Corporate Secretary

(Being trapped in a compromising work situation in which a boss is unable to face up to his harassing behavior leaves Joan in a very frightening predicament.)

This is really hard, um, embarrassing for me to talk about, because it's still so recent. (pause) Well, last year in the middle of a really busy time at work, my boss and I were working late to get out a rush report before a deadline. Most of the other girls had gone home and we were almost finished, just a few pages to go. My boss asked if I would get us both a cup of coffee, which sounded good to me, too, so I quickly got it and brought it in to him at his desk. He stood up, said thanks, and made a pass . . . well, um, he sort of kissed me, um, on the lips and I pulled away and left the room mumbling "You're welcome" or something weird like that. I was beet-red. I could just feel it. What a shock! I could have forgotten the whole thing and called it appreciation or something, but he started doing other things, more embarrassing and more out in the open. Now mind you, I'm no prude, no big moralist, but I just didn't want to get involved with a married man and, furthermore, not my boss.

I finally worked up enough courage to sit down with him one day and tell him that I really liked working for him but his advances were beginning to get in the way of my work. He laughed and said we could talk about it another time. His behavior kept up and became more aggressive a few times. Once he trapped me in his office and started handling me. That made me really scared and angry. After that I made sure I was never in a position to be touched or trapped by him again. But I went home with headaches. And he gave me a lower-than-average performance review for that period of time. Then he told me perhaps I should see a counselor because I was not a very healthy young lady—repressed or something was what he said. Well, that cracked me. I had to do something soon. But what?

Moving to Stage Two

There is no way to predict exactly how each of us will move from one stage to another. Some will take a direct route like this: A ⟶ B, and others will take the circuitous route: A ⊔⌵⌐↳ B. Both paths may take the same amount of time but cover different territory. There seem to be steps in the transition from one stage to another, but we each have our own style of going through the steps. At times the transition between stages seems as long as the time spent in each stage, especially when we're in the middle of the change. I think of the movement from stage to stage as a personal crisis because each person has to overcome some obstacle as well as let go of something familiar in order to move.

Two key personal qualities will ultimately precipitate the crisis or movement to Stage Two: self-esteem and skills. People have to start feeling good about themselves, and they have to have saleable skills. Usually there is a crisis or loss or event of some kind that stops them in their tracks or awakens them to the need to act in order to feel better. That does not mean that everyone acts when a crisis occurs. Some people give up, become hostile, harm others, injure themselves, or just get "stuck" at their stage. This can be due to cultural barriers, lack of access to people, money, experience, or it can represent a lack of motivation to move due to nagging self-doubt, laziness, low risk-taking ability, unwillingness to try, or satisfaction with the martyr or victim role.

Other people act. They may not know how or why, but they feel an inner compulsion to get out of the situation and to survive. I remember distinctly the event that forced me to act within a seemingly powerless work situation. I had to tell my boss that I could not work effectively under the current office conditions. He led me to believe they were all my fault and that he would discuss me with his boss. In a moment of desperation I said that I would discuss the situation with his boss too. To this day I remember how afraid I was to risk talking to his boss and how relieved I was when the situation was understood and appreciated. Two weeks later I had a different job in the organization working for someone else. I would never want to repeat that experience, but I learned how to handle other work situations better as a result.

We all can use the help of others at these crucial times. But we also *must* acknowledge from our innermost being that we are worth the effort and that we will invest in ourselves. I think it comes down to wanting to live rather than die. Gaining self-esteem is difficult if you've been beaten down for years. How one develops it is a critical and complex issue, but self-esteem is possible with help from other caring people in your life.

The signs of increased self-esteem are different for all of us. Think back, if you're over twenty-five, to the first time you decided to take yourself by the hand and make a go of it. Perhaps it was running for a high school office, studying for a test, asking for a raise, going back to school, buying a car. It could have been ten years ago, forty years ago, or yesterday. This experience of going beyond the "I can't," beyond blaming others for our lot, beyond the dependent victim stage is one we face on a major or minor level periodically, even if our home stage is elsewhere. The seduction of the "poor me" syndrome plagues all of us from time to time because our powerlessness feels so real. It takes away enormous energy needed to move on, but it feels good to have the safety from change as well. Sooner or later we realize it is time to move on and to get out of our debilitating victim status.

Whole groups of people who experience powerlessness (the poor, minorities, women, disabled) due to structural blocks in our society need to experience the individual change described above, but often they can do this only by identifying with each other as a group and by fighting "the system" together in order to make change occur. One of the ways powerless people who feel victimized get together for their common good is to form labor unions in business and education.

Listed below are activities that may help you develop more fully through Stage One and on to Stage Two. Some of these will seem appealing to you and others will not. Different people change in different ways, and these are a compilation of the ways in which others have moved to Stage Two.

- Build your self-esteem by exploring who you are and how you get yourself through crises in your life. Consider becoming part of a supportive group who will help you along the way. Resources would include friends, community centers, YM/YWCAs, churches, synagogues, family counseling agencies, and other non-profit organizations.
- Find allies in the organization or in the community who can help you with information or referrals: a network, employee relations people, a community center, advocates of all kinds, other people you know, support groups.

- Name some skills you could develop that would help you become more qualified. Talk to people who have these skills to find out how they developed them.
- List five things about yourself that *other people* like. List five things about yourself *you* like. Do something in the next ten days that shows that you appreciate your qualities, e.g., tell someone about something you have done that was satisfying.
- Talk to someone about your life so far. What major events led you to this point? How do you feel in your life now (happy, sad, afraid, angry, trapped, excited, sorry, joyful)?
- With your support person or group, think of ways to overcome and live more comfortably with your greatest fear. Listen to others share their fears, and give them examples and support for overcoming their fears.
- If you always feel someone else is to blame, ask yourself how you have "bought into" the issue or let it happen to yourself. What can you do to make changes? Discuss the guilt and resentment you feel when attempting to break out of a situation.
- Talk with your boss, if you are comfortable doing so, about the skills he or she thinks would be useful for you to develop in order to grow in your job and in the organization.
- Do you need to get out of your present job in order to gain more power? If so, look around for three other jobs that you are or could be qualified for within the next year. Talk to others about the steps necessary to make a move, e.g., go to a career workshop, tell others you want to move, post for the job, prepare a history of your work, or develop a new skill.
- Are you in a life or work situation in which you are being abused physically or emotionally? If so, talk to someone about your feelings and move yourself with help toward getting out of the situation. Think about getting the other person some help too.
- Find a model or ally in your organization who can teach you about the operation of the organization and how you can become better prepared to move along within it.
- Decide which of your characteristics seems to draw the most discrimination—that you are female, a minority, young, old, fat, bald, unskilled, uneducated, short. Name several features about that characteristic that are pluses or that could be turned into positives for you.

- Close your eyes and imagine yourself as a more powerful person. What are you like? What are you wearing? What are you doing? Whom are you with? Who among your family and friends supports you most? Who disapproves? How do you feel?
- Watch familiar people who you think have more power than you. Observe what they do, ask them questions, try out some of their behaviors for yourself. See how you feel, and observe how others respond to you.
- Organize with other powerless people if you are being unduly discriminated against and have tried consistently to solve the problems using other means. Be prepared for the response by trying to share your concerns as a group rather than threatening the other party. Negotiation is a long, slow process.

Joe, the teacher, who felt burned out and very defeated, finally decided that the system was not going to help him. He got a group of union leaders together with teachers at his school and put together a proposal for teacher renewal programs. Two years later he was the administrator of the program that raised money for teacher-planned renewal projects, from mini-sabbaticals to co-teaching seminars. He found out it could be done and that he could do it.

Todd's story of chemical dependency shows how someone else who cared nudged him to take care of himself.

Joan talked to two other secretaries confidentially and found out that she was not the first person her boss had bothered. She talked to her personnel representative, and with the help of other managers she had met previously she found another job in the company. Her boss has been put on probation for his harassment and has been sent to a professional for counseling.

I'm sure others are in situations like Joe's or Joan's or Todd's, and they will not find a way out or a worthwhile person inside. That is perplexing and saddening as well. Sometimes the impetus for change occurs only when a crisis arises. What do you think will happen to Margaret when her husband dies? What will Andy find when he joins his father in a distant state? Are they building up enough skill and self-esteem to be resourceful?

What Holds People Back?

What do you think will hold people at Stage One back from moving on to the next stage? Probably the most consistent deterrent for them will be fear. And that fear can take several forms: fear of physical abuse or punishment if they strike out on their own, fear of the unknown, fear of being done in again, of failing because of the "system," fear of finding out what they can do if they try, fear of peer disapproval, fear, fear, fear. These fears are real, whether or not they are justified.

The fear itself is not the deciding issue, though. *How they deal with the fear* is what determines whether they move forward. For Stage One people to overcome their fears, even partially, they must get support from others in some form. That does not mean other people should do things for them but that they realize they are not alone in the struggle. That support provides validation that they are capable of doing something for themselves and that they are good people.

We should also remember that for every person who moves out of Stage One there are many who want to move but are not quite ready. When they *are* ready, people at other stages need to be available, as others were for them. It's like passing on to others what we received from someone else at an earlier time.

Woody Allen expresses my sentiments about the fears of Stage One people when, in the last scene of *Annie Hall,* he is talking to his psychiatrist.

"My brother is in bad shape. What can I do to help him?" Woody sighs.

"What seems to be his problem?" asks his psychiatrist.

"He thinks he's a chicken."

"Why, that's ridiculous. Just tell him straight out that he's not a chicken."

"It's not going to be that simple."

"Why not?"

"I need the eggs."

HAGBERG'S MODEL OF PERSONAL POWER

SUMMARY OF STAGE ONE
powerlessness

SYMBOL

DESCRIPTION
manipulation
trapped stage

CHARACTERISTICS
secure and dependent
low in self-esteem
uninformed
helpless but not hopeless

CRISIS OF MOVEMENT
self-esteem
skill development

WHAT HOLDS PEOPLE BACK?
fear

WAYS TO MOVE
Build self-esteem, find allies, get support,
develop skills, appreciate yourself, share
yourself, confront fears, take responsibility,
talk with your boss, change jobs, get out
of abusive relationships, confront yourself

Ask yourself these questions about Stage Two:

Yes No

___ ___   1. Do you watch other people to consciously imitate their behavior, to dress for success?

___ ___   2. Do you have a mentor or role model?

___ ___   3. Is your self-concept solely dependent on how other people feel about you?

___ ___   4. Do you feel that you are learning "the ropes"?

___ ___   5. Are you intensely loyal to a boss whom you would like to work for as long as possible?

___ ___   6. Are most of your social contacts friends of your spouse through his or her work?

___ ___   7. Do you like being around people who have powerful positions, listening to and watching them?

___ ___   8. Do you feel you can see power around you but that you don't have it yourself or at least very little?

___ ___   9. Are you aware of specific skills and knowledge that you are striving to develop in order to progress in your career?

___ ___   10. Are you just beginning to find out who you are inside?

___ ___   11. Do you seek information and advice from as many people as possible?

___ ___   12. Do you feel trapped or "stuck" in your job?

Yes answers indicate that you identify with this stage.

Chapter 2

Stage Two: Power by Association

Magic

What Is Stage Two Like?

Do you remember Hopalong Cassidy? He was a rootin'-tootin' cowboy in the old West and a Saturday morning companion to the children of the '50s. The advertisement that Hoppy lent his name to rings loudly and clearly in my mind; what child do you know who cannot rattle off most of the latest commercials? The ad said, "If you want to be like Hoppy, you've got to eat like Hoppy." I call Stage Two the "be like Hoppy" stage because people at Stage Two usually want to be like someone else. They frequently have a role model or at least identify themselves with other more powerful people.

Stage Two people believe that certain people in the organization have the power, usually defined by Twos as control and influence, and they hope that these people will take care of them, lead them, nurture them, and reward them. For people who've been exploited in Stage One, this can be a "coming out" stage in which they genuinely learn from other people and discover more about themselves. Sometimes in this stage,

19

people tend to emulate these mentors or role models hoping that by being around them, the power may rub off a little. This may be overt like the dress-for-success syndrome, or it may be entirely subconscious. It might even take the form of intense loyalty to the person or the organization, like hero-worship. Bosses take on more significance for Stage Two people than for those in other stages and can have the most long-term positive or negative influence. Since this is such a formative stage, one's boss can be very active in a teaching or coaching role and can guide one into developmental opportunities on the job and elsewhere. Supportive bosses at this stage may be the most significant factor in whether or not a person passes through the stage. Early in my counseling career I had a supervisor who really believed in me and wanted me to grow as much as possible while working for him. He always gave me cases I didn't think I could handle and then worked with me each step of the way to help me gain confidence. At this point of one's career the more responsibility a boss gives with support, the more one can learn.

On the other hand, a non-supportive boss (distant, self-serving, afraid, unfair, racist, sexist) can cause a person to wither developmentally and to start feeling insecure or self-critical. They can erode one's self-confidence by subtly giving the impression that one is invisible or not capable. There is nothing worse than being ignored when one is in need of development or training on the job. Every effort should be made to work with these bosses through suggestions, employee relations, or heart-to-heart discussions. If nothing seems to work, the person at Stage Two must consider finding another boss at some point.

Stage Two people do not have much external or internal power yet, but they can feel the power moving through their office or through their hands. They are apprentices to power. They just can't grasp it. It is elusive, like magic. So power manifests itself at Stage Two as magic, not quite real nor yet available. They are not at all sure how those other people got it, nor are they sure what they would do with it once they had it, but it certainly looks desirable and worth seeking.

If leadership, stated very simply, is the way in which people get things done, then people at Stage Two lead by seduction. By this I mean that they offer people something in return for something else. "I'll give you a good review if you continue to get the job done for me." The bargain is always in effect and usually security or approval is the bargaining chip.

Unsuspecting people can be duped quite eaily by a manipulative Stage Two person.

Some examples of possible Stage Two occupations or situations are trade apprentices, associates in law offices, instructors and assistant professors, marketing assistants or assistant product managers, secretaries to groups or individuals, seminary interns or assistant ministers, women who are married to men more powerful than they, men who are married to women more powerful than they, bureaucrats, people in personnel, appointed officials, new counselors in human service agencies, engineering assistants, or cub reporters. It is somewhat dangerous to describe people's stages by their occupational level because people at the same job can be at different stages from each other. In addition, anytime people move from one job to another or from one career to another or from one relationship to another—even though it's their third or fourth move—they still go through an apprenticeship stage, in which they are learning the ropes. Anyone who's decided on a particular field and is willing to learn and grow to gainful admittance to that field is in the apprenticeship stage. I've had a few career changes in my life, and each time I enter a new field this apprenticeship stage is very apparent to me. There is a new language, a new set of assumptions, new people to cultivate, new associations to join, new skills to adopt. I must gain respect in a whole new arena.

Characteristics of Stage Two People

Learning the "Ropes"

A good description of this stage is the apprenticeship or mentorship stage, in which people are learning the roles, trying on new behaviors, testing assumptions, wearing new uniforms, trying out skills, exploring possibilities, setting up dreams, and beginning self-exploration all as a result of watching and working for others. For some, it's the first time they've really been recognized for being an individual instead of one of the crowd. They now have a clearer sense of their own identity in the organization than they had at Stage One, perhaps even a sense of belonging. Sometimes the belonging feeling is aimed more at a leader than an organization. Some leaders are such strong personalities that they almost demand a following of loyal supporters; and there are many people who like to be part of a loyal contingency. This is most apparent in sports, politics, and show business, but it is also true of charismatic leaders who have ideas that others want to help them fulfill, whether it be in education, religion, architecture, business, social work, or government.

And at still other times the belonging feeling may be aimed at a belief system such as security, political aspiration, religion, or love. Along with the infatuation with power comes the disillusionment phase that people experience in Stage Two when they discover that their mentor makes mistakes, their boss is self-serving, their security falls apart, their religion has no easy answers, their politics fail, or their love fades. This is all part of the process, part of the understanding of power. And this too shall pass, as the saying goes.

For many people the apprenticeship stage of life is the most interesting to them because they like to learn and try out new things. On each new job or with each new experience they strive to learn as much as they can to become skilled. Then when the apprenticeship stage is over they gradually find themselves getting bored and wanting to learn something new again. They may not necessarily be interested in moving up, but they are interested in moving around, to satisfy their curiosity for new learning.

Learning the "Culture"

Stage Two can be exciting, scary, and fun but also tentative. It is a newness stage as well as a loss-of-innocence stage. Along with the acquisition of skills and techniques comes a realization later in the stage that there exist rules, games, barriers, hidden information, informal networks, and a bigger world. At Stage Two people are mostly operating in their own department with a limited group of people, a closely defined job description, and little job discretion or access to information about the larger organization. They gradually begin to see that there are many other departments, fields, and organizations, and that they themselves are in a very circumscribed job. That is not bad, but it opens their eyes to a much broader world of people, ideas, and contacts.

This is the stage at which being in a network of similar people, a professional association, trade association, women's or men's network, athletic club, Jaycees, or a golf club starts to make sense, if for no other reason than support and perspective. Many organizations now have women's groups started by women employees for the purpose of self-education, information sharing, and support. The most successful groups are supported by the women in powerful positions and attended by a wide cross section of women. They have their own board and are self-supporting in the main.

There are groups of people who, for whatever reasons, choose to resist the loss of innocence and to view the world as if it were already the way it "should" be: good, fair, and beautiful. They will not acknowledge and grapple with the other side of life: the evil, the unfair, and the ugly. They may seem like very sweet, childlike, happy people, but one gets a funny feeling that sometime there may be a great explosion or a rude awakening. Stage Five people may behave in some ways similar to the innocent person but with a completely different base—that of understanding the evil in all of us but choosing to go on trusting and living with eyes wide open. I elaborate on these similarities and differences in the chapter on Stage Five.

Dependent on Supervisor/Leader

Supervisors and managers are the main or usual source of information for people at Stage Two. For that reason, the latter people depend on the former's knowledge of the system in order to function successfully. That is why it is important to work for a good boss during the apprentice stage. (If you learn golf from a duffer, it takes a lot longer to unlearn your bad habits later.) People who have good managers tend to outperform those who don't, and they are more satisfied with their work, according to several management development studies.

But some people get so attached to their first manager that they become fearful of ever moving on. That situation may work well for a while, but at some point the manager may leave, retire, be passed over,

become disillusioned or ill, and then Stage Two people can find themselves in a real crisis. This is particularly apparent for secretaries who
move with the same boss throughout their career. They are intensely
loyal, but when their boss leaves, no one knows quite what to do with
them.

As I said earlier, this is a time in which one's boss is central, so it sets
up a difficult situation for people who want to progress but feel forever
like apprentices, even to a good boss. One man I talked with had worked
with the same political figure for twenty years, ever since he had joined
the man's staff out of college. In his mid-forties himself, he foresaw the
possible retirement of his boss, so he spent a year thinking, reading, and
talking to other people about job possibilities. It was frightening
because, even though he was highly respected, he had never had to wage
a job campaign for himself before. He moved to another state and
became head of a non-profit educational organization and is happy and
increasingly confident. He still keeps in touch with his former boss and
friend, but he has made the necessary break.

I have also seen this happen with graduate students who stay in school
for ten years studying with the same professor because of a good working
relationship and perhaps the fear of the next phase, that of finding their
own niche. Others stay on the staff of a well-known person acting as his
or her right-hand person for years, making the person look good and
getting satisfaction in the staff role. Many enter a very uncomfortable
phase after a time, combining loyalty with some confusion and perhaps
resentment. They begin to realize just how much they are needed and
how much of the work they do for the other person, who appears to be
reaping most of the benefits. Sooner or later they leave, either to join
another organization at a different level (on their own merits), or they
start something on their own. This is particularly true in consulting
firms, political staffs, advertising agencies, small businesses, and counseling agencies.

Beginning Self-Exploration

Internally, Stage Twos are just beginning the first phases of self-exploration, trying on the one hand to distinguish themselves from others and,
on the other hand, learning how they are alike in their struggles. They

also learn their strengths and limitations—whether they want to or not. Given the definition of personal power as the combination of externally-derived recognition and action as well as internally-induced reflection and wisdom, Twos are more externally than internally powerful, but possess little of either at this point.

This can be an excellent time for Twos who want to open themselves up to new awarenesses for the first time and try out new behaviors. It is best done within a known or relatively safe environment, for there mistakes can be made and used as learning tools. In fact, not for a few power stages will mistakes be seen again as good learning experiences. That is why membership in trade or professional associations, health, social, or athletic clubs are so useful for Twos. They are good places to practice power.

Some Stage Two people go around hunting for advice from as many sources as they can possibly find. In fact, they go from one to another, looking for a magic way to transform themselves into success models with a minimum of effort. They go from experience to experience, trying to conform in order to be accepted or admired. Perhaps we can all identify with the intense desire to be loved or at least admired by others for what we are.

This need became abundantly clear to me during my divorced and single days when I was once again faced with the problems of dating. My need to be cared about was as strong as my repulsion for the singles clubs. I was caught in a dilemma: Do I try to meet people or just decide to remain single forever? Of course, at that time I saw no middle ground. After eight unforgettable months of "dating," during which I generated some life experiences I can only laugh at now, I decided to give it up and spend the time on developing myself into the kind of person I wanted to become. I became much more relaxed and relieved not to be in such confusion, and soon meeting people and dating was a secondary issue.

A lot of people at this stage take the advice of other people rather than trust themselves. The following fable adapted from Aesop, describes the possible results.

A Man, a Boy, and a Donkey

A man and his son were walking on a road toward town with their donkey.

They met a man who chastised the son for making his poor father walk when the donkey could carry him. So the son encouraged his father to get on the donkey and off they went.

Soon after, they met another man on the road who chastised the father for making his young son walk while he rode the donkey. So the father set his son on the donkey with him and they continued on.

After traveling a few miles, they came to a bridge and met a group of people who chastised them both for riding on the poor donkey who was old and weak. So they decided to get off and carry the donkey.

In their attempts to lift the donkey to their shoulders they got too close to the edge of the bridge, and the donkey toppled into the river and drowned.

PEOPLE WHO LIVE THEIR LIVES ACCORDING TO THE PRE-SCRIPTIONS OF OTHERS RUN THE RISK OF LOSING THEIR DONKEY.

I would like to add just one additional note while discussing self-exploration here, and that is regarding one's physical appearance. Very few people are willing to be honest about it, but if you are confused about why you are stalled in a job, it might be worthwhile to check out your appearance. This should not be your only approach but it is worth a glance. It is a factor that should not weigh as heavily as it does yet it must be taken into consideration for people who want to achieve or move or be accepted in organizations. I do not mean to say that one has to be handsome or beautiful, only that there are very strong norms in most organizations against sloppy dress, unkempt looks, and especially excessive weight. One can dress for success and learn the right words, but fifty extra pounds will be the deciding factor almost every time. Appearance is usually seen as a symbol of an orderly, disciplined mind or as the amount of respect people have for themselves.

Self-exploration can also take the form of volunteering for new assign-ments on the job that will test and push you into new or risky skill areas. One young woman set up an internship with her supervisor's help so she could find out what a first-line supervisor in another department did, thus helping her decide what kinds of skills she would need to prepare herself for that job eventually. Job-related self-exploration can also include reading, conversations, and classes or workshops on topics that will help you learn more about yourself personally. These might include areas such as values, communication, skills, life planning, personal growth, assertiveness, family dynamics, attitudes, personality styles, and group dynamics. Many people say that these experiences of finding out more about who they can be open their eyes for the first time to the ways in which they defeat themselves or hold themselves back in the organization. They also find out that they have many more good qualities than they have given themselves credit for.

Still another way to find out about yourself is to put yourself into environments in which you are the stranger or the inexperienced one. This could include travel to other countries where lauguages and customs are very different from your own, travel to the inner countries of your psyche through counseling, or travel to the wilderness or the mountains to explore the world around you and the wilderness within. My belief is that the strong urge people have to explore canyons, woods, mountains, and rivers brings them near nature and thus closer to their own inner nature. Thoreau said so wisely, "Dwell as near as possible to the channel in which your life flows."

Stuck But Moving

Many Twos experience the career dilemma of feeling stalled in the organization for a variety of reasons: the age of their boss, the number of positions available, the unavailability of further education or training, their own unwillingness to move or change jobs at the time, or "politics." For whatever reason, they probably will not move to any positions of increased responsibility for a long time. In many companies, this is becoming more the norm than the exception. When people feel stuck, they often begin to give up, to be disappointed, or to lose energy in their work because of the loss of motivation. When this occurs the whole organization suffers, and the individual suffers the most. This problem occurs primarily because people have become too dependent upon the organization for their development, their recognition, their self-esteem.

One of the most important things people can do for themselves at Stage Two (or that organizations can assist people in doing) when the stuck feeling occurs is to continue to develop themselves personally and professionally on their jobs, and more importantly, outside the organization. While it may be impossible to chair an important committee inside the organization, it may be very possible to become the program chair for a professional association or to work on a community action project. If another degree may not be useful, then further broadening of oneself through liberal arts classes or just reading widely can be a major developmental move toward becoming a broader thinker. If the external skills and behaviors are as developed as they can be, then the internal realm may be fertile territory for exploration. Knowing oneself better may result in different career moves, like moving laterally, down temporarily, or across to other divisions instead of just moving up in the organization. But changing the attitudes of people about upward mobility—which presently means success—will be very slow in coming.

Two specific groups of Stage Two people illustrate how differently people view themselves at the same stage of apprenticeship. I call the first one the "sky's the limit" group. These Stage Two apprentices firmly believe that Stage Two is but a brief stopover on their way to the top. Some new MBAs, for instance, feel they are actually being "reined in" by having to learn the ropes. Those in large corporations all think they will make it to the top, although they know there are just so many slots at the top. At Stage Two they can be viewed as training for the stiffly competitive stage to follow in which they find out whether they "make the cut" or not. Observed from the outside, it appears that the young thoroughbreds are racing each other for their shot at the big time a few years hence. They are enthusiastic young idealists who are out to make a mark on the world, seeing this stage as the starting gate, and waiting impatiently for the starting bell. For many of them this is the most exciting, though perhaps not the most satisfying, time of their careers.

This predictable apprentice stage has a counterpart in the profession of law and medicine. The newcomers are tested, tried, and then initiated into the "brother/sisterhood" with all the long-standing norms, values, and privileges associated with membership. Those in the middle of the initiation sometimes complain bitterly about the treatment they are being subjected to, but as soon as it is over they seem less eager to fight for change, and some even watch enthusiastically as the next group is subjected to the same treatment.

I see another group of people who are quite different from the "sky's the limit" group. This group I call the "recyclers." They enter a career and try to take on the norms, behaviors, and skills of that job or profession. They find people who they think are successful and try to be around them; they use the jargon of the field, even dress the part, yet they do not "make it" in that field. They do not become accepted, get promoted, or become well-enough recognized. In short, they fail to catch the spark. Or perhaps they get impatient with the process too soon. They move on, continually looking to each new career or job as a magic wand that will somehow touch them and make them satisfied. They have not discovered that a career does not make a person—a person makes a career. They are confused about who they are and how their skills, values, and interests fit into various careers. If the magic doesn't happen, they leave to pursue the next possibility, like Don Quixote chasing windmills. During this erratic process, they fail to accumulate knowledge and experience, and they see no need for behavior change.

We could look at this another way as well. If careers were hypothetically made up of four levels—1-apprentice, 2-practitioner, 3-expert, 4-muse—recyclers would always be at level 1, unwilling to commit their time, energy, or money to move to the next level. Perhaps they fear success. Or perhaps they fear the self-exploration necessary to find out who they really are and where they fit. The cause may go deeply for some, back to childhood experiences and messages or early school memories. Clearly, it is a complex and frustrating situation to be in. Most recyclers are not hiding their dilemma, even though they may think they are. Others can see their patterns more clearly than they can, but others can't do anything about it. Recyclers are not unskilled, just mismatched in jobs or careers that are not congruent with who they are.

The recyclers should not be confused with people who seek new challenges and new levels of accomplishment on their jobs and in each new career. These people have a wide variety of interests and enjoy entering into new challenges. They need variety and change to keep them fresh. They tend to do the job well and to complete their goals or to reach a certain level, and then they are bored, needing the next challenge. They are more like entrepreneurs within organizations, higher risk-takers than most people.

These entrepreneurs usually go to level 2, practitioner, where they get good enough to practice the skill or trade. They do not want to go so deeply into the subject matter so as to become an expert, because they would become bored. This is not bad, although experts generally frown on practitioners. Practitioners who spend their lives seeking to be experts are a frustrated and unfulfilled group. Better to be a good practitioner in a number of areas (a generalist) than to force oneself to be an expert in an area that is no longer interesting. We will get to the experts and muses later.

Let's Meet Some People at Stage Two

Lenny, the Police Officer

(In this example we learn the value of making mistakes and learning from them while in the role of apprentice.)

Ever since I could remember, I've dreamed of being a policeman. Every time the kids in the neighborhood played cops and robbers I was there in the role of the cop, protector of the neighbors against the tyranny of the lawless. I felt it was my duty in life to be strong and to help others. As soon as I graduated from high school I went to school in police science. It was the happiest day of my life when I was accepted as a rookie patrolman in my city. I remember wanting to jump up and down, but I knew it wouldn't fit the image. Well, I set out to be the very best patrolman in the precinct and did it with zest. I thought you just did all the things we read and talked about in school. I had another think coming! It's not quite the same to read about domestic problems with weapons involved as it is to be on the front lawn of a home where a man has just beaten his wife and is threatening you with an old shotgun if you don't leave. So much for trying to get the couple to calm down and talk things over. Oh, I don't mean I didn't learn a lot in school, but it's just more real on the streets. And it can be really boring a lot of the time too. We're rarely in chase scenes or gun battles, or even in grave danger. It's just that anything could happen at any time, and we have to be constantly alert.

Lucky for me, one of the more senior officers on the force took me under his wing the first year and taught me some of the rules before I had to learn them the hard way. I did have one very difficult lesson, though, which I will never forget (nor live down). I was assigned to a stake out, to keep tabs on a suspect that we had been watching for weeks. I was alone in my unmarked car just having to while away the time. Well, it started to get pretty warm in the car and I got a little bit too comfortable. I started to have a harder and harder time keeping my focus on the house. My eyes were very heavy. The next thing I knew I was shocked back to reality by a tap on my window. It was three hours later. The suspect had been picked up and no one could get me by radio, thus causing all kinds of worry. I was embarrassed and frightened by my mistake, falling asleep on the job. What would this mean for my career, for my future? Well, I did get reprimanded and lectured to by my sergeant and my older buddy explained what to expect and how to act in the future. But the razzing from the other officers was the worst. Lullaby Lenny they called me. Thank God my mistake didn't put anyone in danger. Needless to say, it's never happened since, but it was undoubtedly the most memorable event of my rookie year.

Martha, the Assistant Professor

(Martha is a good example of a professional who knows the written rules but is not yet knowledgeable about the unwritten ones or the politics of tenure.)

It is abundantly clear to me which stage I am in at the university. The only power I have is my identification with my discipline of history and with my department. Since I have not yet received tenure, the main activities I engage in are those that will help me to get there, teaching, publishing, and committee work. I feel almost as much an apprentice now as I did when I was writing my dissertation, except now my salary is a wee bit better. I know my department associates are willing to help me, but they also will be involved in my tenure decision. And if I don't make it, I must leave. So I feel pulled between wanting to do a better job at teaching, which I love, and having to keep up with research and committee work, which I am less fond of, having had my fill for a while after my dissertation. And historical research in my special-ty, Tibetan manuscripts, is not very applicable to Introductory

History, 101. I know people say that you must get some visibility in
order to have a more favorable tenure position, but it feels like I am
being told to be excellent in all three areas (teaching, research,
service) at a very early stage in my career. I have a lot in my favor,
though. My educational background is superb, from one of the best
schools in the country, and my department chair seems to be
supportive. All I can do now is press forward with my work and
make a decision about the next phase of my career when I know
about tenure in a year or two.

Ray, the Counselor

(Recyclers can be found in any occupation. By their very nature they
seem to be always looking for themselves outside of themselves.)

I'm one of those people who could never decide what I would be
when I grew up! In fact, I wondered if I would ever grow up. First, I
was a seventh grade art teacher. I did that for three years and
thought I had found my life's work, but then the sameness of
teaching got to me. I also had the feeling of being tied to the school
all day with little adult conversation. The third year, the seventh
grade class was made up of fifty percent delinquents, it seemed. So
I got out and decided to try selling for a while. There was more
money and lots of freedom. That's what I thought. Well, I was
selling educational materials on a salary plus commission basis
and the pressure to make salary was enormous. And did I get to
travel, to *every* school district in the state! It didn't take long to
realize I wasn't cut out to be on the road. I liked the idea of making
money, though, and sales is the place to do it. So I switched to
insurance sales. I took all the training and then I beat the bushes, as
they say, for clients. I called everyone I had ever known. The
turndowns were hard but I kept on going. In fact, I had a really
good record for number of appointments booked. But I had a lot of
trouble in that first year actually closing the deal, asking for the
sale. I was embarrassed to tell anyone, so I said the appointments
were missed. I felt trapped by that mess so I decided to switch.
Besides, a real deal came along. A guy I met was starting a new

venture. He was going to produce wildlife reprints that he claimed every office in the state would buy if they could just see them. He promised me salary plus lots of extra bonuses if I would give it a try. It sounded better than educational material to me so I took it on. Little did I know the volume he was expecting in the first six months. It would have been impossible for a superman. After six months and what I thought were good sales, he closed operations and there I was, out in the cold. (It was February in Michigan.) Now I'm trying something new that might not make as much money but it's more secure. I'm working nights and going to school days to learn to be a counselor. I'm not sure how I'll like it but it's sure worth a try.

Joyce, the Data Processing Apprentice

(Joyce, on the other hand, thinks she has really found herself, thanks to her supervisor who is also her mentor.)

I feel like soaring, I'm so excited. Here I am, young and eager to learn with nothing stopping me. Right now I'm in the technical side of the data processing area of our company, and I'm learning new things every day. I have moved up two grades in fourteen months, and my future looks fabulous. It took me a few years to figure out that data processing was my career, but now all I have to do is put in a lot of time and effort to finish my degree in computer science. That's my next step, and I'm starting back to school this fall, three nights a week at the state university.

I know I can do it, thanks to the wonderful support of my supervisor who is also my mentor. She's really responsible for my new lease on the future. She pushes me and encourages me to go beyond what I'm doing and to try new things, knowing I will make mistakes. And I've made some over the last few years. But she says that's how I learn, as long as I don't repeat them too often. She is such a fantastic manager that I'd like to be just like her myself someday. She is energetic, respected, bright, and savvy. In fact, I plan to work for her as we both rise right to the top. But that will take a few years yet!

Sam, the Assistant Director

(Sam is a good example of someone who used his own "stuckness" as a way to renew himself in his career.)

The economy certainly has a way of changing my career plans. Two years ago I thought I was next in line for a Jewish Community Center director's job, only to find myself on permanent hold because of the cutbacks in social service funding. Everyone became security conscious all of a sudden, and no one moved at all, not even to retire. Well, I thought about the situation for quite a while, considered my other career options and decided on a path that I am very pleased about, now that I can see its effects.

I decided to develop myself as much as I could additionally on my job through skill-based seminars and directed conversations with my boss. At the same time I chose to move into a few select community activities, such as serving on the board of a community health agency and joining a citizen's information group. I also made a conscious effort to meet personally with all the long-term members of our community center to get to know them better.

None of these outside experiences seems to be directly related to my job, but I think I am showing more leadership already after one year on the health agency board than I could get the opportunity to show in my own center. I'm learning new things about myself and I'm meeting some fabulous people. Now as a result of people I've met and ideas we've shared, I not only have a new vision for our community center, but I have other possibilities for my own future. All this happened when I thought I was stuck.

Moving to Stage Three

Not everyone wants to move to another stage nor should they. I have known people over the years who are satisfied and happy in their lives and work who really have decided that the amount of responsibility they have at their stage is about what they can handle and still maintain the balance in their lives. A free-lance legal secretary comes to mind. She likes her work, is very competent, has the opportunity to move to a variety of work settings, makes enough money to travel, has close family ties, and wouldn't change for anything. She has struggled to arrive at her decision, thinking she *should* be doing something else, but she knows her needs, energy level, interests, limits, and aspirations, and she is content. Her hobby of oil painting brings her some extra cash and her free-lance status allows her time to paint and travel. She is developing more on the inside than on the outside. Single working parents with young children often feel that they cannot take any extra time away from the family due to their feelings (guilt, love, obligation), so they choose to put their family first and their career second for a period of time. One young musician turned down an internship with a fine chamber orchestra in a distant city to be with his girlfriend more often.

We all make choices and live with them. The major factor to address in thinking about moving or staying in our present stage is whether or not we can accept ourselves or be satisfied at our stage. There is a propensity in all of us to grow and change but at different rates and at different times in our lives. Some people push themselves or allow themselves to be pushed faster than they can handle capably. We call it getting in over our heads. Others do not push themselves at all and end up being stuck forever. Both can be detrimental.

The crisis that people experience in moving to Stage Three is one of confidence. They know they are doing a good job or that they have certain skills, techniques, or knowledge to do their jobs. They may feel fairly secure or safe in the shadow of their boss, spouse, or mentor. Or they may be trapped in their job with an unsupportive boss or little information about options. The questions in the back of their minds when they are presented with opportunities are, Can I do it? Will I let my boss or mentor down? Am I confident enough of myself to take the risk? Do other people believe in me more than I believe in myself? Will I be able to compete? Am I in a rut? Is this a balloon that will burst? Do I want to make the investment in myself? If I wait, will someone do it for me?

Moving to Stage Three requires you to learn self-confidence and how to take risks on both the personal and the work side. In addition, moving to Stage Three will mean taking on more responsibility for yourself and making a bid for the symbols of power in the organization. It could mean gaining visibility, taking risks, volunteering for new things, competing, being evaluated against others more regularly, working longer hours, achieving more, learning the games and politics of organizational life, getting degrees, leaving the cocoon, depending less on other people, investing in yourself, proving yourself, possibly leaving your boss/ mentor, and being exposed to the harsh realities of organizational life. Most of the popular books on the market about power are written for people who want to be Threes. Titles suggest it: *Power By Intimidation, Looking Out for Number One, Games Mother Never Taught You, Paths to Power.*

For most women, the movement from Stage Two to Stage Three is the most difficult move in the entire personal power model. Stage Two is the stage at which most women are most comfortable. It can be satisfying as well as secure. One can be competent and responsible without having to control others. Just work for good people. The dilemma at this point for women who want to move up is whether they want to do what is necessary: develop their masculine side in order to successfully navigate the somewhat tempestuous waters of Stage Three. Women need to understand their own masculine behaviors and how they can be useful in the organization. The most obvious example is assertiveness, including the ability to say no to or disagree with colleagues or boss; other examples are making decisions on one's own, confronting conflict straight on, showing individual achievement, not showing outward emotion at times, competing with other people and enjoying it, keeping a distance, being rational and analytical, quantitative in thinking, being task-, fact-, and detail-oriented, directed, short-run-oriented, active, verbal, linear, scientific, orderly, objective, and critical. These masculine characteristics seem to come easier to most men and must be deliberately learned or reinforced by women who want to be able to use them. Although women as individuals are socialized differently from each other to a certain extent, we still do have many characteristics in common, some that come much easier for most of us than they do for most men. We will call these the feminine characteristics, recognizing that men, too, can have some of them without being a female.

Many women balk at having to learn to flex the atrophied muscles of their masculine side, saying that being feminine is fine and they don't want to buy into the male-dominated behaviors. They would like to leap mysteriously into Stage Four, or preferably Five, and spare themselves the pain of Stage Three. And they are justified in their reluctance. Far too many women have flirted with their masculine side only to let it completely overpower them, turning them into "honorary men" and losing the essence of what it means to be feminine. The pendulum can swing too far, and for many women it does for a while, a most uncomfortable period of time. Some of my own most embarrassing and awkward moments were those in which I was holding on so tightly to my masculine image that I almost smothered. I remember telling a business client once that I only do business on my terms and that if he didn't like it he could find someone else. He found someone else.

So, obviously, I am not advocating that women become men nor that they accept all the norms of the male-dominated organization. But in order to enter and move through Stage Three and towards more leadership in the organization for the future and for the long run, women need to accept and be able to use masculine characteristics when appropriate, understanding the role those behaviors play in organizational life, while never losing touch with the feminine. I will further develop this theme and introduce the concept of flexibility in sex role behavior in the chapters on Stages Four and Five and in the chapter "Women and Power."

This anonymous poem was given to me by a person in an organization who realized the struggle that people go through to find themselves amidst all the pushes and pulls of contemporary life. It represents the struggle to move beyond Stage Two.

Comes the Dawn

After a while you learn . . .

The subtle difference between holding a hand, and
Chaining a soul.

And you learn . . .

That love doesn't mean leaning and company doesn't mean
Security.

And you begin to learn . . .

That kisses aren't contracts and presents aren't
Promises.

And you begin to accept your defeats
With your head up and your eyes ahead
With the grace of an adult, not the grief
Of a child.

And you learn to build all your roads on
Today because tomorrow's ground is too
Uncertain, for plans and futures have a way
Of falling down in mid-flight.

After a while you learn . . .
That even sunshine burns if you ask too much.
So you plant your own garden and decorate
Your own soul, instead of waiting for someone
To bring you flowers.

And you learn . . .

That you really can endure
That you really are strong
And you really do have worth.

And you learn . . .

And you learn . . .

With every goodbye, you learn.

The dilemma of Stage Two men is somewhat different from that of
Stage Two women. From the perspective of the organization, men must
accept and buy into the norms of power, control, and the cultural
pressures to achieve and move into Stage Three, or they will run the risk
of feeling alienated by the society. Most men are so indoctrinated with
the image of achievement that they don't even question it. They just learn
a trade or go to school to become a provider for the rest of their lives, just
as their parents taught them.

But for another growing group of men, many of whom were products of the sixties, the dilemma is more intense. They grew up rejecting the prevailing masculine norms as their only option. They are, as the title of the book by James Kavanaugh suggests, "men too gentle to live among wolves." They grew up with the Vietnam War, the space age, and women's liberation, among other things. They have been faced with a difficult dilemma: either losing face and being deemed failures by society if they accept the less-than-competitive nature they have culti-vated, or being disillusioned and unhappy in the traditional roles passed on by their parents. They are men whom I would describe as "caught in-between." They do not subscribe to the acceptable norms of men nor do they consistently use their masculine behaviors in relations with others off or on the job. We put men into tighter boxes than we do women today. These men have just lived through a formative time in which their values were developed differently, and so they want different things from life. As a result they may provide some vital links between the traditional male model and emerging male options. More on this in the chapter "Men and Power."

Listed below are activities that may help people move from Stage Two to Stage Three.

- Find a mentor if you do not have one. (A mentor is a wise and trusted advisor who can be objective with you about your life or work.) Ask that person to be a guide for you while you seek out your direction.
- Have a long talk with your friend, boss, spouse, and mentor about your skill areas, strengths, values, personality traits, blocks to effective work, and possible directions in life or in work. Get feedback on your performance that is realistic and that gives you some direction for improvement in the future. This will help you overcome your crises of confidence.
- Work hard on doing a very good job at what you are currently doing. One of the best ways to be seen as a capable and competent person is to be one. Do not rely totally on being discovered for being so competent, but certainly do not overlook it.
- Find out what knowledge and skill you need to move into jobs at the next level in your field or other places in the organization. Look into degree or credential programs that will help you obtain that skill and

knowledge. Find programs that work to your schedule and expect time to be very tight for a while. It's worth the effort in the long run if you've chosen the program carefully.

- Get to know your organization in depth. You can do this by talking to people, looking at printed material, and getting yourself into a broader network. Name the top people in your organization and what department each is working in. What path did each person use to get where she/he is? What are the unwritten norms of your organization? Who really makes decisions? What kind of behavior is rewarded? Whom do you have to know or be recognized by? How can you get extra assignments that will give you access to more people in the organization, e.g., committees of all levels of employees, a centrally located department, a volunteer activity?

- Name some things about your organization you like and some you don't like. How can you capitalize on those you like and work around those you don't like? A complaining person without solutions is not appreciated in organizations for long.

- Decide to do at least two new things that you have never done before and that constitute some kind of a risk for you. Record how you felt in preparation for them, during the event, and after. What were the results? What did you learn about yourself, about taking risks?

- Develop your network. Name three professional or trade associations that you could join to meet more people or learn more about your profession and its leadership. Absorb as much as you can from the meetings you attend and stay around afterward to talk to people who work in different organizations from yours. Name some people you know already who could be information sources or supportive people in your life and career.

- Learn to take care of yourself in case others don't. Try not to be disappointed when you realize that there is no magic in the world and that most of what people get they work for. If the magic has left your life, get with other people who can help you bolster your own self-confidence once again. Practice making your own decisions and living with the consequences.

- Start your own business. One good way to find out how you would function in a risky environment is to run something on your own. Many people who are very unhappy in organizations because they feel uncreative or unappreciated are frustrated entrepreneurs. Look into what it would take to start your own business by talking to others who have done it.

- Examine your dress, language, and habits to see which of these may be getting in the way of imaging yourself as more satisfied or powerful.
- For women, name the masculine behaviors. Check those that you are comfortable with, circle those that you aren't comfortable with. Plan ways you can develop the behaviors you think are most important on the list. Talk to other women and men about this. Take some courses, model other people, practice the behaviors in safe settings, and get feedback on your results.
- Work out to the best of your ability any relationships you have with bosses, spouses, or friends who are unsupportive. Use every means you can to remedy the situation. If all else fails, remove yourself from the situation and learn how to take responsibility for yourself.

Martha, the assistant professor, decided that she was not progressing toward tenure in her all-male department as she wanted to, so she joined a women's faculty club. By discussing her situation confidentially with some insightful tenured professors, she formed a plan for tenure that included both the objective and subjective sides of the issue. She joined some different committees, co-authored articles with some people, had candid conversations with others, became a board member in her professional organization, became more collegial with her peers, worked diligently on her teaching, and sailed confidently through to an affirmative tenure decision. Lenny, the rookie, is now in his tenth year with the police force and chooses to remain a street patrolman: "I don't want to sit behind a desk or go out on raids. I like being with the real people, the average person who needs me and appreciates what I do at least once in a while." Ray is wondering what to do with his counseling degree, and Joyce is in the middle of her college work, still glowing with enthusiasm. Sam wonders why he ever wanted to be a director. He has much more time in his present job to do the outside things he wants to do.

What Holds People Back?

People at Stage Two will have to overcome their need for security if they are to move to the next stage. It's so comfortable to be learning from others, to have the way paved by another person who believes in you. Now it's time to try out the unfamiliar, the new, the next step. Most find it helpful to do so in familiar territory, though, with others' assistance. That way you have change within some security, and you can examine your fears realistically. Others find the only way for them is to change abruptly, to move or leave or put themselves under some stress to get going. Whatever you do, find and use resources and start taking risks, small risks and then larger ones. Try one new thing and see how it works, like going to a professional group meeting in your field. If you go again it will be easier. Before you know it, you'll be an officer. Try to move the sense of security from outside yourself to inside yourself without being overwhelmed. Think of yourself as a butterfly emerging from a cocoon that has been holding you. Remember, you can usually go back to the place you left (in some form), so ask yourself "What's the worst thing that could possibly happen to me if I go ahead with my plan?"

Above all, don't try to do it alone. Get into a supportive environment or with a group of work associates who believe in you and will help you grow.

SUMMARY OF STAGE TWO
power by association

SYMBOL   **DESCRIPTION**

magic

the "Be like Hoppy" stage

CHARACTERISTICS
learning the "ropes"
learning the culture
dependent on supervisor/leader
new self-awareness
stuck but moving

CRISIS OF MOVEMENT
confidence

WHAT HOLDS PEOPLE BACK?
confidence
need for security

WAYS TO MOVE
Find a mentor, get feedback, be competent,
get credentials, get more involved, find
solutions, take risks, develop networks,
take care of yourself, do something on your
own, examine your image, take on the
masculine if necessary, work out
relationships

Ask yourself these questions about Stage Three:

Yes No

___ ___   1. Do you feel competitive about almost everything you do?

___ ___   2. Do you make a conscious effort to appear confident?

___ ___   3. Do you feel that you really have to prove yourself because you have been given responsibility?

___ ___   4. Do you think that power is finite, i.e., there is only so much to go around?

___ ___   5. Do you think you've acquired a lot of knowledge and now you ought to make use of it?

___ ___   6. Do you understand the political games that people in organizations play?

___ ___   7. Do you sometimes think that you have "arrived"?

___ ___   8. Do you usually ask yourself first, "How will this affect me?"

___ ___   9. Are symbols extremely important to you, like salary, titles, material possessions, office placement, or number of supervisees?

___ ___ 10. In the game of life do you feel someone has to win and someone has to lose?

___ ___ 11. Do you think success will make you a better person?

___ ___ 12. Do you believe power means being in control of others?

Yes answers indicate that you identify with this stage.

Chapter 3

Stage Three: Power by Symbols

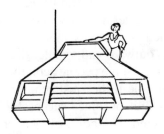

Control

What Is Stage Three Like?

Stage Three is the dynamo stage. It is exciting, grueling, challenging, outwardly rewarding, competitive, oriented to winning and to self-promotion. People at Stage Three are in the thick of things. They operate according to the unwritten rules and roles of the organization. They are learning or have learned to play the game, and for the most part they are rewarded for it. Stages Two and Three are the most prevalent in most organizations. Thousands of people at Stage Three have been led to believe all their lives that "this is it!" They have striven for degrees or positions or salary levels or sports cars or homes in the suburbs or luxury vacations, and now they have attained them. Stage Three people love symbols of success. These could include appropriate body proportions, a great tan, birth of a child, an award, certification, The Stanley Cup, tenure, the position of head minister, bishop, best-selling author, vice-president, millionaire, Executive Director, Senator, Most Valuable Player, Chairman of the Board, best all around, or manager. The list could go on and on. Not only do they like the symbols, they want others to notice them. So they will hang the symbols in their office, drop them into conversations, wear them on their lapels, leave them on their coffee tables, drive them to the office, use them on stationery, have people over to see them, wear clothes that show them off, and be impressed when you remember them.

You see, Threes interpret the symbols as signs of their worth. Way down deep inside they wonder who they would be if they didn't have their symbols. This is particularly true for men, who have been socialized to believe that success is outward and visible, like scores, titles on doors, and size of homes. In fact, some people actually think they will automatically become ideal people if they just achieve "success." To see how false that notion is just think of some "successful" people you know who are abrasive, self-centered, paranoid, or even crazy. Of course, not all Stage Three people are like that either. It's just that many Stage Two people think there is some magic in symbols, so they continue to strive for these Stage Three successes.

The description of power at Stage Three is control. It is the word that comes up most frequently (along with influence) when I ask an audience to say the first word that comes to mind when the word "power" is mentioned. Control suggests that one person has more of it than others, that the buck stops somewhere. Control suggests the possible use of force to ensure certain results. Control suggests discipline and persistence. Control suggests nonemotional responses and being well defended. Control suggests regulation and comparison against standards.

So who exactly are Stage Three people? He or she can be anyone who has achieved some sought-after external recognition or reward, whether it be position, status, credential, material possessions, salary level, or stage of expertise. And these are obtained by a variety of methods: hard work, degrees, luck, inheritance, being in the right place, looks, or competence. The prize is external and recognizable and makes the person feel that she or he is more worthwhile as a result. The person is achieving the prizes for being successful in our culture. For many there is even a sense of initiation into Stage Three. Sometimes a ceremony occurs to mark the occasion, e.g., public recognition, an award ceremony, or graduation. More often the initiation consists of the first meeting of the new managers, the purchase agreement, the letter of promotion, the diploma, or the first results of the election.

Characteristics of Stage Three People

First of all, let me reiterate that Stage Three is the most masculine of all the stages; so, many of the characteristics described may apply more to some males and may disturb some females. Many women think, however, that in order to move up in the organization, they must become just like men, usually Stage Three men, and that is why they get stuck at this stage. (More on this later.) It is probably the easiest stage to understand because it is so much more predictable than the rest, and the expectations on the surface are so much clearer. Stage Threes are rewarded for being strong, decisive, expert, organizationally savvy, and competitive.

Egocentric

Stage Three people have learned an important lesson somewhere along the way: discover your strengths and capitalize on them. They adhere to the power of positive thinking philosophy, and they are always trying to become better. They have achieved a fairly high level of self-confidence and are willing to take on the world sometimes. In fact, it may appear as if they are at times proving to the entire world what their strengths are. But they do have many skills and considerable knowledge by this time that have been recognized by others. They have worked long and hard to get where they are and they are proud. Partly as a result, they have a consistent characteristic—to think about themselves first in any situation. How will this decision, program, or person affect me? Will this be good for my career? Will this get me recognition or visibility? Most Threes have highly developed egos that tend to affect the way in which they view themselves and other people. They can run the risk of being unusually self-centered or driven. Sometimes their egos appear to be strong but are indeed fragile, which may cause them to do such things as hide their mistakes or weaknesses in the organization, or make it look as if the mistake is someone else's fault. Making mistakes is hard on

Threes. They really like, almost more than anything else, to be right, which ultimately means to be perfect.

Realistic and Competitive

Threes know more about the rules and the games by which the organization functions than those at other stages. They make it their business to know. And it is important, because they have some external power now and must take their responsibilities seriously. In fact, if they are accepted over time by people above them, Threes may even be included in making the rules. The rules at Stage Three usually involve playing to win, beating the competition, and being the best. Otherwise you are considered weak and vulnerable to others who will surely take advantage of you.

In order to effectively move up in the organization, Threes must know who needs to know what and whom to have on their side. Even if they pretend to know, they can get by because they have become accepted. It reminds me of the old union leader who was talking to a younger member. He said "I don't care if you like the board members or not, but you've got to get them on your side to pass a motion." They operate on the reality, not on what ought to be. Some people call this company politics, while others refer to it as the only realistic way to get things done.

There is another group of Stage Threes who are a little more ruthless in the way they see the game. They play "hard ball," as the saying goes. They compete strenuously, volleying one person against another. In some organizations this method is the only way to stay alive because unfortunately, that's the only game that's played. But people don't last long in those organizations. Another "power player" is always at the top, and heads are rolling again. One organization fired its entire marketing department one day because of a wrong move by the director.

There is yet a third group of Threes, and they are most prevalent in organizations. They are the people who play only by the prescribed rules, say all the right things, wear the right clothes, go to the right places, entertain the right people, join the right clubs, chair the right community committees, cover the right mistakes, and take the right risks. But way down deep they're shallow. They have no depth of judgment or clarity of opinion. They just know that the name of the game is win-lose, and they are out simply to win. Without rules and roles they would flounder. An executive who has learned how to work with these people coined a wonderful term for rule players, whom he says he can always pick out at a meeting. He calls them "suits." He says the suits always say the expedient thing without thinking through the implications. They mouth the rules. A few years ago I heard a "suit" give someone advice on her doctoral dissertation: "Do whatever your committee says. Write exactly what they want you to write, even if you hate it. Pick something that you can finish in a year and grit your teeth. The important thing is to finish and get the piece of paper." The other person's response was that life is too short.

Expert

Many people have arrived at Stage Three because they have accumulated a lot of knowledge or expertise. Their symbol is the capacity of their mind or their depth of study. They gain control because they know more than others do about certain subjects. And they often use this to their advantage, for instance, by asking detailed or specific questions of others at meetings or by citing obscure facts and concepts from their store of knowledge. Lawyers, doctors, college and university professors, and ministers generally rely on this symbol for their power. In corporations engineers and financial analysts generally consider themselves the professional experts. Experts tend quite often to be responsible and hard working because that is what they have always been rewarded for. They can put out volumes of work and come up with intricate plans in a very thorough manner.

It becomes apparent sooner or later, however, that expertise in a particular subject does not suffice if one wants to gain more decision-making power (control and influence). Organizations are run by people who can manage well. Experts may think that to move up in the organization they must move to the management side and lose some of their expertise. Most organizations reward technical expertise quite highly, if it's kept up to date. But not all experts make good managers. At any rate, it is a key decision in their career. Choosing to remain in an area of technical expertise is in many cases a better decision, but it represents a perceived limitation in organizational power and takes reflective and introspective thinking to accomplish successfully. And these are qualities for which experts are not particularly noted.

Ambitious

It seems as if Stage Three people are perpetually in search of new challenges. This is as true of their personal lives as it is of their work. They love being given a problem that looks insurmountable, for it means that the opportunity as well as the reward will be greater. And the more visible the challenges are to others the better they feel. They may even thrive on taking risks. It gets their adrenalin going and gives them energy. In fact, they take enormous pride in their energy level and their ability to handle many projects or problems simultaneously.

One of the ways in which this sense of challenge emerges most interestingly is in Stage Three persons' choice of leisure activities. That same driving need for challenge permeates their choices in leisure, and they participate in the most unusual, demanding, or visible sorts of activities. Each event must be somehow greater than the last. Canoeing must be in whitewater; hiking must be in the mountains of some exotic place; being in nature must be at a survival level; running must be a marathon; driving must be racing; reading must be devouring best sellers. The event itself is exciting to Threes, but even more exciting is the opportunity to tell others about the experience.

Certain people in many organizations (mostly corporations) epitomize Stage Three and particularly identify with this idea of challenges and risks. This group is made up of people who move in the fast lane. They are highly visible, and they stand apart from other Stage Threes because they have been selected or programmed to move up. The pressure is on them to maintain their momentum, to take risks, to perform at a high level so they will not disappoint their sponsor or someone else, but most of all themselves. Since many of them are bright and well trained, they will not be satisfied until they have gone as far as they can go. It's as if they marry their work. They probably received their success programming as children. For the boys, it was not enough to play football, they had to be the most valuable player; not enough to be good, they had to be captain; not enough to be a good player and captain, but chosen all-conference; not enough to be chosen all-conference, but given a full football scholarship to a prestigious school. For the girls, it was not enough to get good grades, they had to be popular; not enough to be popular, they had to be cheerleaders; not enough to be cheerleaders, they had to be homecoming queen; not enough to be a queen, they had to date the football captain. It goes on and on, and carries over into their adult life. The pressure is enormous. But many "fast trackers" seem to thrive on it. The more action the better.

Success or perfection programming can be readily observed in the behaviors of parents. For instance, two fathers of high school students were talking to one another at a basketball game. The one said to the other, "Where did your son do his earlier work?" Another example comes from a newspaper article on sports, from the father of a ninth grader who had just pitched his fourth no-hitter of the season. He said "It was a good game, but I told Arthur not to let it go to his head. He can always do better."

In many ways the fast lane people are the most ironic of all Stage Threes because they appear to be the most successful, yet they have the most to lose. What happens to those who don't hold up, who break under the pressure, who suddenly get passed over because their sponsor fell out of favor? They may recoup, but generally the bruises are worse because they also have a longer way to fall. For all those who make it to that supreme goal—whatever it is—there are just as many who don't. The death of the dream is a very difficult experience to come to terms with. Sometimes their dreams fade when they lose their families due to neglect along the way, or the dream may die when their health fails them. Perhaps the most confused group are those who do make it to the top of the ladder and look over the landscape, only to discover out there the tops of other ladders and a lot of emptiness, as in the wonderful little book by Trina Paulus, *Hope for the Flowers*. Let me tell you yet another story with a different twist, of a woman in the fast lane from way back in history:

The King's Seamstress

Long ago in a faraway land lived a young woman who gained a reputation far and wide by being the finest seamstress in the country. She could make rags look like velvet and thread look like golden strands. She was very happy with her family and friends and loved her work. One day the king who had heard of her fine work asked to see her and some samples of her most elegant garments. She was elated and scurried to find her most superb coats and gowns. They were strewn with beautiful jewels and cords and were soft and luxurious to the touch. The king was pleased and asked the young woman to become one of the court seamstresses. Her dream had come true. She would be famous and would be able to serve the king and queen directly, with all her needs attended to. She was told that her family could not accompany her, and it was a great distance to her home from the castle. Still, after long thought, she could not pass up an offer to sew for the king. She packed up, said a tearful goodbye to her family, and started her new life in the castle of the king and queen.

All went well for several years. She was busy and made new friends among the seamstresses in the castle. She was so busy that she did not have time to visit her family, but she was in a different world now and they would have a hard time understanding her life. After one particularly complicated robe project she began to notice that her fingers were stiffening in the joints. It was harder and harder to do the fine detail work she had been known for. She became less and less adept at even the regular sewing. Eventually, the king had to make the difficult decision to dismiss her because she could no longer serve the court well. He was very kind and thanked her for her work, telling her that she could now return to her family and friends in the country.

When the time came for her to return home she was nowhere to be found. The whole court searched for the woman but to no avail. Finally a young boy who was playing among some remnants in the corner of a unused room came upon the woman wrapped up in a ball as though she were hiding. He told her that people were looking for her and that it was time for her to go back to her home. She tucked herself desperately under the fabric saying to him, "Please don't tell anyone where I am. Just leave me alone. This is where I want to die. Leave. Pretend you never found me. Please! Please!"

"But why?" the young boy said. "You can't stay here. It is time for you to go home."

"That is impossible," she wept. "I don't remember where I came from!"

Charismatic

Last, but certainly not least, there is a group of Stage Three people who get things done by the sheer force of their personalities. They are charismatic, which means having an inspired quality that captures allegiance and devotion. They can inspire people and even nations to follow their direction because people believe in them, and seem to want to be influenced by their ideas and vision. At times they may even seem divinely inspired. They leave a distinct impression on people they meet. We often project charisma on other people if we want to be inspired. I call it making people larger than life. This has happened most with people in political life and in sports.

But there is also a dangerous side to charisma. There is a thick line between people whose charisma comes from deep within and those whose charisma is a surface device used to get power or to control other people. Ego is the primary distinction. Stage Three charismatics are those who know they can use their personal qualities (or have developed qualities) in order to subtly control or direct others. And they can be very subtle.

This charisma occurs not only in business. It can occur wherever there is an opportunity for a following: among college professors, coaches, athletes, ministers, or parents. Often an unspoken message is behind their words: I will like you if you do this; I will give you good grades; I will take care of you; I will protect you; I will favor you. Often a subtle sexual message lingers somewhere behind their words, but they rarely admit to it. The message can also become overt, a request for sexual favors in exchange for personal help from them. It is particularly damaging when this sexual control is attempted by persons in the helping professions (counseling, teaching, ministry, etc.), because then these charismatic people are dealing with others when they are most vulnerable. Those in the helping professions should try to understand what kind of power they have over other people and how to handle it responsibly. It should not be abused, especially for the sake of building one's own self-esteem or ego.

Women and Stage Three

Women are certainly capable of operating at Stage Three, but they have had to make a conscious choice, a deliberate move to take on their masculine side in order to do so. For many women this is frightening, even a bit distasteful. They may think of it as giving up part of themselves rather than taking on a new part. As a high-ranking woman in a Fortune 500 company said, "Act like a woman, but think like a man." Unfortunately, some women also act like men at this stage, and they buy totally into the rules and games of the organization, thereby losing some of their own most worthwhile qualities. This is not to say that women cannot compete with men, but that they can do it in a style that represents another model, another way of being. Otherwise they are once again dependent upon men for their acceptance; being one of the boys is their goal. Women need to step back and look at themselves periodically to see if they have outwardly become someone who is incongruent with their inner selves.

Women need to *understand* the games—perhaps even respect them— but do not need to *play* all of them. They need to *understand* men in the organization, but do not need to *become* one. It is difficult because sometimes women feel they may fall behind if they don't get in there and "do battle." In the short run that may be true, but not in the long run. An example of this comes from two women managers in an organization who both worked for the same male boss. He had confided in each some disturbing news about the behavior of the other woman towards her. They were both confused because the behavior did not seem like that of either of them. After several days of thinking, one of the women went to the other confidentially to ask whether what she had heard was true. The other woman was very surprised and then related what she had heard about her colleague. They then figured out that they had been pitted against each other deliberately. It was one of the organizational games, or at least their boss's game. They decided they didn't like to operate that way, and both went together to speak with their boss. His initial reaction was, "I can't believe the two of you talked to each other about this!" Now he would have to find a different way of managing them because the old ways were not sufficient.

Stage Three is the biggest struggle for women in organizations, but they really can't afford to get stuck there. One way to avoid that is to talk regularly with women who see the larger picture, who have not lost their feminine side, and who are respected in the community and in the organization, no matter what their positions are. Test out ideas, moves, confrontations, dilemmas. Listen and learn. Resist the urge to know it all. Because women have not been pressured as greatly to "arrive" at

Stage Three, they may be the greatest hope for organizations to learn to move their leadership on to higher stages.

Men and Stage Three

Most men have been taught that they should "arrive" at Stage Three. It is considered the epitome of success. For many it is indeed a satisfying juncture. They have attained what they were aiming for. They fought the good fight, obtained the degree, achieved significance, won the race. They are ready for the next challenge, the next salary level, the stiffer competition. For some, work success is the only thing in life that matters, and one hears the tired and sad line, said to a lonely spouse, "But I'm only doing all of these things for you." That is difficult to swallow when it means one's spouse is never home, never has time for family events, always lets organizational priorities prevail. "Doing it for you" really means doing it for me, even if I think I'm doing it for you. Some men work to make a living, rather than making a living work.

Other men in Stage Three acknowledge that there is much more to life and many other arenas in which to achieve success: family, community, personal, intellectual, emotional, and political life.

And then there are the gentle men discussed in Chapter Two who struggle with the societal pressures to achieve Stage Three when it holds little appeal. Some of them truly are afraid and need to be supported to learn how they can be Stage Three men without totally buying into the predominating rules. Their issues are different from women's because women were mostly socialized to be at Stages One or Two, and to go beyond represents progress in our society even though some women would disagree. For men not to strive for Stage Three, which they've been pushed towards, means to settle for less or not to have succeeded in society's eyes—a more difficult pressure to withstand.

Let's Meet Some People at Stage Three

Pierre, the Foundation Executive

(Pierre gives us a glimpse of the still unquenched drive for success. He is confidently and hastily climbing the career ladder and will not stop until he reaches the top.)

I love my work. I feel like I'm married to it in all honesty. I eat, drink, and sleep work. What happens to this organization while I'm the director will mold my image in this community for the future, and I know the top jobs in the big foundations only go to people who have a strong track record. I intend to have more than that. I want a strong track record at a young age. I want to usher in a new era of foundation philosophy, but I can only do that when I'm at the top with enough power to pull it off. Right now I feel very successful, and I need to really capitalize on the areas of foundation work that will give me the most visibility. Right now that is in the area of evaluation models. The board is very interested in this, and I intend to become even more of an expert along the way. After we try out some models successfully I'll give a presentation at a national meeting on our experiences with evaluation. That will help the foundation, and it can't hurt me at all.

You know, I like being the head of something—in charge. I enjoy the challenge of managing other people and working with clients, the board, and employees. A clear distinction I've noticed about being at the helm is that other people's image of me changed. People defer more to me, listen more when I speak, and some try to stay on my good side more. I also get more flack, just because I'm the one who is in charge and who gets the blame for things. But I especially like the position I play in the community. I represent an enormous amount of financial power that other people want to benefit from. Essentially, they need to persuade me and my staff that their cause fits our mandate and the criteria we have for funding projects so we in turn will persuade the board. That very fact gives me a great deal of control, too much at times, over the direction of events and organizations. Sometimes what I say goes just because of my position. Now there is a discomforting side to that too. I can't tell from how people treat me whether they're being nice to me because of my position or because of who I am personally. Would they be different if I were not in a powerful position? I don't know, but as long as I like it, why worry about it?

Andrea, the Entrepreneur

(This entrepreneurial success story exemplifies how much success can breed a thirst for more. Some people get success only to be bored and eager for new challenges.)

> In a lot of ways my story might be typical of most business ventures. I was working for someone else in my mid-thirties. The work was OK, but my ideas went beyond where that company was at the time. It just so happened that I inherited a very small amount of money, but enough to suggest a risky venture. It was now or never, I thought, and the ideas I had for new products were sure to sell if I could get the capital to back me. I got my business plan together with the help of some financial wizards and started manufacturing a prototype in my basement because I was still working on my old job. I worked for months getting all the investors (including the bank) informed and relatively secure about the success of my venture. I recruited a management team and we waited and talked and persuaded. I'll never forget the day we signed the final agreements and we were official. I thought I had died and gone to heaven. Not for long though, because the real work was ahead. It took years of blood and sweat to make a success of our product and we did it. That all started nine years ago. Now the whole situation looks different to me. We grew pretty fast the first years, and, as many companies do, we sold out to a larger corporation. Now I'm miserable. All those years I'd been my own boss, making my own decisions, and getting instant feedback and rewards. Now I'm working for someonne else. They have the last word and all major financial investment are approved by them. There is no challenge left for me, and I'm too stubborn to kowtow to bureaucrats. After all, I made this company what it is. Now I feel like I'm being gently put out to pasture. That's not for me. I'm looking for something new to dig into, some new and bigger challenge, some mountain to climb. As soon as my obligation is over, I'm on my way.

Susan, the Minister

(Susan gives us an example of some of the questioning that occurs about

new careers and risk taking at Stage Three. She is breaking new ground
and testing whether her values and ways of solving problems fit with the
organizational culture.)

> No one told me in seminary that churches were so political. It
> makes corporations look mild by comparison. I was expecting to
> come and teach, preach, baptize, bury, and counsel people who
> would thank me and tithe generously. Those ideas were shattered
> during my internship year. Now that I've had my own church for a
> while, I must admit that I thought I could change some of the
> factors here that lead to politics and strife. I'm beginning to believe
> that it is the nature of life in the church. Now don't misunderstand,
> I like the ministerial functions very much and feel quite competent
> in them. It's just the extra administrative duties, heated committee
> and board meetings, budgets, and personality clashes that I wasn't
> ready for. There is always a small vocal group that disagrees, that
> wants control, that wants its way. I'm learning quickly how to listen
> better, negotiate, and stand firm in some cases. It's further compli-
> cated for me because there is a faction here that doesn't believe a
> woman can be a minister. They don't expect me to stand up for
> myself, to challenge them, or to be able to be a true sympathetic
> ear. Yet when critical events occur in their lives they are forced to
> involve me because I am their minister. It's a clash of traditional
> and new ways and it's difficult. Another example is that some men
> withhold financial information from me because they don't think
> I'll understand it. My ministry is giving me real opportunity to
> show my people that I am up to the challenge. I've got a plan and
> I'm determined to follow through with it. Right now, I'm just very
> conscious of being competent but different, capable yet outside. I
> know it'll just take time, but it can be exhausting along the way.

Pete, the Engineer

(Pete is an expert who is at a turning point in his career, wondering
whether he ought to go the technical route or the more seductive
managerial route that arrives closer to the top.)

I consider myself a top-flight engineer. I've had many good job assignments here and I am very loyal to this company. After all, I put in a lot of my time to prepare for this and I wouldn't want to change now. Too much water over the dam to do that now. But I'm at a real decision-making point in my career. I have always identified myself strongly with engineering. I've received recognition and rewards for my expertise in this field. Now that I've had success I look at what's happened to other guys like me in the past. If I continue to pursue the engineering route I will become more specialized and narrower but more of an expert in my work. And that track, even though it looks inviting, is not rewarded as much nor looked on as highly as the other managerial track. At least that seems to be the perception. On the other hand the managerial track is more of an unknown and more of a risk because it requires people management skills and less technical expertise. It feels like I'd have to start over in another field. And if I don't do well, I'll be obsolete as an engineer. I'm confident though that I can manage well. I'm just not sure what I want and what will be best for me. I want to weigh the risks but go beyond where I am to new challenges, whether it be on the engineering side or the managerial.

Marsha, the League of Women Voters President

(This example points out the joy and excitement that occurs when a person discovers new areas of confidence and learns to capitalize on them.)

When I first joined this organization I did it to get out of the house, frankly. And little did I know that lurking in there was a leader, wanting to get out. I quickly moved through the committee structure the first few years, doing a good job at every position and finding out all about the power structure of the organization. (I learned early on how to have a say in the league: Be in charge of a project that people support and which has high visibility, and do a good job.) Next thing I knew I was elected to the board and now had a role in the policy making and financial aspects of the league. There was a tricky year in there in which I wanted to run for vice-president (president-elect), but I didn't want to come out and ask for it. What happened was partly luck, partly planned. I had lunch with two influential board members, and during our conversations I briefly outlined for them my personal plan for the organization's future. They both figured strongly in my plan. When the discussion came up several weeks later about appropriate vice-presidents, one of them asked me if I would be willing to consider it. I said it looked like a lot of responsibility but I would like to give it a try. Now that I'm in the middle of my term, I look back and wonder how I could have considered anything else. The question is, where do I go from here?

Allen, the Product Manager

(Allen knows the rules and intends to play by them to WIN.)

There is a formula for success around here. You go to the right college, start out in the right department, and get a good boss. Then you work your tail off to prove how much you can work and how smart you are. Along the way, you get to know and be seen with a few influential people in and outside the company by playing sports, joining a country club, and being on a community board. The only other thing you need is a couple of lucky breaks. I think there are three rules for successful movement into the next job: observe the rules, don't cross your boss, and always be willing to take on more than you can handle. This means your work is number one and must remain so until you have reached the level you're aiming for, retirement as chairman of the board. After all, someone has to be at the top. I figure, why not me? There is nothing you can't have if you know how to get it. And there's always a way. The closest I've felt to this before was my high school hockey championship team. We were so good and so prepared, we knew we couldn't lose.

If you are intrigued with the symbols of power and the meaning they have in organizations, turn to Natasha Josefowitz's wonderful symbol list in her book. It describes the office location, space, desk size, floor covering, use of secretary, type of clothing of each level of management. Her book *Paths to Power* is a good description of the various responsibilities of different levels in the organization and how to attain them. Also Rosabeth Moss Kantor's book *Men and Women of the Corporation* gives an overall view of organizations and a guide to finding one's way through them, based on research and practice.

A Turning Point in the Personal Power Model

The movement from Stage Three to Four and beyond marks a distinctly different move from any that have preceded it. The first three stages have many trends or characteristics in common, and the last three stages do as well. It may be useful here to illustrate the main differences between them, so that as you begin to read Chapter Four you will understand why it will seem like such new territory—or a turning point.

Building Up, Then Letting Go

The first major difference between Stages One through Three and Four through Six is called "building up, then letting go." In Stages One-Three you work quite diligently at getting to know who you want to be, acquiring basic self-esteem, feeling good and confident, seeking recognition and affirmation. You find, capitalize on, and promote personal skills and strengths as well as any new skills and experiences you can accumulate. All these things build normally and naturally into the self-confident image of the Stage Three person. It's as if you've been filling a pitcher all along the way and now it is getting full.

In Stages Four through Six the story changes. Stage Four people begin to go deeply inside and encounter intense personal questioning and reacquaintance with their true selves. They begin to question the value of the full pitcher and even the value of the pitcher itself. After this crisis of integrity is understood they can proceed, as they move to Stages Five and Six, to letting go of having to be seen as strong, confident, perfect, and competent. They have found a deeper source of self-esteem that does not depend on external signals. Again, this reiterates that Stages One-Three are more externally-oriented even when it comes to inner journeys, while Stages Four-Six are more internally-oriented, but in touch with the world.

Finiteness of Power

Another major difference between Stages One-Three and Four-Six is the "finiteness of power." At Stages One-Three power is seen as *finite*. Remember the gold coin analogy? There are only so many to go around. If I have twelve coins and you take six, I will have only six left. I've lost power. Someone wins, someone loses.

At Stages Four-Six the idea of power is changing. It now appears to be *infinite*. Accepting that may take a little doing, which is why Stage Four is a transition stage in this respect. But infinite power suggests an ever-filling well from which to draw power. If I have twelve pieces of gold and by giving six away it not only increases your power but increases my own as well, then the win-lose status of power is lost. Empowering other people is a way to increase the total potential of power and spread it around. No one loses. Stages Five and Six people see themselves as conduits only, as channels of power to other people. They have no need to hang on to any of it themselves. It is like love: The more you can channel it to others, the more it multiplies.

From Tangible to Intangible

Another main distinction between Stages One-Three and Four-Six is that the first stages result mostly in tangible rewards, while the later stages reward people with intangibles. Skills, degrees, jobs, titles, material possessions, elected positions, salary, and homes are examples of Stage One-Three rewards. Intangible Stage Four-Six rewards might include understanding one's life purpose, integrity, empowering others, enjoying quietude, and thinking long term, peace of mind. That is why it is difficult to motivate Fours, Fives, and Sixes in traditional organizational ways. The motivations and rewards do not have the same meaning they used to.

Cultural Encouragement and Discouragement

Lastly, the culture is a strong influencing factor in the decisions of most of us when it comes to personal power. We are either trying to meet the cultural expectations and aspire to the positions that our socialization encourages (Stage Three for men, Two for women), or we are trying to rebel against the culture and deliberately change the goals that have been instilled in us. Either way we are still controlled by Stage Three ideals and models in our advertising, in our family, and in our social lives. Beyond Stage Three the situation gets more confusing. Because the predominant culture (laws, mores, customs, rewards) does not encourage or reward Stage Four-Six behavior, moving to these stages becomes more of a personal decision, a commitment to purpose, to service, to inner principles. It is a lonelier and less charted course, and most of the work goes on inside long before the behavior is apparent to people on the outside. It feels as if you are being asked to give up many of the things you've learned to want and strive for all these years. It's an about face in many ways. And you have to look inward before you can look outward again, not in a narcissistic way but in a self-healing way as is elaborated in the chapters on Stages Four and Five.

Moving to Stage Four

Contrary to what many of us would like to believe, you don't just sit down one day and decide to move or grow into Stage Four. Moving to Stage Four is more of an event than it is an achievement. Usually a change of this magnitude requires a crisis to precipitate it, especially for men who've been taught all their lives that being successful, strong, rich, famous, perfect, and masculine is the highest goal and reward in life. The crisis in moving from Stage Three to Stage Four is one of integrity, inner and outer congruity in life. The event that initiates it can be of internal or external origin, but it triggers a whole series of deeper, more serious questions, which are extremely painful to answer. They are questions such as, Who am I, really? What am I doing here? Where do I fit at work, home, in the community? Do I want to work? Can I trust myself? Can I remain (or get) married? Do I have more capability or am I plateaued? Who cares? The event may be a major or sudden illness (heart attack), being passed over for a promotion, losing at sports, discovering total boredom in life or on the job, falling out of love with your spouse, a significant birthday, losing energy, chronic depression, or it can be developing Inner Kill, which I call the art of dying without knowing it. Whatever the event is, it invites or propels the individual to enter the inner realm of self-knowledge and integrity. Integrity is simply a quality or state of being of sound moral principle, honest and sincere. The move from Stage Three to Four, because of the nature of the crisis, is perhaps the most critical turning point in one's life.

One man told me that he didn't realize until he was lying in the intensive care room following emergency heart surgery, that he never wanted to be in the successful family business that he had been in for twenty-five years. For the next several years he twisted and turned his life around, trying to find out who he was and what he wanted. Everything was up for grabs. He tried another line of work, had an affair, sold his house and lived on a beach, read a lot, wrote a lot, and tried a variety of counselors in the attempt to peel back all the crusty layers that had grown up around the real person he was inside. He caused himself and others a great deal of pain in the process. But he was determined to get the questions answered for himself before it was too late for him. He and his wife, who was, of course, having her own struggles during this time, survived these events and are now building a new life for themselves, more realistically and more genuinely than ever before.

I have just described one man's mid-life crisis. Not everyone will experience the events he did during the transition, and dramatic outward events are not required to prove what's going on inside. Nor can a mid-life crisis guarantee that everyone will take that opportunity to look at themselves closely and allow that experience to really change them. However, the mid-life crisis often coincides with a stuckness at Stage Three—the inability to get out of the trap and the added confusion of not knowing which questions to ask. It can be a frustrating and bewildering time for people who've ordinarily been competent, energetic, reliable decision makers. They don't trust their own judgment any more because they can't seem to focus enough to make decisions. They don't know what they really want or where they want to go. And the more others push them to get the answers, the worse it becomes.

It takes a courageous person to take on the struggle of knowingly moving from Stage Three to Stage Four. Men sometimes think just the opposite. They believe that introspection and discovering fears and other emotions are women's traits and are soft and weak. Being out of control is one of the worst things that can happen to a man. Many men will fight, ignore, shun, or ridicule the whole idea of discovering the fearful and wonderful world within. They will choose to stay in Stage Three by diving into their work to reach a higher level of success or by pushing themselves physically to prove their prowess. Or they will become drained and bitter over the confusion and lock up the inside, never to hear from it again. The pain of feeling is so great they turn off their feelings altogether. "Inner Kill" sets in; they withdraw from life and work; and then they die from the inside out both physically and emotionally.

To move to and through Stage Four men need to let go little by little of their stereotyped view of themselves and their prescribed roles in the world and cultivate their true feelings. They need to develop the qualities that they have not understood or have undervalued, qualities such as the ability to have deep relationships, to nurture others, to see longer range issues, to give to and cooperate closely with others. Men tend to negate personal growth, quality-of-life questions, values, feelings, intuition, flexibility, and adaptability. These are the qualities that will help men balance out their masculine side with their other side (the feminine side) that has been dormant for so long. This does not make them weak; it makes them whole.

Another man shared his transition story with me illustrating another view of the change. He felt that he was being controlled in a negative way. He was possessed by his job and his habits. He noticed this one night when he couldn't get himself up from watching TV, even though he wanted to. He observed the same things about work. He set appointments to do recreational things and then let work infringe on them frequently, even though he didn't want it to. Success at work and the power it brought compensated for the lack of meaning in his life.

First he gradually withdrew from TV, newspapers, and other controllers like coffee. That only made matters worse because now he craved TV and coffee constantly. Finally he had to admit the craving was overwhelming. He went to talk to his priest about the escalating problem. He recognized that his was a spiritual struggle, that power for him covered the fear of confronting death. Now he had to let go of his expectations for his life and start afresh. It was difficult, but he says that "in letting go totally, everything came back in a fresh form, my work, my life, my family." He spends more time alone now, is better balanced, understands his other side better, has moved to a new position with more responsibility but less weekend work, laughs at himself more, is calmer, and is excited about life.

To move to Stage Four women have to reconfirm themselves, their sense of the balance between the masculine and the feminine. At this point they have had some recognition or success at Stage Three and have been acknowledged by the system sufficiently to feel they can compete in it, but not so much that they drown in it. They now have to balance the behaviors they took on at Stage Three with the inner qualities of being a woman and find the style that suits their real self. Some women have told me that this means they have to move to another company to capitalize more effectively on their competence, or it may mean splitting off from a mentor or model who is no longer necessary. More often it means being involved in a broader sphere of activity in which they can develop their style without so much pressure from their part of the organization. It means getting a broader view of themselves. It's time to establish who they are, apart from everyone else. Some women may experience some lingering doubts at this stage because they may wonder whether they are the token woman or whether they really are respected for who they are and what they can do. At this point it is helpful for women to seek leadership opportunities inside and outside the organization that will broaden their visibility and base of influence, like community boards, organization-wide committees, professional groups, or broadly based civic groups.

At Stage Four, both men and women move beyond jobs and titles to credibility, respect, reputation, and experienced judgment. You begin to develop and trust your own personal style which capitalizes on strengths and acknowledges weaknesses, for both are there. Your spheres of contact become broader because you are less afraid of people who are different from you. You see them as people to learn from, not people who might be trying to outsmart you.

Here are some specific ways to move to Stage Four:

- Learn how to be alone with yourself. Go on a long day trip by yourself and see whether you fill it with activities or have some quiet moments to think about larger issues.
  - Learn to sit quietly and listen to your thoughts without having to get anxious.
  - Learn to express yourself through a journal in which you can write anything and everything.
- Do some serious self-assessment.
  - Ask yourself whether you want to be the person you represent at Stage Three. If so, fine. If not, admit to yourself that you aren't who you want to be.
  - Ask yourself the questions that were mentioned in the middle of this chapter, on page 63.
  - Read books or attend seminars on the mid-life reassessment time: *Seasons of a Man's Life* (Levinson), *In Her Time* (Sangiuliano), *Transformations* (Gould), *Passages* (Sheehy), *Middle Age Crisis* (Fried), *Against the Grain* (Moitland), *The Inventurers* (Hagberg, Leider).
  - Make a list of the things your parents would want you to do with your life. Circle the items you don't want to do. Think through the implication of this for your present life/work situation.
  - Learn to be honest with yourself.
- Try new things that will make you think differently. Read widely in the arts, literature, and science to stimulate your creative mind. Keep an open and active mind, especially about things you think you know a lot about.
  - Create or rent a crisis in your life to get you "off the dime."
  - Push yourself into an experience in which you are out of your element. Try a workshop, a trip to another country, a physical experience. Do it quietly, not with the gusto of a Stage Three. Examine its effect on your thinking. Reflect on it, write about it, and let it sink in.
  - Get out of the rut of daily activities you're in. Develop a hobby, read in new areas, get on a board in the community, write a column for the newspaper.
- Get support if you need it.
  - Start a men's or women's group to talk about work or personal issues.
  - Find a new mentor or begin being a mentor to others.

- Seek out a counselor, priest, minister, rabbi, or a good, patient friend to talk through the things you're feeling. Choose someone who is beyond Stage Three in your opinion.
- Build on your networks.
  - Broaden your range of contacts in the organization and outside the organization by getting yourself on broader organizational committees and tasks. Think quality, not quantity.
  - Keep track of old friends and contacts in the organization so you can help them out whenever possible.
  - Test out your leadership skills in professional or civic association leadership positions, being who you really are, and then let your management see how you are respected outside the organization too.
- Concentrate on the present and not on the future.
  - Build on the reputation you have secured in order to work on projects you like and are good at. Don't take on things that will move you ahead in your work if you sincerely are not good at them or do not like them.
  - Accept the challenge of broadening your job and deepening yourself rather than fussing about not moving or looking around for other jobs.
  - Have a long talk with your boss about what you do best, like best, and can learn from on your present job.
- Reflect on the types of people who are at Stage Four.
  - Write the names of people you know whom you respect the most for the quality of their judgment and their personal integrity. Are these the same as the people in your organization who have the best jobs? What qualities of the most respected people would you like to have that you don't have now? Talk to one or two of them about how they acquired those qualities.

In an article entitled "The Things You Know After You Know It All" John Gardner says:

The things you learn in maturity seldom involve information and skills. You learn to bear with the things you can't change. You learn to avoid self-pity. You learn not to burn up energy in anxiety. You learn that most people are neither for nor against you but rather are thinking about themselves. You learn that no matter how much you try to please, some people are never going to love you—a notion that troubles at first but is eventually relaxing.

As you can imagine, Allen, the product manager, Andrea, the entrepreneur, and Pierre, the foundation executive, are still madly climbing. Marsha, the league president, has decided to go back to school to study public administration. She enjoys the practical side of running an organization and now sees her children getting to the age where she can invest more concentrated time in school. She hopes to manage in government or be a director of a non-profit agency someday.

Pete, the engineer, got himself involved with a management assessment center and found out that his people skills would have to be developed extensively to compare with his fine technical expertise. He decided it would be too much of an effort to do that at this stage when he is just getting into the enjoyment of his expertise. He's decided to stay in project engineering and broaden his professional base by presenting more papers and getting on the board of his professional group. He's also going to take a month-long vacation to Europe with his wife this fall.

Susan decided to have a series of long-range planning sessions with her church board to help get her plans into effect. There were some very tense times along the way when she sensed people's doubts about her abilities, but enough strong people supported her to turn the tide. Now she has to get the plan implemented.

What Holds People Back?

People at Stage Three are most frequently stuck because they think they aren't. They think they've made it to the top or are on their way, so they don't need to move anywhere but up. They are very comfortable and do not want to be upset or stopped. One man said, after hearing the stages, "I don't want to know anything about Stage Four or Five. I like it at Stage Three, and I'm not finished with it yet."

The second major factor that interferes with their move—but only after they know they are dissatisfied with Stage Three—is confusion over everything. Confusion is a blinding light that they can't switch off. They have hidden their weaknesses and covered their other side (males especially) for so long that the process feels at first like excavating in a very old and deep mine. The confusion is perplexing; it lasts far longer than their patience or time permits; the solutions seem to come only from inside; and no one else can tell them what to do. The only redeeming quality may be that others have been through it and usually find themselves better off after it's over. One woman said, "One of my friends reminded me when I was in the middle of all this that it was a great growth experience. It's hard to see that when you're in the middle of it. Ask me in a year whether it was a growth experience or not."

But eventually the confusion subsides and life takes on a vastly broader potential after the hump is crossed at Stage Three.

SUMMARY OF STAGE THREE
power by symbols

SYMBOL

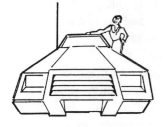

DESCRIPTION
control
the dynamo stage

CHARACTERISTICS
ego-centric
realistic and competitive
expert
ambitious
charismatic

CRISIS OF MOVEMENT
integrity

WHAT HOLDS PEOPLE BACK?
not knowing they're stuck
confusion

WAYS TO MOVE
Learn to be alone and to seriously reflect on yourself, try new things that make you think differently, get support from a Stage Four, Five, or Six person, build networks, concentrate on the present, be reflective about the next stages

Ask yourself these questions about Stage Four:

Yes No

1. Do you take pride in your solid record of competent work?
2. Are you consciously choosing to be a mentor to other people?
3. Do you feel as if you have a life going on inside of you that is distinctly different from the one on the outside?
4. Have you consciously chosen to act with integrity?
5. Do you think beyond your current job and peers as part of your base of influence, i.e., community, professional leadership, political arena?
6. Is it important for you to have a natural and personal style that is yours and not what the organization expects?
7. Have you had a major crisis or triggering event in your life that has challenged the way you think about life and work?
8. Do you find that the symbols of success do not flatter or motivate you the way they used to?
9. Have you learned to admit weaknesses and mistakes readily?
10. Do you acknowledge both feminine and masculine behavior as useful, depending on the situation, and use them appropriately?
11. Do you ever feel you are different from or out of touch with others in the organization?
12. Do you speak out when you are asked to do something you don't believe in?

Yes answers indicate that you identify with this stage.

Chapter 4

Stage Four: Power by Reflection

Influence

What Is Stage Four Like?

Power by reflection. What does that mean? "Reflection" itself suggests at least two different meanings. The meaning of being a mirror or image is especially fitting to Stage Fours. They reflect more accurately than ever before their own competence and their own style of operating, as opposed to the organizational style. They are more congruent. Also people who work or live around them begin to mirror or reflect their behavior as well. They trust Fours and often choose them for mentors. Fours have a solid reputation of honesty, fairness, sound judgment, and follow-through—in a word, *integrity.*

Reflection also means contemplating or pondering. Fours are entering into a self-reflective stage that will not be readily apparent on the outside. As a result of whatever experience or crisis they had in moving out of Stage Three (and usually it was a personal crisis), they will never be the same again. In fact, the more accepted and respected they feel for what they are doing the less important it becomes and the more confused they are. This is a stage of confusion on the inside and assuredness on the outside. I think of it as the sandwich stage, because Stage Fours feel caught between their own outward show of competence and their inner dilemmas, just as they are caught between clear and straightforward Stage Three and mystifying Stage Five. And so the problem that needs to be addressed is one of integrity, i.e., soundness or wholeness.

Stage Fours no longer want to play by all the rules, for they realize it doesn't reward them as much. Now that they are developing their own style and way of being, they wonder if they are out of touch, too different, or fooling themselves. They have not yet emerged as inwardly confident people, yet they look very polished and competent to others. They are undergoing a reassessment, which causes them to be a bit more humble and possibly more tentative. A good analogy is that of a trapeze artist. A Stage Four person is in the precarious moment of the trapeze act when she or he has let go of one swinging bar and is floating through the air, waiting for the other bar to come swinging along. He or she has not yet completed the act and is filled with expectancy, a bit of anxiety, and confidence.

Stage Four people have become more secure primarily because they have established a record, a long history of competence, expertise, respect, honesty. They are not living from one promotion or raise to the next, because life seems too short for that. They generally trust themselves and others much more and rely on informal contacts within the organization more than on any formal reporting structure.

The symbol for this stage is the reflective thinker, which emphasizes the importance of spending time reflecting and thinking, listening and questioning—mostly inside. It is a time for deeper exploration, for raising questions about self, life, and work that may have been lying dormant or have never been raised before. Stage Fours may even appear at times to be taking a sabbatical from work or life. Fortunately, this does not go on forever and the Four reemerges slowly as a more integrated person. The outer and the inner begin to integrate through this struggle.

Stage Fours have influence, and that is the definition of power at this stage. People respect their advice, come to them for counsel, want their recommendations, and invite them to plan with them, no matter what level they happen to occupy in the organization. One's reputation can spread several levels upward in the organization just by casual reference.

However, the appearance of influence or reputation alone should not be mistaken for Stage Four behavior. Stage Fours influence people because of their fairness, follow-through, honesty, and unwillingness to be self-serving.

Compare this wise-counsel type of influence, for instance, with the type of influence that we call political clout, that which is obtained through large contributions to political candidates or by rubbing elbows with those in office. Although that is one form of influence, the more substantive influencers in politics are those who keep themselves out of the limelight and help the candidate see both sides and the long-term implications of issues so as to make the best decision for the greatest good. Partisanship can get in the way of making difficult decisions, especially for politicians who seek the good of the constituency over their own parties or egos. One governor recently stated, "Until I decided not to seek reelection, we could not get the two parties to work together on some difficult budget decisions. I decided it was the price I had to pay to get a fair solution."

It is impossible to describe Stage Four people by the positions they hold within the organization. They cannot be identified by symbols or specific status but by how they interact with others. For instance, it would not be unusual to hear this comment about a Stage Four person regarding an important committee assignment: "If you are serious about that committee's objective, make Jane the chair. She won't be shoved around, but at the same time she is fair and listens to everyone. She always seems to forge compromises that almost everyone can live with because she has no flag of her own to wave." We've all heard words similar to these. Someone else may be technically more qualified or have more prestige, but if you want it to be done fairly, give it to a person who is not unduly biased and who will listen.

At Stage Four true leadership occurs, separate from position or status leadership. People in status positions *can* be leaders but are not automatically leaders because of their positions. Stage Four people are known for being natural leaders, those who just emerge from the group but are not the self-promoting types. Fours emerge as leaders because they have integrity as they plan, organize, listen to others, help work out solutions, and think up good ideas. True leaders must have a true followership, who will follow because they trust the leader's integrity, not because they were manipulated by threats, theatrical persuasion, or by the power of a position that forces them to follow. True leaders have long-term followership because they give more and more of the power to the followers, and are not short-term, self-perpetuating people.

Characteristics of Stage Four People

Competent

Stage Four people have proven beyond most doubt that they can be counted on to get the job done well. They follow through on tasks, they are honest and sincere, and they do what they say they will do. This is unusual in many organizations. That's why they stand out. Certainly they may be conscious of the fact that they may be promoted if they do a good job, but they do a good job mostly because it is a mark of personal pride. They do things because they are the "right" things to do, and because at the same time this way of acting brings its own rewards. If they feel strongly that they are being asked to do something they don't believe in, they usually have enough courage to speak out. On the other hand, they are not petty perfectionists, who never finish anything because it could always be better. They have learned the art of delegation, and they know the balance between undereffort and overkill. So Stage Fours are respected by others because of who they are over the long run. Someone has said they're like high-quality classic cars. They may not be the most glamourous cars, but they are made better, last longer, and don't go out of style. And they give a good return on one's investment over the long term, even though they seem to cost more initially.

Because they can be trusted, Stage Four people usually have or can get access to more resources and information in the organization, particularly through the informal network. Generally, they are trusted with information because people know from experience they will not use it against them. This is true at all levels for Stage Fours, whether they be secretaries, managers, or directors. Even though Stage Fours are impatient with power plays and organizational games, they see politics as the way many people get things done in the organization. They don't choose to play along totally, but they are not naive. They recognize the maneuvers, and they act according to their own best judgment. They know the rules, but if they don't choose to follow them, they also take responsibility for the results. They can say no and be unafraid of the risk it represents. They no longer have the same stakes as they did at Stage Three.

Reflective

Few are aware of the battle that goes on within Fours. It is fought between their outer reputation and their inner questioning. Since the movement from Stage Three to Stage Four was precipitated by a reassessment, Fours find it difficult to escape the gnawing internal questions: How can I be more myself in this organization? Now that the old goals are less intriguing, what do I want next? What will my peers think when they find out I'm more vulnerable? How can I find more *balance* in my life—to let family, friends, and community become more important and work take a more realistic place? How will I live up to the trust that people have in me? Do I want to stay here? How will this new person within me behave? Can I admit my weaknesses now or even laugh at them? Can I be helpful to this organization with my newfound sense of self, or will they think I have lost the spark? Am I too driven? These and other questions will continue to be asked all through Stage Four despite the competent behavior that may appear on the outside.

The armor has cracked. The true self is beginning to emerge. The old rules are changing, and the new rules are being written from inside. Most of the growth and change occurring at this stage is on the inside. And it can be a roller coaster experience: One day the world all fits together; the next day it all falls apart. The consistency on the outside is mocked by the confusion on the inside. It's like being in a revolving door with one half going out, and the other half coming in. The outwardly firm direction and decisions are backed by a cloud of gray at times inside, yet the balance for most people is maintained, and the debate is largely a silent one. This is especially true for men who, while feeling more open and questioning, have not been taught how or given permission to talk about it. This results in brooding, moodiness at times, seduction by distractions that will help to avoid the issue, easy solutions, frequent changes of inner plans, long fantasies and daydreams. People tell me that if their peers knew what they were thinking, they would be shocked and amazed. Some say they feel they're losing their stuff, shrinking, drying up, even dying. They believe they have nowhere to turn and no one to understand them. Admitting to limitations, truths about self, pain, sadness, fantasies, need for care and love is extremely difficult for us all, but men struggle more with themselves at this stage.

This ability to admit to human limitations and to be able to let go of the need to be in control is one of the major factors that distinguish Stage Fours from the previous stages emotionally. The impulse to be in control, to take charge, is still strong, and Fours constantly struggle with it. Running things has always been their practice, and it has worked well most of the time. But now they are learning from a slow inner process that life and work are really not controllable ultimately, and they are beginning to feel there is a different way to be. Unfortunately, Fours are not certain what that way is; so they let their reputation speak for them while they sort it out. (We'll see later that the obstacle is mostly a matter of ego.) But eventually a slow acceptance of humility and patience appears that has never been felt before. One man said, "I felt as if I had a flat tire and no way to fix it, so I had to learn to walk or take the bus. I couldn't race around as much, and I learned a lot about myself and other people in the process."

Men are going through a process that includes taking on their feminine side, of accepting themselves as whole persons with the warmth and emotions, intuition and inner strength of the feminine as well as the analytical, competitive, intellectual qualities of their masculine side. When men take on their more feminine qualities—sensitivity, nurturing, intuition, thoughtfulness, long-range thinking, caring, giving—they sometimes feel as if they are "going soft." This is a particular dilemma until they realize that there's nothing wrong with having softness in your repertoire. For men, the pendulum seems to swing toward the feminine so far that they sometimes fear they will lose their identity in a world that rewards the masculine so strongly.

For many women, another movement is taking place. Women have lived longest in the most feminine stage (Stage Two), have taken on the masculine (Stage Three), and now they must reaffirm or accept in a different way the feminine in them to avoid becoming "honorary men."

Again like a pendulum, women make a swing to the masculine side in Stage Three, then at Stage Four they struggle to return to a more comfortable place. It may feel to them as if they must give up some of the rewards of Stage Three, but women find the rewards of Stage Four more satisfying. If they were able to manage being *in* Stage Three but not *of* Stage Three they can now move on and restore their balance more quickly at Stage Four. They are now able to use both masculine and feminine behavior appropriately, depending on the situation. This comfort with flexible behavior does not occur in men until Stage Five.

Whereas men were teachers or models for women at Stage Three, women are teachers and models for men at Stage Four. The wisest men I know have said they learned the most important things about themselves—both personally and interpersonally, as adults—from women. Some say this is because it is less threatening to talk to a woman or that men do this to seduce women or to feel taken care of. These are possibilities. But also many men seek or crave inner strength in women at Stage Four and beyond. Men know there is something more there that goes beyond the stereotyped roles in which they can get stuck, but they truly do not know how to find it on their own. This is why it is so sad to see women content to be "honorary men," stuck at Stage Three forever. It's an interesting case for choosing different counselors and mentors for different stages of one's own development. For example, female mentors might understand better how to move from Stage One to Stage Two, whereas male mentors might be more helpful when learning how to move to Stage Three. Beyond that, the most critical consideration is that the home stage of the mentor be beyond one's own.

This struggle for identity can be equated in some ways to the apprentice stage, Power by Association. One may again sense the feeling of new learning, dependency, watching others, discovery, unsureness, or tentativeness. With Twos the outward skills and behaviors dominate, while with Fours the newness is deep and internal. Fours are in a training period preparing them for another real turning point, but they have the advantage of an organizational front that shields them from the vulnerability of Stage Twos.

Strong

Fours are perceived as strong, nearly invulnerable people. They are seen as solid and usually consistent. People know them and trust them. Fours can afford to be forthright and honest with people because they feel little fear of reprisal and much outward confidence in handling situations. Because they've been through several stages they may understand more clearly the motivations of people at Stages One through Four. That is a distinct advantage for them in managing others if they are at all alert. The president of one company said, "There are certain people I talk to who I know will always tell me what they think I want to hear, and then there are those I can trust to tell me what they really think. Get as many of the latter working for you as possible."

Fours are still greatly aware of themselves and their role in the organization. They are a part of the system and must be aware of whom to help and in what ways, but they may not act it out as blatantly as at other stages. Fours are learning to increase their influence and reputation by broadening their base of contacts into the community and by sharing power with selected people. They are still aware of power as control, rules, and games for many, and they haven't fully accommodated their emerging belief that power is infinite. A good way to describe them is that they have self-esteem, but they are not guided as closely by their ego as they were before.

The following story fits Stage Four people for a variety of reasons. The king, the witch, and Sir Gawain all illustrate some aspect of the stage in different ways. Saying more will spoil the story. You think about it. The story is very old, so we will have to overlook the female imagery to get to the broader message.

King Arthur's Dilemma

Long ago, King Arthur ruled the land. He was out riding one day and was taken by surprise by a horseman, who came out of the woods and knocked him from his horse. The enemy knight was about to behead him when he noticed it was the King. He thought for a second and offered the King a reprieve from death if he could find the answer to a riddle and return in one year with the solution. The King gladly consented to the offer and asked what the riddle was.

"I want you to find the answer to the question, 'What do women want?' " said the knight.

"Well, that shouldn't be impossible," answered the King. So he went back to the castle pondering how he could solve this riddle.

(Before you read on, stop and think about that riddle. What *do* women want? What would you say is the correct answer?)

King Arthur wasted no time in calling in Sir Gawain, one of his most trusted knights, to tell him of the surprising task they had to fulfill. Sir Gawain was amused and quite confident that together they could find the correct answer to the riddle. Gawain set off across the land to ask all the people he could what they thought the answer to the riddle was. He went to the wisest people, the street people, the hunters, and the priests. He searched everywhere for the answer. He searched for a whole year without ceasing, and at the end of the time both he and the King had to admit that no single answer seemed to them adequate to answer the riddle. They were crushed.

They started off together on their journey to meet the knight, thoroughly discouraged and perplexed. As they were riding slowly along, out of the woods came a strange figure. As they got closer they could see that it was a witch. And what a witch! She was so ugly she had warts on her warts. And she walked all scrunched over, carrying a big black crooked stick.

The witch stopped them and said in her scratchy voice, "I hear that you are looking all over the land for the answer to a riddle."

"Yes, we certainly have been," offered the King sadly, "but we have given up at this point."

"Well, I have great magical powers. I know right now the answer to your riddle," said the witch.

"Well, do tell us," answered the King, brightening up a bit.

"But I want the hand of Sir Gawain in marriage if the answer I give you is correct," said the witch, looking directly at the knight.

"I could never ask that of one of my most trusted knights," the King retorted. "That would be like sentencing him to life imprisonment."

"It's your choice," replied the witch.

At this point Gawain broke in and said, "King Arthur, the choice is the possibility of your life being lost in a duel or my life being altered by marriage to this witch. There is no alternative. Allow me to marry the witch in exchange for the answer to the riddle."

"This is very hard for me. I will only go along with it if it is truly your wish and you are being honest with me," responded the King.

"Yes, this is truly what I wish," stated Gawain soberly.

"All right, you get your terms." The King turned to the witch. "Now tell us the answer to the riddle."

"I would like to wait until we meet the knight," said the witch smiling once again.

So off they rode, the three of them each pondering a different thing in their minds. They arrived at the assigned place, and very shortly the knight arrived. He looked surprised that three of them were there.

"Well, King, do you have the answer to the riddle, 'What do women want?' " asked the knight.

"Yes, we think we do," offered the King, glancing at the witch.

"The answer to your riddle," droned the witch, "is simply this: Women want sovereignty, to have independence and the ability to make choices."

"I am amazed," responded the knight. "That is exactly correct."

King Arthur and Sir Gawain were elated that the answer was correct and were anxious to start back and announce to the people that the King's life had been saved. Then they looked at the beaming face of the witch and it sank in. Now she was to be the wife of Sir Gawain. But, refusing to go against their honor, they put her on their horse, and they all started back to the castle.

It was a glorious return. The story was told throughout the land, and there was celebrating everywhere. But soon came the time to go through with the commitment that the King had made to the witch.

The marriage was performed right there in the castle. And Gawain weathered the whole thing quite well. Alas, their wedding night came as it was bound to, and Gawain was about to perform his husbandly responsibilities. But just then, the witch stopped him.

"Now, you know that I have supernatural powers," stated the witch. "Let me pose a dilemma for you on the eve of our first day of marriage: I will turn myself into a beautiful woman for you, one of the most beautiful women you have ever seen. But you must make a choice. Either you can have me beautiful by day and a witch by night, or you can have me beautiful by night and a witch by day. Which will you choose?"

(Before you continue, what do you think Sir Gawain will choose? What do you think most men would choose?)

Sir Gawain sat back and pondered the choice for a while. He thought over what had gone on in the recent past and mused about his future briefly. Then he said with a twinkle in his eye, "I would really like for you to choose which you would most like to be, beautiful by day or by night."

The witch was obviously pleased with his response, and she too reflected on the events and the decisions of the last days. Then she looked sweetly at Sir Gawain and said with the same twinkle in her eye, "Because you have given me the choice, I will choose to be beautiful both by day and by night."

(This King Arthur story is a pre-wedding story passed on from one generation to the next.)

Comfortable with Personal Style

Stage Fours have developed or perhaps accepted their own personal style of doing things that may or may not fit with the most prevalent organizational norms. This may emerge in the hours they work, their management style, demeanor, or sense of humor. In fact, many Fours have now become respected and accepted despite their obvious differences in many areas. These would include age, sex, race, personal appearance, working habits, educational background, level of income, and length of membership. They know more who they are and are more comfortable with it. One woman remarked, "I was so relieved when I realized that classic clothes are really me. They're feminine but serious, comfortable and understated. I don't have to worry about being in or out, just clean and pressed. It's a little more boring but so much less bother. I spend only thirty seconds deciding what to wear and devote more time to other more important things."

For some Fours their style becomes part of their trademark. Clothes, briefcases, demeanor, voice, hairstyle, laugh, sense of humor, and mannerisms become part of the portfolio of the person. People at other stages have a style too; they try out various styles or change them frequently, attempting to find what the organization rewards, as opposed to what suits them. But their style is frequently not as congruent as is the Stage Four style.

Fours can do at least two things better than people at stages preceding them. First, they can admit mistakes without having to be found out first. They may have to think about it for quite some time, but they can handle the loss of pride in being able to admit mistakes to others. Second, because of their style and respect, they can take more risks and be more courageous. There are few heroes in organizations any more because

people are generally too oriented to power or security to take risks. Stage
Four people have the confidence, reputation, and competence to be
heroic. They'll take the risks in a different way than they would have
before. Taking risks means feeling scared, not knowing the outcome.
And it could mean losing. Stage Fours don't have as much to gain or as
much to lose as they did before. They think about the outcomes more
broadly than win or lose. They think about the change that will occur
either way. Stage Fours can disagree, stand alone on issues, give in, if
necessary, without harboring as much resentment, and build support for
others. There are more alternatives available to them and more chances
for true heroism and leadership.

Stage Fours need to be continually aware of two dangers. The first is
represented by a behavior that occurs among some Fours who are
struggling deeply inside to shed Stage Three and looking with more
vision toward things to come. They subtly accumulate power for themselves, even though their outside behavior may appear to be in support of
others. It is alluring to use the old rules and the new respect to quietly
build larger spheres of influence, that is, more and more people who can
be obliged to them. It assures them that if the new way of being doesn't
work, all will not be lost.

Influence and coalition building on the one hand are a good way to get
things done far more effectively than force or coercion, but some Fours
fall into the trap of making a Stage Three type game out of the use of their
newly emerging influence. In the end they emerge as the star, having
been seduced by their own goodness, and the power has not been spread
around at all. This occurs mainly because they become fearful of going
deeper, of really touching beneath the surface, of asking themselves
once again who they really are, how they want to live and work, and what
is important in their lives. Fours learn very deeply at this stage that one's
reputation is all one has in life; it is easily damaged and not so easily
regained.

It is important for Fours to build worthwhile and common sense
coalitions or networks in and outside the organization or family, because
these webs of support are necessary for leadership. These networks
include community, professional, social, religious, and political contacts and are most effective when they involve real issues that are of
interest or importance and where solutions can be found for problems.

It's also these networks need to be nurtured continually or they will weaken.

The second danger that Fours need to be aware of is more difficult to describe because it can grow out of behavior that appears to be altruistic. Many Fours have a need for continuity, for things that are less transient than most things in life appear to be. They have a need to build something that extends beyond themselves. This could be the development of a program, the planning of a strategy, the purchase of equipment, the starting of a business, the donation of time and money to a project, the chance to reorganize a department, the building of a company, or the writing of a book—something that will represent them and carry on at least in memory after they've moved along.

Stage Fours are seeking more meaning from their work than they get from position, promotion, and money. They want to know that what they are doing makes good sense and that it will be worth the effort. It's not enough to follow directions and have little personal investment any more. So Fours choose their priorities well, and they discipline themselves to work toward those that have the most usefulness and assurance of long-term continuity. It may take time and much patience but it's worth the effort. The danger then comes in the results of their work. They may inadvertently put themselves on a pedestal or allow others to do so if they are not careful. Others may begin to idolize them, emulate them, and generally attribute unreal characteristics to them. While this may be rewarding for a time, it can eventually hurt these individuals and make their projects appear self-serving. Those same people who have built the pedestal often grow to resent the person on top and begin to chisel away at his or her feet. One woman described this as being a "thermometer" for other people. When people felt good about themselves they felt good about her, and when they felt bad about themselves they resented her. She hadn't changed, but was feeling the pain of others' perceptions of her. Fours can take themselves off the pedestal by sharing more of their humanness, their foibles, their goals, and their pains with others.

Skilled at Mentoring

Fours make very good mentors. They still have stakes personally in the organization, but they can be fairly objective with individuals—

especially those at apprenticeship stages. And they are probably willing to be a mentor to a variety of people, not just those who are racing to the top. Mentors are wise, objective, and gifted advisors who can look at work and life from a broad perspective. They desire the fullest development of the other person, yet they do not plan an exact path to follow. Mentors ask hard questions but do not always expect answers. One of the most rewarding experiences of a Stage Four is mentoring. It not only provides Fours with challenges and occasional successes but also a larger network of influence. Women at Stage Four find they get satisfaction as well as visibility by mentoring both older and younger poeple at all levels in the organization. Notice I said individuals. While Stage Threes are busy getting known by the *positions* they hold in professional and community groups, Stage Fours are respected for the *personal* effects they have on individuals in these arenas. Gaining respect takes longer this way, but it is longer lasting. You can see that longevity becomes increasingly a factor for Fours—being around for a longer time and working through proven competence. It is difficult for a person who is moving from one job to another all over the country every two years to become a Stage Four person.

Stage Fours may go beyond mentoring to become personal counselors for people who are going through the crises and questions of life and work. This can be useful to a point or it can be problematic. Being a good listener, a sounding board, or a catalyst for personal change may be helpful, but one must recognize when one is no longer professionally qualified to help or when the help has become a block or hindrance. One boss I talked with had become involved as a counselor in the personal problems of an employee only to find out they went much deeper than he thought. When the employee tried to commit suicide he felt guilty and responsible. It was a difficult lesson to learn, but now he says he knows when he should cease being a listener and advisor and become a referral agent.

Because Stage Four people have started taking the inner road, they may be quite misunderstood by others when they try to explain what's happening to them. It's difficult to explain in understandable terms to a Stage Two or Three person the process of letting go, of reevaluating goals, of getting to really know oneself. First, these are not the major motivations and values of persons at Two and Three, and second, trying to explain the process somehow sounds trite, easy, or even shallow. Many Fours find one or two persons to act as their mentors and then resolve to live with some loneliness for a time as a result. In fact, the loneliness becomes a friend and changes to aloneness—the feeling of being alone and feeling all right. Unfortunately, many former friends (and some spouses) are lost in the move from Stage Three to Four because of the rather dramatic shifts that are occurring inside, especially within men. All these factors make this stage the most difficult one for men.

Showing True Leadership

Stage Four is the first stage that can be labeled as *true* leadership as opposed to traditional *position power* leadership. The word leadership is about as misunderstood as the word power; there are several kinds of leadership just as there are several kinds of power. In order to determine which people show the characteristics of higher stages of leadership we must ask leaders who they are promoting: themselves, others, themselves at the expense of others, both themselves and others? In this context, although some people lead others at each stage, a truly non-self-promoting leadership does not begin until Stage Four. Fours have survived the integrity crisis and have emerged as more whole, honest, principled, reflective, and secure people. Stage Threes may be in charge or up in front, but their leadership is chiefly concerned with their own egos, prestige, and control. In contrast, Fours think more about other people and the longer range effects, therefore taking a broader approach to the issues and to leadership.

True leaders can follow as well as take charge, but from a base of strength, not weakness. Stage Four people are just beginning to see the power of turning things over to others or working more through people. They look at implications and weigh alternatives. They incite differences of opinion because they know it fosters better thinking. And they are more personally powerful because they have less to lose. But Stage Four leaders still feel some pressure to calculate to whom they tell what, and why. They are organization conscious and quite influential. They are trusted and respected for their judgment, not only for the hoops they have jumped through. But they are close enough to the hoops to remember the grinding pressures; therefore they must be careful that their judgment is not unduly affected by their prior experience.

Michael Maccoby writes skillfully about the types of people I am describing at Stage Four in his book *The Leader*. Whereas the gamesmen operated well at Stage Three, now a new organizational character is emerging who embraces the "self-development" ethic. The Fours he describes are more tolerant and flexible, willing to experiment with new ways of relating at work and at home. The health, learning, and development of others is important, an ethic grounded in human rights, not in unquestioning loyalty to the organization. They have a strong need for meaningful relationships and productivity in the work place based on equity, respect, and cooperation (p. 49). Work should not insult people's dignity, Maccoby asserts, nor demand excessive sacrifice of their emotional life, but be a way of developing abilities, contributing to society, satisfying human needs, gaining new experiences, and meeting different kinds of people (p. 53). He says gamesmen fit America during a time of unlimited economic growth and the career ethic, but now we are in need of new leaders who can operate in limited growth situations showing caring, integrity and a vision of self-development that creates trust (p. 51).

Although the six leaders he describes have some qualities of the gamesmen, they have more. They can feel emotions, show empathy, and live in a world of emotional reality, not fantasy. They use their heads *and* their hearts. As Maccoby says, "The head can be smart but not wise" (p. 85). They are at all levels of the organization. They are concerned about profits and costs, but they want to work in an environment in which everyone can contribute and is equitably rewarded. It is no surprise that the qualities of caring, competence, trust, and friendship emerge as important to the new leaders. They will not sacrifice basic values to get to the top, and they are willing to share their power with others. They spend more time in planning with groups to build consensus and less time reacting to mistakes and misunderstandings (p. 223). They can assert authority on issues, but their self-worth does not depend on winning every contest. And they are broadly read in ethics, psychology, history, and literature. Within the six scenarios Maccoby includes women, men, and minority leaders, at all levels in the organization.

The following anecdote regarding one of the new leaders describes succinctly one of the finest characteristics of Stage Four leaders: A union official was running for head of his union against one of his close friends. After a careful scrutiny of the skills needed in the next decade for the effective managing of their union, he supported his friend for the position. He was not looking for a seat of power. He was looking, rather, for a way to continue to operate on a one-to-one basis, listening and helping to solve problems. He could do much of what he wanted to do in his present position, and he was able to teach and travel as well. He was modest, dedicated, and principled. His philosophy was to abide by the golden rule.

Let's Meet Some People at Stage Four

Lamon, the Mayor

(Lamon represents the struggle that Stage Four people have being in public life. He is a professional public administrator, not a politician.)

My job gives me a good chance to put into practice my philosophy of public administration. I consider myself somewhat of an expert in the area with two degrees in the field. I would be lying to tell you that I'm in politics for nothing but service. I have a hard time with anyone who believes that. I like being in the limelight, being the center of attention at times, but there is a serious academic side to me that not everyone sees. I hate campaigning, for instance. If I could get out of it I would. It's not that I don't like people but you just don't get to really talk to many people on the campaign trail. I'd rather avoid big crowds where I must be dynamic for the audience, and just talk one-to-one for an hour or two so I can really hear people's opinions and reasoning.

I've always felt that the finest political people have had the loneliest jobs, not the most exciting, as some people think. It can be lonely because you are aware of all the powerful special interest groups, and you also know the amount of stretch in the budget. Added to that you have the philosophy of your party, the influence of your leaders, and most important, your own reasoned judgments about what would bring the greatest good for the city as a whole. These views might all be at odds with one another, and juggling them all is a real trick. You are elected to serve the city, yet each group or organization wants you to see them as an exception. That may not be wise for the times or the city. So every time I make a decision I ask myself, "How would I decide on this if after the decision I would be placed in the shoes of one of the parties involved, but before the decision I wouldn't know which party's shoes I would be placed in?" I try to make decisions as if I were not going to run again although that is much easier said than done.

It's hard to be an enlightened mayor without an enlightened electorate. I'm not complaining, because my city has had a long history of wise decision makers and educated voters, but I am illustrating the reality of the multiple pressures on a public decision maker. I quickly realized that the most important thing I could do was to gather a staff around me all of whom excelled at what they did. I couldn't afford to use only party supporters or less experienced people who would not threaten me. The way I continue to grow in this job is to be challenged and to continue to look at longer term solutions to our city's problems. If I can't say of my terms in office that major development occurred, unemployment issues eased, and clean air was guaranteed, I would not feel I had done this city justice—but not without a balanced budget. So in addition to my other duties, my team has set out to form coalitions in all sectors to push forward on these three projects, providing ideas and resources but depending on the vision and leadership within the community to carry out the programs. That's what makes all this worth it to me.

Jeanne, the Certified Public Accountant

(Jeanne exhibits the confusion resulting from success that is not meaningful anymore. She experiences a crisis in her work that helps her clarify her values, experience a new way of being, and start her on a different path. She may be seeing purpose as more than an extension of ego.)

I was a classic example of an organizational success story. I went to college right out of school and joined the accounting firm with the best track record. I put in all the overtime I could in those early years, because as a woman I wanted to prove what I could do. Of course, being one of the youngest to get my CPA helped a lot. The partners noticed me and promoted me consistently along the way. I was really riding high even though I was always tired. I thought I was really making it.

At a conference a few years ago I began to talk to some other women CPAs from other firms. We were just laughing and comparing notes. One woman in particular asked us some very hard questions like, where were we headed? why? and then what? What else did we have in our lives that gave us meaning? Her words and my answers started sinking in very slowly, so slowly I hardly noticed. But over the next year my subconscious noticed. I started to feel the pressure of tax time more strenuously, the promises of promotion seemed like carrots on a stick, and some of the practices of the organization that I had always accepted and taken for granted started to bother me. For instance, we had few small businesses as clients because we had to charge too much for our time, yet small businesses were my best and most interesting clients to work with. I churned and wrestled with these disconcerting thoughts and finally took a three-week trip to Nova Scotia all by myself. By the time I came back I knew I was going to leave the firm and start my own practice specializing in accounting and planning for small businesses. Well, scared as I was, I felt like a huge load had been lifted off of me. And that was two years ago. Already I'm convinced that this was the right thing to do, although it was one of the most difficult decisions of my life. Starting a business is not easy. And no one taught me how to run a business in college. It's more than numbers. I know that for sure. My banker has been invaluable, believe me. I am so much happier even though I frequently work just as hard. I am helping out small growing businesses, I am making a difference, I am in charge of my life. And I like myself better. I have a social life, and I build in break time. You know, I even considered building a firm out of this, but then I laughed because two years ago I left a bureaucracy. Why start another one?

Someday maybe, but not for a while yet. I'm too busy wallowing in developing new clients and in establishing a name in the field. And I want to be careful not to burn myself out even if I love what I'm doing. When it's time to grow I'll think about it.

Riley, the Musician

(This example shows us how the stereotypes of big success can be deadly. Giving up what you've always wanted because you now know what's more important is one classic characteristic of a Stage Four person.)

I'm a funny kind of guy, and I know other people don't understand me, nor do I fit the stereotypes of professional musicians. The only two goals I have in life are to play good music for people to enjoy and to encourage young people to participate in music. I don't stay out all night, smoke, shoot or snort drugs, nor do I yearn for the travel circuit, wait to be discovered, nor work on a best-selling recording. What satisfies me is knowing that when I sit down at the piano, the sound is mine and the quality is grand. I want to please people with my music. I have had the unfortunate experience of being discovered and being cajoled into recordings, TV shows, and the like. But the offer necessitated moving, uprooting myself without my family, and living a very stressful "successful" life. I tried it for a year and decided that being famous right here is just enough for me. And teaching kids is the finest reward there can be. If people want me to record my music, that's fine, but I am not about to take on the required lifestyle of those who are aiming at the top. Life is just too short. And my music is not as good when I'm under stress, either. Now do you see why I'm considered a strange dude?

Don, the Procurement Manager

(Don has accepted his strengths and limitations and is comfortable with the balance between his work and his personal life.)

You know, I'm about where I'm going to be in this organization and I know it. Last year I was offered the position of department head, and after thinking long and hard, I turned it down. They brought in a younger guy from one of the other divisions. For a while I thought I had made a big mistake, but the long talk I had with my boss's boss helped. The department is in need of an overhaul, and plenty of energy would be required to do that. I've been gradually pulling back on extra assignments at work ever since our third baby was born. Having a blind child takes so much extra time and attention that I just can't do it all. I know management sees me as competent because of all the awards and good appraisals I've had. But I had to accept for myself that at this point in my life I would probably not be up to this large a challenge. I've really made my own choices, and they've been tough ones. It's a lot to give up and I may not have another chance. That is the harsh reality of it all. I must admit that the activity I enjoy most is developing my people, not reorganizing the department. I get the biggest kick out of seeing someone move from a lower skilled status to a more satisfying position or from a life crisis into self-confidence. I like to place my people all over the company so they can get better experience, and they always remember to keep in touch, so I have cronies in all corners.

Judy, the Writer

(Judy had to overcome obstacles that plagued her for years. She had to discover slowly in herself the writer that was there hiding all along.)

They told me I wasn't really going to make it, in their opinion, in the writing world. I just wasn't able to grasp the nuances of the language and provide sufficient poetic imagery to arouse my audience. I was young and naive and I believed them. And that was a big mistake. Now they were just being kind, and they were quite accurate about my skill in fiction writing. It stinks. But they never suggested that I try any other kind of writing. So I quit trying to write and I went to work on regular jobs with publishing firms and educational institutions. Just by accident someone asked me to do an article for a newsletter on a program at my alma mater. I said I would and started in on it. Well, that was all it took to unleash the trapped writer inside me. I devoted hours of my free time to developing my writing ability. A mentor helped me immeasurably, encouraging and challenging me along the way. Now I write non-fiction of all kinds, and I am making a living at it. I just had to find my own style and quit trying to be the greatest novelist of the twentieth century. I think I've found myself through my writing too because I feel creative, relaxed, rejuvenated, and alive when I write, rarely bored and dulled like I did in my other jobs. And I am choosing to write about things that are useful to people, that help them to develop and discover their inner selves as well.

Hank, the Corporate President

(Hank is struggling with a deep question: "What is my purpose in life?" He thought it was work, but success in his work was not as satisfying as he thought it would be. Now what?)

You know I've got to admit, just between you and me, that I really used to genuinely enjoy all the perks, the applause, the admiration of my employees as a result of my position. We've been lucky to have a great management team or we never could have pulled off the continued growth in this company in the last seven years. We've exceeded all of our expectations and there seems to be little that we can't do if we set our minds to it. So the challenges are all there, just for the picking. But I've been suffering lately from a malaise that I don't seem to be able to cure. I know that I could move to some other very lucrative positions from where I am now, and my successes could stockpile, but somehow that seems like an empty challenge. It sounds to me like more of the same. I really have been spending some long hours thinking about my life and work lately. Of course, a few days at home with a cold will do that to you, give you a forced sabbatical to think about some of the other things in life. To be very candid with you, what I came up with is that what I really lack in my life is a purpose around which all the other things revolve. Or maybe it's that the things that used to serve as purposes for me have lost their savor. I just don't want to die in my eighties with my accomplishments being only at work. That raises all kinds of other questions, of course, like what is my purpose in being? What's worth enough to me to invest time, energy, and money on? Can I find my purpose in or through my work, or is it broader than that? What do I want to be remembered for most? What do I want my kids to say about me after I'm gone? Am I passing on traits and qualities in my management team that I will be proud of in the long run, or are we just following the rules? I know I'm known for being quite people-oriented, but how could I do something really significant with my company that would make a difference in individuals' lives? Can my purpose also be the company's vision? Am I ready to be a visionary leader, courageous and willing to lead into unchartered waters where few models have been attempted? What have I got to lose? Is this crisis of purpose the cause of my malaise? Whom can I talk to about this?

When I read about wise people, principled people of the ages, there are certain characteristics that seem to be true of them. They knew what they were, they knew what they wanted, they were ultimately disciplined, they suffered disappointments but kept on going, and they inspired others through their selflessness. Do I have the fortitude to follow any of their leads? Could I even take a stab at learning more about commitment and dedication to principles and purposes? Where do I start?

All these people represent some confusion between their own personal characteristics or values and the expectations of the profession or organization. They are all finding their own way of doing things, of living with themselves so as to achieve some sense of balance and continuity within themselves. Everyone chooses a different way to do this and experiences varying levels of crisis along the way. Because Stage Fours have begun to be more reflective and introspective, it is more difficult to pinpoint exactly how the transitions occur for them, for they proceed on the basis of their own inner experience.

Moving to Stage Five

In moving to Stage Five the perplexities of life begin to take on daily significance. Everything seems to have an equal and opposite side, including oneself. Self-acceptance may sound familiar to a Stage Four, but Stage Fives know what it really means down deep inside.

The crisis in moving from Stage Four to Stage Five is a crisis of ego, one of the most challenging crises any of us can experience. We've been told that all our lives we have been putting ourselves down, thinking negatively, and expecting the worst. So we do an about-face and work diligently to build up a healthy, strong, and stable ego. Some of us do such a good job we have ego to spare; others of us never quite get to that point. Still others wallow in guilt because they know they could be rich and successful if only they could work harder at it. In fact, it is useful to practice positive thinking, especially if you have learned to carry on a largely negative dialogue in your head about yourself. Positive thinking is a start to a more integrated way of thinking about self but cannot be substituted for healthy, honest self-appraisal. It is most useful for people at Stages Two and Three but not as useful for people at Stage Four moving to Five.

The goal in moving to Stage Five is to let go of control, of having to know, of planning all the time, of building a subtle base of influence. Letting go of one's ego means looking not at the personal advantage in a situation but at the advantage to others, the organization, or the larger vision. It means not winning while another loses, but finding ways for everyone to win. Have you ever tried to do that and still avoid becoming a martyr? You can't unless you have a strong, healthy ego. In other words, you have to possess a strong, healthy ego before you can relinquish it.

Fours have begun the move to the inside, but are largely narcissistic at this point, dwelling only on their own inner dilemma, their own personal growth. Once beyond Stage Four they will begin to *live* the results of the Stage Four reflections. They will operate more intuitively. They will still need quiet time, but less time to think about themselves because they're more accepting of both themselves and others.

Stage Fours need to give themselves a personal sabbatical somewhere along the way, a time to stop temporarily to rethink their destination and their life purpose or mission. Stage Five people have a different vision than Fours. They come out of the self-reflective cocoon. They see beyond the self, the department, even the organization to a broader view of the world. They ask hard questions and don't know the answers but they don't seem upset about not knowing either.

Fours need to learn to be less and less dependent on the external rewards and more oriented toward internal rewards that are not ego-oriented. If no one were to ever know what I have accomplished, could I still feel good about it? Am I starting to fit my work in the organization into the larger framework of my personal life goals? Do I feel any sense of consistency in the way I operate at home, in the community, at work? Can I drop some of my role behavior and accept myself, all of me, then make sure I'm not headed in a direction that makes poor use of my skills? Can I get past the point of proving myself, of overcoming obstacles, of working on my weaknesses? There will be enough other people reminding us of these anyway.

Stage Fours need to let others (either a person or a group) who are wiser guide them into Stage Five or suggest things for them to think about. These people are usually not bosses but people from wider ranging disciplines who can broaden their vision and stimulate their thinking and their creativity. This is very difficult for Fours to do because they pride themselves on having gotten to where they are largely on their own merits. It is indeed a humbling experience for leaders to admit that they need to let someone else lead them, but that's one of the paradoxes of moving to Stage Five.

It gets more and more difficult to describe what people can do to move to new stages because change becomes even more individualized as we proceed to the advanced stages. But I will attempt to summarize some general themes that emerge for people. And here are some specific things that Stage Fours can do to move to Stage Five:
• Forgive others.
People tell me that they couldn't go on to Stage Five while blaming parents, bosses, or spouses for their own problems. So they sincerely forgave others, put away all grudges, and began taking full responsibility for their own behavior.
• Expect a deep personal crisis of ego.
This began with the move to Stage Four but deepens during this stage. It could be a struggle with death, illness, loss of a love, career crisis, or personal fears. It involves letting go of what one thinks of as "me."

People who describe this say they went to the bottom of their well and then slowly returned again in a new frame of mind, not to take over the world but to live and love more simply and realistically.

• Enjoy a period of silence.

Some have said they sit absolutely still for long periods of time, just being ready for direction. They do not rely on mantras, although that is a useful way to begin the quiet process. This may last for days, months, or even years off and on. They are listening for that still, small voice inside them that begins to be heard. It can only be heard when the noise of the mind quiets down.

• Let go.

Control in Stage Five people transfers to some other source of egoless power, whether it be the universe, a principle, one's inner voice, a master teacher, or some other spiritual force. This is not to be confused with being blindly led by dogma, but is a more personally responsible, integrated action that permeates one's way of living without imposing rules or roles.

• Prepare for a sense of loss.

There is, for some, a true mourning and grieving, a deep cleansing period due to the acceptance of not being able to have things the way you've known them, including success and achievement. What will replace these is not yet obvious.

• Anticipate glimpses of wisdom.

There are glimpses, moments in which you know more than you think, can look beyond what you can see to a much calmer, more global view of life—a certain wisdom. You hear yourself say things you didn't even know were in your repertoire. You get insights that amaze you, and you wonder from what source they come.

You cannot go to classes to learn Stage Five behavior, nor can you buy a kit that will turn you into one. You can be around Stage Five people and observe how they are or read about them, but no techniques will get you there. The only way is by inner and personal experience, and it is usually done alone, though guided by another person. Anyone who assembles big groups and charges large sums of money to teach growth in these areas is usually misled, ego oriented, or just plain dishonest. You cannot learn Stage Five behavior from Stage Three people. And you cannot buy life purpose and broader vision.

In order to move to Stage Five, you must sincerely want to drop your ego and be prepared for the excruciatingly wonderful process to follow.

What Holds People Back?

Two major factors stand in the way of Stage Fours. First, they have not experienced a need for a meaningful, other-oriented life purpose. They are inner-directed, but they have not sat down quietly to ask themselves why they are alive. Not just whether they are living, which was asked in Stage Four, but *why*? What is their reason for being, beyond themselves in the world? This can only come out of an intense and honest inner conversation in which life's priorities are set. Buckminster Fuller spent two years without speaking following a suicide attempt before he launched into his life's mission—to serve the world through useful design.

The second, but perhaps primary, obstacle is that Fours are still controlling and controlled by ego, which can be tied to parents' expectations, perfectionism, overcoming insecurities, or a need to be loved and not abandoned. Whatever the source, Fours who are struggling with ego run the risk of continuing to care, however subtly, that in the end their good deeds will be recognized, their name included, they'll be paid for the work, they'll make others indebted to them, they'll be depended upon and more developed as a result. There are still strings attached with Fours. They cannot let go because they will lose control.

SUMMARY OF STAGE
FOUR
power by reflection

SYMBOL

DESCRIPTION
influence
the sandwich stage

CHARACTERISTICS
competent
reflective
strong
comfortable with personal style
skilled at mentoring
showing true leadership

CRISIS OF MOVEMENT
letting go of one's ego

WHAT HOLDS PEOPLE BACK?
letting go of one's ego
no need for life purpose
ego control

WAYS TO MOVE
Forgive others, experience the loss of
"me," have long silent times, let go,
experience loss, glimpse wisdom

Ask yourself these questions about Stage Five:

Yes No

___ ___ 1. Do you care as much about other people's development as you do about your own?

___ ___ 2. Are you comfortable with yourself enough that other people's opinions of you do not affect you?

___ ___ 3. Do you have a life purpose that reaches beyond yourself and your organization?

___ ___ 4. Do you have a deep inner core of spirituality?

___ ___ 5. Do you genuinely enjoy being alone?

___ ___ 6. Do you operate out of a quiet, inner sense of calm?

___ ___ 7. Is your ego getting smaller and less significant all the time?

___ ___ 8. Have you lost track of the organizational ladder?

___ ___ 9. Do you consciously give power away by empowering others?

___ ___ 10. Do you feel your work and your life are becoming more integrated, less splintered?

___ ___ 11. Do you believe power is infinite?

___ ___ 12. Do you often laugh at your own foibles?

Yes answers indicate that you identify with this stage.

Chapter 5

Stage Five: Power by Purpose

Vision

What Is Stage Five Like?

Stage Five is unlike all of the preceding stages. Its uniqueness lies in the strength of the inner person relative to the strength of the organizational hold on that person. The guide for behavior in Fives is the inner intuitive voice. They trust it more than they trust the rules. Stage Fives are different internally *and* externally now. They are more congruent because they no longer have to live two separate lives as Stage Fours do. And it is even harder to spot Fives because they don't care if they're ever spotted. In fact, they may even hide a bit.

Fives have a life purpose that extends beyond themselves. This has resulted from a deep, inner churning, a long, slow, or painful evolution in which the old rules have dropped away temporarily and old allegiances, ideas, and people have been reevaluated. These people have encountered themselves head on. And they are finding their inner truth, a life purpose, a moral imperative that goes beyond themselves. As the button-maker says to Peer Gynt, "To be yourself is to demolish yourself."

Stage Five is giving away power, letting others lead. It is letting go of the written or organizational rules and living with a sense of inner justice and order. It is learning to strive for others or more often for principles. *Above all it is not ego oriented.* That is why Stage Fives are called the irregulars in organizations.

The symbol for Stage Five is one person passing power to another. Stage Five people believe that power multiplies infinitely. The more power you can give away, the better. Power is like love: You can't have it truly until you give it away or let it go, and the more of it you give unselfishly, the more it multiplies. Fives know that love or power given away comes back full circle but not in the same form in which it was given. They do not attempt to gain or accumulate power because they find the other forms in which it reappears, like caring, appreciation, and friendship more rewarding.

An example of this unselfish behavior in a community might be this: Joe decides to nominate Charlene for a community service award because she is truly a significant contributer and highly deserves the recognition. He has no motives other than wanting her good work to be rewarded. He writes a very well-documented, concise, and engaging application for her, remaining anonymous himself. Charlene never finds out who nominated her, but she is very touched by the nomination. Years later, when she and Joe are on a task force together she asks him if he nominated her. He smiles and only says that he knows the person who did. Stage Threes in this case would be anxious for Charlene to know who nominated her, so they would be recognized in return; Stage Fours would nominate Charlene anonymously but let it leak so Charlene could reciprocate in the future if she chose; but Joe at Stage Five made sure Charlene was rewarded because she truly deserved it, and he remained anonymous. A Stage Five does the thing even if he or she knows there will be no personal return.

The definition of power at Stage Five is vision, which has many connotations and elicits marvelous images. Stage Fives have keen vision. They can see beyond the obvious and look with an inner eye. (The eye is an ancient symbol for inner vision and wisdom.) And this vision includes and goes beyond the self and even the organization. Although Fives may be involved in organizations, their self-image is beginning to extend to the larger world. They see themselves paradoxically for the first time: On the one hand, they are insignificant and, on the other hand, tremendously important in the larger scheme of things. Since they are now emerging from their long inner struggle of definition and self-acceptance—which takes years for some and a lifetime for most—they can concentrate on essentials, the things that give meaning to them, and more important, to the lives of others. They can walk humbly and do great things for an individual or for the world because both are equally important to them and require the same dedication. A Stage Five person made this telling remark about his work: "I used to complain about all the interruptions in my work until I discovered that the interruptions *are* my work."

No particular jobs or positions necessarily lend themselves to Stage Five behavior. To have arrived at Stage Five means that some symbols of the external stages have been achieved and, more important, that much inner work has been accomplished. In fact, Fives and Twos may some-times look alike and thus confuse observers. They both may appear unassuming or non-ego driven. The difference is that Fives consciously give away power, influence, and information they have accumulated, while Twos have not yet tasted power. You can't give away something you don't own. Letting other people control you without knowing first how to control yourself, which is more typical at Stage Two, usually occurs as a result of fear or insecurity, not self-esteem. One example of this would be dependence on a manager who acts like a controlling parent.

Another confusion that arises is expressed by people who *feel* the Stage Two/Stage Five split. They are experiencing a deep inner journey in one part of their lives (Stage Five), but in areas like work or rela-tionships, they are at Stage Two. So they feel pulled in two directions, with their home stage generally at Stage Two. I usually recommend that they apply the same process they used to get to Stage Five in one area of their life to the other areas, i.e., if you've learned to be honest with yourself and to let go of control in your family situation why not try to do the same thing at work? Or if you have learned to take leadership in the community, why not take a little more leadership in the family?

Stage Five people have experienced the inner struggle and evolution as a totally individual experience and do not feel that others must have the same set of experiences they did in order to find inner peace. Also people need not reach a certain level in the organization to experience

Stage Five, as long as they have received some of the recognition of Stage Three and have then looked inward to learn the meaning of themselves at Stage Four. Many people who hold positions of external power or prestige in organizations are firmly entrenched in Stage Three. They may lead exciting lives with lots of activity and challenge but at the same time are caught in the web of unending expectations with no larger vision beyond their own ultimate success. They do not have peace of mind and inner calm.

The kind of power that is emerging in Fives, that of power from the inside out, is described by Rollo May in *Power and Innocence* as "nutrient power," that is power *for* the other. It shows caring and giving with respect, not manipulation. As examples he cites teaching at its best, healthy parenting, political statesmanship and diplomacy. Nutrient power wishes other people well and does what is within its influence to develop or provide for them (p. 109).

You may be thinking that Stage Fives sound too good to be true. In some respects they are. But not always and not in an arrogant way. They are disciplined in their inner life, and their detachment from the things that run most people's lives sets them apart, but not by design. They live from the inside, not from the outside.

Characteristics of Stage Five People

It is more difficult to describe the behavior of Stage Five people because so much of what goes on in their lives is totally hidden from view. Also Stage Fives do not seek the limelight, and they share their inner processes only to a few as an illustration or an empathetic gesture. Therefore, you may know them more for what they don't do than for what they do.

Self-Accepting

Stage Fives are perhaps the most genuine and human of all because of their near total self-acceptance and their tight grasp of reality. Stage Sixes for some seem out of reach, mystical, or too advanced to be understood. People at Stage Five know their strengths and limitations and clearly accept both without continuing to work at transforming themselves. That is not to be confused with a flexibility and *willingness* to change, which they also have. But they are not devoted to self-development or personal growth. Their changing goes on inside with a clear acceptance of the traits that probably will not change or will take too much energy to change. Instead, a Stage Five person will remove him or herself from situations in which those traits get in the way or will simply laugh at those situations in which their ineptness is shown. I know several people who are the most assured, competent people professionally in their work, and can speak comfortably to large groups of influential people but who are totally inept with fifty people at an informal social gathering. They laugh about sitting in the corner or hiding gracefully behind the nearest plant, pretending to be invisible. People at Stage Five can laugh at themselves; in fact, they get quite a kick out of their incapacities. And it is wonderfully comforting to others who've not yet learned to admit to any weaknesses lest they be used against them. Stage Fives are frustrating to others, though, who feel one should always be working on oneself. To hear Stage Fives say they will probably always be critical, or messy, or late distresses self-developers.

Calm

Along with self-acceptance comes a beginning kind of calm that is a mark of Stage Five people. They're usually not in a hurry to get places because they are content with their situation and life. In fact, their internal calm can be sensed even when they are in tense and frightening situations. They are not blocking the feelings, but their reservoir of serene feelings is deeper. Their calm is like a faint perfume that scents the air; it is emitted non-verbally to the surrounding environment.

This calm content behavior is not to be confused with that of shy or quiet people who may indeed be tense inside or afraid to speak, nor with judicious types who are quietly analyzing the situation to appraise its worthiness. Calm people can be outgoing or quiet. What they emit from the inside makes the difference.

Visionary

If Stage Five people are valued in an organization they must be nurtured and protected, usually from the Threes. Fives are not only beyond the traditional rules and norms, they do not always fit well into the accepted culture of the organization. And what's worse, they really don't care a whole lot. Since the symbols no longer persuade or motivate them, other forms of motivation must be considered if they are to be kept in the organization as useful contributors. Why then would anyone want to keep Fives around, if they don't fit? For precisely that reason. They can be visionaries for the organization at all levels. They are not afraid to ask difficult questions, to present preposterous arguments, to be creative, to suggest alternatives that go against the rules. And they are deliberately non-self-serving. They give away ideas, find ways to promote others, and do not usually bid for more responsibility. They tend to be more naturally creative, in a form that fits their style and background. They are the people who are dragged kicking and screaming into leadership positions because they have the necessary vision, and yet they frequently want nothing to do with being at the helm. They would rather lead from behind.

Stage Five people, though different from the norm, are still in touch with reality in the organization. Fives provide a different model or basis upon which to operate, which is useful but not easily tolerable to Stage Threes, who want to control all the variables. Stage Fives are not predictable, they ignore politics, and can be counted on to disagree if they think it is justified. Most people can't figure them out, can't find their vulnerable spot, can't motivate them with money or threats. They usually can't be "had." As a result, most organizations can tolerate only a limited number of Fives.

Some officers of progressive organizations say they can specifically identify their Stage Five people because they give wise counsel and respond reflectively on almost any issue. The employers admit to having to protect these people at times, or at least explain to others why they continue to keep them around. In one organization, the presence of a Stage Five person was described by a fellow employee like this: "I'm not at all sure what Al does on his job any more. All I know is that long before any major decision is about to be announced in this place, there is a steady stream of important people to his office."

Stage Fives do have vision, but it goes beyond money, profits, and position, to asking and answering questions like: What is the best long-range strategy for this organization? What is our role in the community and in the world? What are the most important issues we will face in five years? How do we develop our people to be self-motivated and productive? How do we tolerate differences in our leadership? How can the work place be more humane and provide more equality? Where do we fit into the emerging world economy? What kind of a say do employees have in our future? Are we in the wrong business for the wrong reasons? Fives are the conscience of the organization. They call the organization to do what is right, even though it may be uncomfortable. For example, they will call attention to any discrepancy between the organization's publicly stated goals and the way those goals are actually pursued.

Humble

Probably the most critical variable affecting Stage Five people is the lessening of their egos. This one characteristic distinguishes them in an astonishing way from other people. Diminished ego, however, does not mean loss of self-esteem. On the contrary, persons with less ego who have consciously given it up often exhibit more self-esteem than others. Fives make a conscious decision to transfer the energy expended in struggling with themselves and their problems to other arenas—people, ideas, organizations.

Their reduced ego sometimes makes Fives hard to understand. This is because they are not generally motivated by the usual things and therefore can't be as easily figured out or manipulated. The more consistent and integrated Stage Five persons are, the more profound is their influence on others. Some people have said they have been influenced by Fives simply by observing them or being around them. Their operating style appears and is expressed in the way they process information, the kinds of questions they ask, the breadth of their knowledge, and the depth of their awareness.

Since this ego reduction is one of the distinguishing characteristics of Fives, it would be nice to describe how one goes about obtaining such a trait. Unfortunately, there is no course or credo that offers a magic way to achieve this. It is a development that occurs deep within the person and is often not even shared with those closest to them. In fact, the more that is spoken, the less authentic may be the experience. It may be just one more strategy for building up the ego. And ego reduction may in fact be a by-product of other things Fives do or experience, not a goal unto itself. It may be like happiness in that respect. One does not seek it for its own sake, but enjoys it as a result of an experience, thought, or event.

Several other qualities seem to develop either along with or because of the loss of ego. I hesitate to even describe them lest they be misunderstood. Just because people acquire one or all of these qualities does not necessarily mean their egos will be diminished, only that I have noticed them in people whose egos are reduced. The first of these qualities is a tremendous need for solitude, for time alone to respond to the power within and beyond and let it wash over oneself. The solitude refreshes, awakens, and clarifies. The ability to be totally quiet without reading, writing, or thinking is a gift and one to be savored in this frantic world. Fives seem to be able to do that in the middle of a day, even, strangely enough, in a group or on the go. They carry solitude with them, like a cloak, yet they can be easily with people.

The second quality is an increased willingness to listen to their inner voices and to distinguish between intuition and wishful thinking. They have learned that having generated it, wishful thinking will always be consistent with their will. They also know that intuition tells them what to do and does not always agree with their will or their reason. They receive intuitive messages through their small inner voice, which only whispers and is rarely wrong.

The third quality that develops in Fives along with a lessened ego is a different kind of humor. They have no need to put others down, make them look stupid, or use sexual connotations to demean them. Whereas Fours are just finding their own style of humor, Fives find their humor by laughing gently at their own foibles and by observing the silly, ordinary things of life, like children's antics and lowly puns. Their humor is fresh and honest, not sarcastic or angry. They have little need to elevate themselves by putting others in an inferior place. In fact, some people don't even develop a true sense of their own humor until Stage Five. They're either stern or serious or they adopt the humor of the marketplace to fit in. Their own humor has been buried for years, only to resurface at these later stages. It's a joy to be around people who can laugh at themselves and mean it.

Yet another quality of Fives resulting from a lessened ego is their apparent innocence. Rollo May once again sheds light on Stage Five behavior by describing this quality of innocence in personally powerful people. It is "a way to confront powerlessness by making it a virtue. A conscious divesting of his/her power . . . not in a harmful way but free from guilt . . . and with no evil intention." He describes the quality in some artists and poets as a quality of the imagination that gives a childlike clarity in adulthood, a freshness, newness, color. These people reflect the awe and wonder of spring that leads one toward spirituality. They preserve their childlike attitudes into maturity without sacrificing the realism of their perception of evil nor their complicity with evil. They are authentic (*Power and Innocence*, pp. 48-49).

The second-to-last thought is particularly important in our discussion of Stage Five people. A distinguishing feature of theirs is their knowledge of the shadow within themselves, their dark traits. They do not hide from these traits any more but realistically watch them to keep them from being overwhelming. And they see and accept these traits in others as well, for they are not so naive as to deny evil intentions. Stage Fives allow themselves to be human, and as a result can be more trustworthy or honest with others. One person was lamenting to a friend that she was not a very forgiving person and the friend made a wise observation: "You equate forgiving someone with liking them. Perhaps you could forgive them if you agreed with yourself that you didn't have to like them." That sounded somehow more realistic and a great relief to her as well.

There is a danger to the quality of innocence, and it is described by May as "pseudo-innocence." Stage Five people can be vulnerable to this danger but Stage Two people are even more so, for they are looking for answers through magic techniques and the avoidance of conflict or reality. Pseudo-innocence is a danger in the New Age and other movements that rely on positive feelings and images, the elimination of power and other organizational evils to bring back the Garden of Eden. May describes pseudo-innocence as a defense against having to confront the realities of power, including status, prestige, and the war machine. It can become a shield from responsibility and growth. It protects us from new awareness and from identifying with the sufferings and joys of people (pp. 63-64).

Pseudo-innocence means capitalizing on naiveté, says May. It is childhood never outgrown, fixation on the past; childishness not child-likeness; it is utopianism, closing our eyes to reality and persuading ourselves we've escaped it; it makes things simple and easy; it means not coming to terms with the destructiveness in ourselves or others; it cannot include the demonic and therefore becomes evil; it is a Garden of Eden mentality. It lacks the dialectic movement between yes and no, good and evil. It is the denial of and absence of good power. Pseudo-innocence hopes there are no enemies, which is to deny history (pp. 49-64).

Stage Five people are acutely aware of the other side of themselves, of all people, and of organizations. Living with it daily, they know people can be evil, good, greedy, and warm simultaneously. Yet Fives are especially able to walk the tightrope, adjusting continually to the necessary balance not with naiveté but with innocence renewed—a suffering innocence. This innocence is born not out of fear or lack of responsibility but out of a new sense of accountability. Their self-acceptance is not a declaration that evil is good but that it must be recognized and confronted. So Fives understand others and feel a connection with them through their suffering and joy as well.

The following story describes what happens when people live their lives with no role for humanness or reality. In a small business partnership, two women worked together diligently for several years. During that time the business went up and down as businesses do inevitably. One of the partners had an enormous fear lest anyone ever find out there were any problems or that the business was struggling. She made a point of telling people how well they were doing and how on top of everything they were. Their image far outweighed their performance. When particularly bad economic times hit one year, the one owner could not ask for help even though they needed it, and the other could not confront the issue with her partner. The situation got progressively worse, but the one partner still talked as if it would all turn out fine. Their business failed financially because they could not admit they needed help. Their pride may have been a major factor in this business failure. The appearance on the surface and the protection of image was more important than accepting the facts and working on the issues together.

Generous in Empowering Others

Stage Five people cannot help but affect others. Since they know this, they have consciously chosen as a way of life the empowering of others. Not only is it a healthy discipline in reducing ego but in the long run it's always the right and just thing to do. Empowering others gives them dignity and does not diminish the giver. So everyone wins.

The ultimate objective of most Fives, whether stated or not, is to empower others: to raise them up, love them, give them responsibility, trust them, learn from them, and be led by them. In fact, Fives exhibit leadership by empowering others. They feel they are merely a conduit of ideas, energy, and power that is to be given out or passed along. This comes through in their lives and their work. Alexander Graham Bell was heard to say, "I feel like my discoveries come through me, that I am a channel for forces greater than my self."

Fives do not need to be in charge. More often now, they choose not to. They prefer to be behind the scenes. They would rather participate as good team members in an organization and develop others' leadership. Frequently they are encouraged to assume leadership positions, but if those positions do not specifically fit their life purpose, they will usually decline. There are some basic reasons why Fives are such good behind-the-scene leaders: First, they are not afraid of change. In fact, they welcome warranted change and see it as a way to learn. They often find ways for the change to help each individual person, or they help each person to see the change as an opportunity. Second, they have vision. They will look longer range and see the bigger picture. And third, they are less fearful. Since they have less at stake in the organization, they are not continually covering their tracks or worrying that people will use them or their information.

To empower others Fives usually choose the least obvious and public ways. For instance, when a Five becomes a mentor for another person, it is usually inconspicuous. More often, they simply sense a need for mentoring and respond to it. And being mentored by a Five does not mean being told what to do or given their model to follow. In fact, getting information from Fives about their life and career strategies is difficult. They'd rather tell wonderful stories or metaphors for you to figure out. So the best way to learn from a Five is to be in a more casual relationship or setting with them, learning from their style and listening to their conversations, rather than asking for procedures or posing questions on technique. Then later, perhaps years later, you'll hear yourself make their kind of response to a question or situation. They're wonderful in that long-term mentoring capacity. You can feel their presence long after they're gone.

Another important way in which Stage Five people empower others is to give everything away: ideas, titles, responsibility, leads, solutions. They have no strong inclination to hold on to these ego-building things. This trait is confusing to others, however, who wonder how someone can freely give up the things that are supposed to mean so much. But this gets progressively easier for Fives because they find great satisfaction in selfless giving. They've discovered that to diminish oneself is to know oneself. Their deeper, true-to-nature traits emerge more authentically when they remove the armor. And all their fears—fear of reprisal, of failure, of loss, of being alone—are taking a less central place in the whole life of Fives.

Yet another way Fives have of empowering others is to use them as teachers. Fives are intuitively curious people. They have a depth of knowledge or expertise in some area but have also developed a breadth of interest in addition to that. They are not afraid to wade into areas of knowledge foreign to them and to ask simple or basic questions of others. This broad interest and curiosity in turn gives them new insights into their own field and allows them to be more creative. The persons teaching them also gain: a sense of self-respect and satisfaction through sharing their knowledge and an increase in the knowledge of their field by having to explain it in understandable ways.

Stage Five characteristics can be viewed from the perspective of another culture very different from our own. The following are nine principles for learning the way to highly develop oneself, according to Miyamoto Musashi, in his Ichi School of Oriental Training. The characteristics of highly developed people in our two cultures are amazingly similar.

1. Do not think dishonestly
2. The way is in training
3. Become acquainted with every art
4. Know the ways of all professions
5. Distinguish between gain and loss in worldly matters
6. Develop intuitive judgment and understanding for everything

7. Perceive those things which cannot be seen
8. Pay attention even to trifles
9. Do nothing which is of no use

(A Book of Five Rings, p. 49)

Confident of Life Purpose

Stage Five people know what their life's purpose is and seem to be able to wed this to their lifestyle and their work. From deep inside they have naturally evolved what has always been waiting to be recognized. They now have a sense of mission or vision for their lives. Usually their life purpose can be stated in very simple and straightforward terms, e.g., to help people, to love, to obtain peace, to wisely lead. The exact thing or idea they choose really doesn't matter, except that it comes from within and is the reason they get up every morning. They may not think about this purpose every day, but ultimately it is their underlying reason for living. They may devote time, money, ideas, work, or a lifetime to their purpose once it can be articulated, for it brings internal rewards that cannot be measured in tangible ways. If you were to ask them what their purpose is, they might be embarrassed to talk about it or may tell you something very acceptable. It is not important to them that others know, only that they themselves know that their purpose is worthwhile, respectful of others, egoless. Reinhold Niebuhr said in one of his most quotable observations, "Nothing that is worth doing can be achieved in a lifetime; therefore we must be saved by hope. Nothing which is true or beautiful or good makes complete sense in any immediate context of history; therefore we must be saved by faith. Nothing we do, however virtuous, can be accomplished alone; therefore we are saved by love" (from *Tomorrow Is Now* by Eleanor Roosevelt).

Here is an interesting story about a man's life purpose, which affected others around him in varying ways.

Tales the Silent Watchers Tell

Once upon a time, in the Village of Man, one of the many

began to dream of his homeland and became full of
longing.

In time, the others became concerned and, thinking it would
be a kindness, called on him to tell of his dreams.

The one was at once pleased by their interest and readily told
them, in glowing terms, of such a place as they had never
seen and could not imagine.

The more he told them, the more uneasy and confused they
became until suddenly they broke in upon him declaring,
"There is no such place as you describe. You are ill and
raving! Return to your work and dream and say no
more." They then turned from him and thereafter avoided
him.

In time he withered and died, and they said it was a strange
disease—one that first maddened and then killed him.

Later, by a clear stream that passed near The Village, the
Silent Watcher heard two of the water carriers saying,
"I wonder how the one could describe so vividly a place we
say does not exist?"
and
"How could he know about such a place, if as we say, he
could never have been there?"

Still later, a shepherd was heard to ask of his sheep,
"What made us turn from the one?"
and
"Did he not die of loneliness and not madness?"

One evening, a fire-tender was heard to ask of the fire,
"If the one had denied or kept silent about his homeland,
would he yet live among us?"

A star-watcher was heard to wonder of his star,
"What if we are the ones who are mad and this ever-the-
same life of ours is our death?"
and
"Did not the one in dying return to his homeland?"

After the Silent Watcher had carefully recorded this tale in The
Journal of Man, he noted:

A man died—others had turned from him and avoided him.
A man withered and died—his difference was not welcome
among others.
A man died; others became thoughtful.
Thus Man learns.

                                                    Hugh Harrison, 1977

Spiritual

The word "spirituality" makes a lot of people squirm. They describe it as
non-rational, anti-intellectual, dangerous, manipulative, holier-than-
thou, ego-feeding, or as a substitute for responsibility. It can be all of
those things for some people, but not for Fives. For Fives understand
spirituality as the acceptance of and respect for a non-human, non-evil
power that is greater than they are and that gives them strength. The
power can be a master guide, a universal force, a principle, or God. It is
broader than a specific religious belief or dogma. It may be the quality in
Fives that allows them to let go of finite external power and turn finally
and trustingly to the infinite inner power source. People at other stages
certainly can have a spirituality or a faith, but it would have a different
meaning to them. Those in Stage One through Three equate spirituality
with religion. They see it more as a way to feel secure, to possibly escape
from life, to have clear, unquestioned direction and identity, a way to get
things and ensure success, or a way to save souls. Fives think of
spirituality as the source of fuel for all of life, and they believe it cannot
be tied to dogma.

People will describe their path to that spiritual source differently. The
key idea is not how one gets there, but what one believes about the source
and how one behaves based on the inner core of spirituality that underlies
and pervades their lives. They trust their intuition because it is not
grounded in ego but is fueled by their spiritual source. They do not talk
much about their spirituality, they just live it. Since their egos are
diminished and they are secure, they can participate in any number of
activities or events and feel a consistency and purpose. What kind of
work they do no longer matters. What matters now is how they behave
and treat other people and how they live out their inner faith. Their
associates can feel the depth of their commitments and can sense their

integrity without even having to discuss it. In fact, Fives are somewhat reluctant to talk about their spirituality because they know how easy it is to get caught in their own rhetoric. They generally would rather talk over with close associates their life issues, such as how they are struggling with the inconsistencies of their lives. They realize that life is just one humbling event after another.

Let's Meet Some People at Stage Five

Ruby, Describing Sally and Ken, Parents

(This example reflects the effects that a disabled child can have on the lives of its parents, enabling them to deepen spiritually in the process.)

> I am very close to Sally and Ken and lived through with them the experience I am about to relate. Although it did not happen to me I will try to do justice to the effect it had on them. Ten years ago, Sally and Ken's lives appeared to be over. Sally gave birth to a child who had cerebral palsy. She was so scared and disappointed, so despondent that she thought of ending her life right there and then; yet somewhere deep inside, a small flame of love for this infant of theirs caused her to go on for just one more day. They sought counseling and support from parents of cerebral palsied children, and slowly, I mean inch by excruciating inch, they moved along. Ken was very busy with his work at the time, being a new super- visor in an electronics manufacturing firm, so he felt pulled in all directions at once. They had a four year old as well, so Sally was kept busy without trying. The first thing they learned from the group meetings with other parents was to try to talk openly together about their fears and frustrations as well as their joys. Some parents just needed to let off steam or feel sorry for themselves, and others talked about how much they were learning about themselves through their child. At that point all Sally and Ken could see was that they were learning survival. After one frustrating evening at the group meeting, another couple asked if they wanted to have coffee with them. That evening was the beginning of a long and deep

friendship that they consider one of the most special things in their lives. The couple shared their struggle with Sally and Ken in such a realistic way, yet all the while sharing the joys and the growth that occurred in each of them and in their family. Sally and Ken now know exactly what they meant. Their lives are different. They care about Bobby's welfare and Susan's too, but it calls them both to search out the deeper meaning in their lives. They're grappling with questions such as, What really makes us human—success or suffering? When all is said and done, aren't our friendships one of the most lasting things we have? How could we go on without faith in a higher power who understands the complexity of our lives?

Carl, Describing June, the Banker

(This example shows the way in which an employee views the behavior of a Stage Five bank president.)

I know June won't talk to you openly about what she's up to, so all I can do is describe her for you since I think she is rather exemplary. June was shocked into adulthood at age thirty due to the sudden death of her parents in a plane crash. She was left with the family bank and a lot of grief. She had been educating herself to move into management in three or four years, but at the time she was a loan officer for a major bank. Needless to say, she had a dilemma on her hands because she was in no mood to even work. The stress was enormous. She hasn't told me the details of that part of her life, but I know something very important happened inside. She emerged from that experience a different person, and it shows in the way she runs the bank.

She did decide to take on the management of the bank with help from several mentors. And there were some rough times. June believes that her community bank is there to serve the community. She spends as much time out in the community as she does in the bank. She delegates responsibility to bright and competent people whom she encourages to challenge her; and she has opened the board to a broader cross section of people who can bring her fresh views and more educated opinions. She is willing to learn but is also willing to take responsibility. She is particularly strong in her beliefs about people and work. She shares the profits and losses with the employees, encouraging each of them to feel part of the entire bank image and success. In fact, she is helping us all to redefine what success is, beyond financial growth. She is honest and rewards others who are. The honest bearer of bad tidings does not get punished in this bank, but encouraged. She wants to be informed, even if the news is bad. How can you work to change if you're not aware of the need? she would say. She feels she as an individual is expendable, but the group is not. She relies on all of us and expects us to run the show. In fact, she gives the impression with her quiet self-confidence that she's really the invisible leader, only there to remind us of principles we've agreed on or to ask questions we've overlooked. And she gets right to the heart of the matter without leaving us shattered or embarrassed. She always wants to know if our customers benefit from our plans as well as the bank, not just whether the plan helps us compete with other banks. In fact, she has a community advisory council to raise issues in the bank and the community that need to be addressed.

You just get the feeling that she is secure enough not to be threatened by much at all. And that makes her very powerful in the bank and in the community. Not powerful in a negative sort of way but in the sense of being able to free other people to do their best for themselves, the bank, and the community because they don't have to be afraid of her or fight her. It's hard to describe her without making her sound perfect, which she's not. But when she feels a mood coming on or is not in a good frame of mind to talk she will postpone the meeting, turn it over to someone else, or remove herself from the discussion. She regularly takes time to reflect and think. You really ought to meet her to see what you think. I've been working for her for eight years and am content to stay another eight because of all I've learned.

Jed, Describing Sam, the Conscience
of the Organization

(This example shows how a person's role in an organization can serve as symbol of Stage Five—a conscience. In this case, the person may not need to be at Stage Five himself to have this effect.)

There is this guy at our church whom many people would like to ignore but whom I consider one of the most important people around. Now, I can't say what makes this guy tick, because he appears to be pretty weird, but I do know that he acts as our social conscience. He's been through about every experience imaginable in life, and he isn't shy in telling about it. If I had been able to survive half of what he has and remain sane I'd be happy. Nevertheless, he's a weird duck. He dresses strangely, he looks strange, and he acts strangely. And people don't know quite what to do with him. But he has unselfishly dedicated his life to working with the street people through whatever means necessary. That's why I call him the conscience of the church. Here are some of the things he does that make us squirm. Almost every week he brings people with him to church who just happen to be living with him until they move on to permanent quarters. Regularly he manages to entice a few members to get involved in some prison project or a support group of some kind. Of course, we always get more out of it ourselves than we feel we give to others. Another thing he does is to arrive at church meetings ready to challenge us on the way we spend our money or the ways in which we measure success. He even needles the minister, suggesting that he encourages the status quo or caters to the wealthy. He is relentless, but he and the minister are still dear friends. The very sight of Sam reminds me that there is more to life than my own and my family's comfort. Sam stands for dedication to simple principles and a clear purpose. He is not sophisticated or suave. He is love personified. He has been around the block several times, but he has been plucked out of the mainstream to lead a different kind of life. He raises the hackles of people, but in the end his style confronts us sincerely and allows us to think about the critical things in life.

Bill, Describing Martha, the Problem Solver

(The role of a Stage Five person in an organization may be to remain

titleless but to be available to do the things one does best and the things
the company needs most at the time.)

I think Martha's been around here since this place opened. And
she's probably had most of the jobs as well. But when a company
grows as fast as we have in the last fifteen years, you need people
who can wear all sorts of hats. Martha started in manufacturing and
soon became a supervisor. She's been in accounting (learned it on
the job), procurement, personnel (she started that office), and a few
others. She just learns so quickly and accomplishes things so well
we kept giving her different assignments. A few years ago she'd
covered most of the new territory, and we were at a loss as to the
next direction for her. We thought seriously about making her the
manager of a group of departments, but she was aboslutely against
that. She said that managing others was not the skill that she
wanted to use, nor was she particularly rewarded by managing.
Martha came up with her own solution. She wanted to be the
"Problem Person," she said. That meant to me that people anywhere in the company could come to her with problems, and with
her background, her ability to gain people's trust, her wonderful
contacts, and a great mind she could help solve them. Well, let me
tell you, it was the greatest idea by far. She has no title because she
wants none. She just goes to her office or wanders around the
company until she finds a problem or until a problem finds her.
Then she goes to work. She doesn't threaten anyone because she's
not their boss and she gives them all the credit. She's the most
dearly thought of person in the entire company. I found out by
chance that she has instructed the compensation people to hold her
raises. She doesn't want to move to her next tax bracket and she's
having too much fun to have to start managing more money at her
age. Amazing.

Lois, Describing Stuart, the Teacher

(When people find out who they are and that the absolute love of their
lives is in their work, this discovery is its own reward. This example
speaks for itself.)

I know Stuart would be embarrassed to have himself cited, but I really feel he is an example of someone who has found his true self and his purpose in life. Stuart was in Korea during the war and never forgot the look on the faces of the children who had lost their parents or who were hurt in other ways. He really had a hard time adjusting to civilian life after he returned. He went to business school on the GI bill and worked for several years at a large company. From what I know he did fine, but he says he wasn't happy most of the time. He just couldn't get those faces out of his mind. As I recall he said he just dropped out for a while and searched for himself and his future. Along the way, he needed money, so he worked part-time as a teacher's aide in his local school. Slowly he recognized in those children's faces some of the same sadness behind the eyes, the same searching in the stances, the same joy in a response. He decided to start over, to pool his money and open a candy store in a poor neighborhood. He knew it was the right decision no matter what it would cost him. And he was finding out more about himself through the children every day. Now he's been a candy store owner for twenty years, and he's stayed in the same neighborhood. Every fifth year he takes off three months so he can refresh himself. But while he's working he serves as a friend and father figure for many of the kids in his neighborhood. He makes sure they have shoes for dances, suits for graduation, contacts for jobs. They bring their spouses and kids back to see "Pops," which is their nickname for him. He has such a large amount of love and energy for them that some people are curious if he's on some wonder drug or something. Oh, he has his bad days, but he tells me that he's found the purpose of his life in the changes he sees in those faces when they are cared for and loved by another person. He says that all he wants is to touch the lives of children and I believe him.

Cal, Describing Maya, Community Activist

(Acting as a catalyst but not as a ringleader is often the mark of a Stage Five person. In this example Maya clearly put the good of the community ahead of her own good.)

I'm not even sure what Maya does for a living, although I know she leaves work early sometimes to come to meetings. All I know is how much she does for this community very quietly and with determination but with no interest in thanks or recognition. She decided about five or six years ago after a TV report on the high incidence of drug use and the increasing number of broken homes that our community was not looking after the welfare of all of its members adequately, and she feared it would get worse in the future. She decided to see what the energy of one little person— with the help of lots of others—could do to rally the community. She went personally to the mayor to get a task force set up on family solidarity. She chose not to chair it but instead got a prominent citizen who was respected by all. The task force represented all partners in the issue including parents, school officials, teenagers, business people, youth agencies. They came up with a multi-year plan to work on the top three issues they had identified, which would involve all the groups represented. The plan was not limited to drug information sessions but evolved into family retreats, employment training programs, emergency counseling and referral, and community pride campaigns. The entire community was touched in some way or another by the program because of its pervasiveness. And in every part of the program Maya worked she pulled strings but moved into the background. She told me laughingly that it had nothing to do with humility, it just wouldn't have worked any other way. I haven't seen her for a while, but I assume she's resting up for the next challenge in meeting unmet needs.

Moving to Stage Six

The crisis that people experience in moving from Stage Five to Stage Six is that of understanding the cosmos. No longer does the individual matter in the larger scheme of things, and yet the individual is all that matters. That paradox, once understood, accepted, and humbly loved, moves one toward wisdom. In fact, coming to understand paradox as a guiding force in life is one of the clues that a Five is moving to Stage Six.

A paradox in the move itself is that Fives do not seek to move anywhere; they just love and may or may not emerge as Sixes. It doesn't really matter. And that may be why they become Sixes.

Life becomes a true mystery as people evolve beyond Stage Five, for just understanding their place in the cosmos is in itself mind-boggling. But increasingly, their knowledge combines with their intuition to create wisdom. Wisdom goes beyond knowledge or intuition and adds an extra dimension that comes from deep within. People who are moving from Stage Five are content to wait for wisdom, for they know it is gained through a deep understanding of life and death.

Beyond Stage Five, people begin to see the role of death in the scheme of life, and they become friends with death because they have seen beyond it. Again, this is a mystery to be lived and perhaps not totally understood, but it allows them to see the world in different ways and to live more calmly and genuinely. How this occurs is impossible to explain because it is unique to the individual, but once it occurs, one can never again live as if one didn't know it.

Stage Five people in transition are connecting with several dimensions that go beyond the ordinary ways of perceiving, knowing, and being. In our culture they risk being considered crazy or too far out. So for support and acceptance they must look to something beyond ordinary reality. Once they have learned this and experienced it regularly, they cease to need cultural inclusion. They can be committed but detached. The energy and inner power they have is almost totally fueled by another source.

This life stance allows Fives to give up anything and everything of worldly value and to be about a larger universal purpose. Fives in transition sometimes find their lives taking slow but strange turns so that their way of life begins to merge with their purpose. They may be poor by many standards but rich in those that matter most.

Fives cannot move beyond that stage on their own. They feel a slow, inner drawing toward Stage Six wisdom, and they discover teachers along the way who they least expected could lead them. But they are content to let themselves go and to learn another way of approaching life.

What have people done in moving to Stage Six?

It would not be wise to try to describe how to obtain wisdom. As the old saying goes, "he that breaks a thing to find out what it is has left the path of wisdom" (J. R. R. Tolkien).

What Holds People Back?

Most people will never know why more Fives don't move to Six because people rarely talk of experiences at these levels. If they do, it's usually for the sake of instructing others. In fact, when people freely offer the information that they are Stage Five or Six people, they probably aren't. It's another one of those paradoxes. One woman told me with a broad smile that she had moved from Stage One to Stage Six in one year. I responded that I was simply amazed and that I hoped she would not stop there.

The main reason people won't move to the most developed stage of personal power is usually a lack of faith. They just can't let go of assurances in order to get to the final step of living with no fear, deep spirituality, and true paradox. It is too ambiguous, or it is too frightening or unpredictable. Another reason people won't move to Stage Six is that most have too much to give up. We've lived for varying lengths of time accumulating reputations, possessions, knowledge, and know-how. Stage Six people have to be willing to sacrifice all of that if they are truly to live the integrated life. They must even consider giving up their lives in some cases. Can you imagine Sister Teresa asking what kind of return she will get on her investment? Usually the very things that we hold most dear are those things we are asked to give up in moving to Stage Six. We cannot be attached to (get our life's meaning from) things or people and still operate fully in Stage Six.

SUMMARY OF STAGE FIVE
power by purpose

SYMBOL

DESCRIPTION
vision
the irregulars

CHARACTERISTICS
self-accepting
calm
visionary
humble
confident of life purpose
generous in empowering others
spiritual

CRISIS OF MOVEMENT
understanding the universe

WHAT HOLDS PEOPLE BACK?
understanding the universe
lack of faith
too much to lose

WAYS TO MOVE
in individual ways

Ask yourself these questions about Stage Six:

Yes No

_____ _____   1. Do you see all of life as a paradox?

_____ _____   2. Do you understand the interrelationship of all things?

_____ _____   3. Is service to the world of individuals your "work"?

_____ _____   4. Do you operate on an inner set of ethical principles that pervade your life?

_____ _____   5. Are you committed yet detached?

_____ _____   6. Are you unafraid of death?

_____ _____   7. Do you frequently ask unanswerable questions?

_____ _____   8. Do you have a life purpose for which you would die?

_____ _____   9. Do you feel complete peace of mind?

_____ _____   10. Are you considered a sage?

_____ _____   11. Do you enjoy long periods of solitude and silence?

_____ _____   12. Are you nearly perfect?

Caution: This is a trick quiz.

Yes answers to these questions *do not* necessarily mean you identify with Stage Six.

Chapter 6

Stage Six: Power by Gestalt

Wisdom

What Is Stage Six Like?

Being at Stage Six is like floating in a balloon that is circling above the earth and making occasional landings. Many times Stage Six people are perceived as being out on a jaunt, alone with their musings. But when they are available, they are certainly not untouchable. In fact, they can be warm, inviting, and nurturing. But they live in domains that are not totally accessible to others. Their habits generally include long periods of solitude, silence, and reflective thought. During these times Sixes are refueling, relaxing, recharging. They need to do this because they are so oriented to giving, to being available, to listening intently that they can become depleted without being aware of it. The energy they possess comes from a source beyond themselves, so being continually open to that source is part of the way they live their lives.

Sixes are sages. They may be well known or unknown. They may be persons who touch only one life profoundly, or they may be internationally known heroes and heroines of centuries past and present. They

129

are godlike without being gods in the flesh. They can be one's grand-mother, the owner of the local candy store, a philosopher, a day-care administrator, a boss, or a poet. All of us have a bit of Six in us, just as we have a bit of the other stages, and just a few people live more congruently in this stage. The description of personal power at Stage Six is wisdom. Part of the mystique of Stage Six people is that they may not fit all of our preconceived notions of how wise people ought to be. We may have an image of what wisdom is, and we may indeed have had a relationship with a person we considered truly wise, but we saw them in a subjective way. In other words, a person who appears wise when you are in Stage Two may look very different to you when you are in Stage Four. It doesn't mean the person wasn't really wise; it means your understanding of wisdom has changed. No wisdom figure I know would admit to being one—and that's part of the paradox. They would laugh at taking a quiz to find out whether they are wise. They might, in fact, answer all the questions no because they are so humble. So if you answered the questions yes, you are probably *not* at Six yet. (That's why it's a trick quiz.)

Sixes are fearless, especially when it comes to death. This is because they believe their life's work is so important that sacrificing their life would only further that work. In order to operate at Stage Six, this basic human fear must be met head on. Sometimes having a near-death experience introduces people to Stage Six. Sometimes experiencing the death of another gives us a new wisdom. Stage Six people are thankful for whatever life experiences they have, and they have accepted the fact of their own death. They are no longer trying to defy or ignore it, as most of us do.

Power by Gestalt suggests that Sixes see the whole picture. Gestalt means more than the sum of the parts. The whole has a dimension that transcends the total, and Stage Six people see this. Thus, they can ask questions that seem to be on a higher or broader level or that call into question some underlying assumptions. But Sixes do not try to one-up others or embarrass them. They merely share the insight or vision that comes to them, if appropriate. Sixes exude power of an inner origin.

The symbol for this stage depicts a person whose personal power pervades the surrounding space. They have some undefinable quality about them, which may vary from person to person, that permeates the space they occupy or touches the people they are with. Their presence comes from an inner well of calm, of quiet strength, in which they live. And it may be disconcerting to some who are not used to it or are anxious themselves. One wise person I've observed is very quiet while people are talking to her; in fact, at times she will close her eyes to be able to listen more acutely. I watched her do this with a highly verbal person, who became very disturbed by it, since eye contact was an important part of the conversation to him. The scene became almost humorous as it continued. The speed and the intensity of the one-sided conversation increased until the wise person said, "Let's continue this chat over a lemonade." Her peacefulness and attention made the other person nervous.

Although disconcerting at times, the gestalt of Sixes affects people positively. They want to know more. They are intrigued. I am told of a well-known actor who exudes personal power when he walks quietly into a room. He consistently and genuinely cares about serving others instead of himself and his career. He purposely takes himself out of the limelight and supports and trains others to go beyond him. People around him say that he is a wonder to behold. The more selfless he is the more people admire him—though that is not his aim—and it makes him very uncomfortable. In fields in which stardom is the primary goal (which could be almost any field), it is sometimes more difficult for the brightest shining stars to move beyond that role. They have too much to give up, too much to lose. The nagging fear of being forgotten or dismissed haunts them, so most of them never get past Stage Three.

Power by Gestalt also leads to the concept of transcendence meaning, "beyond the limits of human experience or knowledge." The Stage Six person can tap a source of power and insight that is infinite and all-knowing, yet not to be plumbed in modern ways, only in the ways of the ancients. Their source becomes a way of life, a part of their being, a peace of mind, not a technique or a costume. Some Stage Six people may not obviously exude personal power or affect us right away, but after a while they astound us with their presence in our lives. We hear their voices when we least expect them.

Stage Six people are not hermits. They don't hide in caves or cloisters. They are out among people. That is not to say they do not spend time in solitude, but the model I am presenting requires that Stage Six people be in relationship. Stage Six people, involved and active in the world, get their energy from a different source now, and their activities serve others almost entirely.

Sixes are not limited to any one setting, type of work, or way of life. So one does not become a Stage Six by engaging in a certain type of work like political activism, social service, health, business, or the ministry. And there are relatively few Sixes around, no matter where we look. They may be the very people we least expect to see as wisdom figures, so how can we recognize them? One man related the experience of "meeting wisdom," as he describes it. He was on an airplane flight a few years ago and happened to sit next to a frumpy looking older woman. He hesitated to engage in conversation with her, but when he finally did he was astonished. In her gentle way she gave him wonderful new insights about himself and the world. "She tapped into my soul," was his conclusion. He has never seen her since, but he will never forget her.

We might all identify with this man's experience in some way. When we are around wisdom figures, they touch a part of us that has experienced wisdom, that—at least momentarily—feels as if everything fits, that all is interrelated, and that there is a larger plan for us. All of this gives us peace of mind and a reason for being. This part of us peeks out occasionally and surprises us or makes us yearn for more contact, but we are not able to hold on to it for more than brief periods of time, nor are we even sure that we want to. Most of us have never thought about it. So when we are around Stage Six persons, this unfamiliar, neglected part of us is touched and uplifted without our full awareness—until later, perhaps. Because this part of us is so strange, it may frighten us when it emerges, and the Stage Six persons who have caused it to surface may frighten us as well.

Stage Sixes operate at a level of power Rollo May calls integrative power or power *with* other people. They certainly do not need nor do they want the limelight. It is the kind of power that invites criticism and feedback because ideas develop best when they are digested and reworked. A prime example of this simple and mystical kind of power is the nonviolent resistance of Gandhi and Martin Luther King, Jr. The nonviolent method has a way of disarming its opponents by exposing moral defenses. It works on the conscience and on the memory. The opponent has to live with himself or herself after injuring a nonviolent person (*Power and Innocence,* pp. 110-111). So working with Sixes may draw criticism or even hatred because they are not playing by the rules. Being with them requires a real commitment. They will never manipulate others to join them.

Sixes see life as a paradox, as opposites balanced in tension with one another. And they themselves are seen as paradoxes to others: They are calm yet can be passionate, patient yet vexed, complex yet simple. But somehow they still seem integrated as a whole. Life is a wonder to behold, a mystery to be lived, and a miracle to be appreciated.

The manifestation of power at Stage Six is wisdom, of which we have already been speaking. Wisdom is a complex concept and open to several interpretations; however, to me it is a quality of being that goes beyond information and even beyond knowledge or intuition. It is a quality of sageness that is so deeply embedded within each person that it takes on the nuances of that person's total integrated style. A wise philosopher gave me this definition: "Wisdom is a practical power of the whole person. It is not to be equated with knowledge if, by knowledge, is meant information, expressable in propositional form. In simple language, wisdom might be a love for what is good, not devotion to good in general, but to what knowledge and disposition lead us to do in light of the circumstances" (John Knox Coit).

Characteristics of Stage Six People

Comfortable with Paradox

Through most of the power stages we struggle to find the answers, to separate the right from the wrong way. And we may come to some conclusions only to find they don't necessarily work for all circumstances. Then we go through a period in which there seem to be no answers at all, just lots of confusing questions. Slowly, we find that there are lots of answers to every question depending on our view, and then we decide which view we want to take. Stage Six people aren't concerned about answering questions at all. Asking questions is more interesting, and they do not need answers. Things can be amorphous, ambiguous, and abstract. And almost everything seems to be a paradox, a combination of opposites or contradictions.

Some of the paradoxes that Stage Six people live with might be:

The more we know, the less we know
Continuity is change
The question is the answer
Humility requires deep self-love
Commitment means detachment
Evil and good are siblings
Our strength is our weakness, our weakness our strength
Everything is interrelated; everything is separate
We are all significant; we are all insignificant
Everything is simple and complex
The transcendent is the real
Active is reflective; reflective is active
Everything matters; nothing matters.

Sixes are not perfect by any stretch of the imagination. In fact, they accept their humanness more than most other people. The main difference is that they have gone beyond the acceptance of their qualities (strengths and weaknesses) to the point of integrating and in fact appreciating their quirks and their shadows, as Jung describes our negative qualities. Some folks fight with or run from their shadow all their lives, fearing that it will take them over. If we can accept and then befriend our shadows, they can become useful companions, keeping us in balance and our life in perspective. This sounds easy, yet it may require a lifetime of reflection, work, and pain to accomplish, often with professional help. One reason this is such a task is that we must become vulnerable and honest with ourselves, admitting to lies that we and others have perpetuated, before we can move on to more authentic living. The paradox of our shadow is that frequently it is disguised as our strongest positive trait, and we can't believe that it would "do us in." Take for example, the strong, emotionally stable people whose strength isolates them from feeling or experiencing personal human tragedy; or the beautiful people whose beauty precludes them from being taken seriously or becomes a defense against understanding the ugliness in themselves; or the perfect people whose compulsion leads them to the height of anxiety. Because Sixes have learned to incorporate their shadow and even have a sense of humor about it, they can disarm and even intimidate others, but with no pretense. Sixes may appear to be idiosyncratic or individualistic, but this usually reflects who they really are rather than a need to become unique. And there is a big difference between the two. Threes and Fours strive to become unique, while Sixes are content to be who they really are. An anonymous author said, "Maturity consists in no longer being taken in by yourself."

Not only have Sixes integrated their shadows, they have also come to a new realization of their mind-body-spirit relationships. There is a heightened perception in Stage Six people of the unity, the gestalt of the mind-body-spirit dichotomies. They think of themselves as more of a *process* than a person; they are more like conduits than receptacles. Through them flows wisdom. They have combined their being with a much larger universal wisdom that puts all things and events into a larger perspective. It is as if they can step back from their linear life lines and observe the whole cinema—past, present, and future. For instance, Stage Six people may experience an illness or some emotional stress. Instead of fighting it or overanalyzing it, or blaming themselves, they recognize that they may also see some meaning in the event from a broader perspective, or they may take the time to do some reassessment. When a loved one dies, they do not deny the anguish and the pain, but at the same time they realize that this is the beginning of a new relationship with the person on a slightly different plane. This event has been an abrupt break in the continuity of the relationship, but they believe it may resume after a time, in a different way.

Unafraid of Death

Possibly the characteristic most comforting to Sixes and most baffling to others is their lack of fear of their own and others' deaths. Sixes have experienced sometime in life a dress rehearsal of their own death or have in some other way deeply prepared for it. It could have been physical, mental, or emotional but it was real to them. The event changed the way they view life. They see themselves as part of a longer continuum. Elisabeth Kübler-Ross and others have conducted extensive research on the subject of death. Their conclusions suggest that in most cases death is not a frightening but a calm experience. Most people reporting the observation of their own death or near-death experience have said it was not scary or evil or awful. Instead they claim that it is hard to come back to reality because it is so much calmer and lighter on the other side.

A woman relates her experience regarding her physical death. "There I lay on the hospital surgical table all broken apart and bleeding. That was one part of me. The other part of me, the spirit, I guess, was floating above the table watching the goings on. I was calm and rather amused at all the effort they were going to when I knew that I had already died and gone to the other side. I had been broadsided in a terrible car accident. I was rushed to the hospital but I knew it was too late because I had already left my body and was greeted by a wonderful person on the other side with a shining light. Then as I watched I began to feel tugs pulling me toward the table. I didn't want to go back, but the tugs were stronger all the time. Finally I gave in when I could no longer resist and the next thing I knew I was recovering in the intensive care ward. I have never been the same since. I now have very little fear of death. In fact, I am almost looking forward to it. But apparently, I have some other things to do."

Having met death, Sixes find it's their constant companion and helps them put life into perspective. Their values change now because of what they have learned about values on the other side. No wonder material possessions—status, jobs, titles, control, fame, money—cease to matter. What matters now may be very different for each Six, but it is usually the intangibles: caring, love, service, giving, peace of mind, wisdom, integrity, and beauty.

This acquaintance with death and with people who have died is one way to account for transcendent qualities or a sense of the gestalt in Sixes. They have a source of contact beyond human experience. Another explanation is their strong spiritual tie to a universal supreme being. Whatever the source, there is indeed a contact point or a bridge between these people and another plane of existence. They draw frequently or continuously from that plane for their energy and insight, claiming none of these insights originate within themselves. In a sense they have given up both their external and their internal power to draw from their higher power. Their goal, if any, is to avoid being an obstacle in the path of that power.

This spiritual sense of other-world contact is not to be confused with popular trends and quasi-self-actualizing experiences in the psychic realm. After the encounter group era of the '60s and the narcissistic era of the '70s, the next attempt at self-realization for the searchers is in the spiritual and the psychic realm. People are getting religion and super power now in the way they were getting sandals and long hair in the '60s. There are classes in magic of all kinds, from meditation and dance to out-of-body training, automatic writing, and clairvoyance. I criticize these things not because they are particularly bad in themselves but only because they can be substituted for the real and difficult work of deep self-exploration. In fact, most of these experiences can distract the person, if only temporarily, from the central work, that of knowing one's real self and one's connection to the central pervasive force of life. If these experiences do less, then they are distractions. In fact, some of these psychic or even religious experiences can be dangerous for individuals who are vulnerable or emotionally unprotected.

Any experience that promises powers that sound too good to be true or that requires discipleship to another should be suspect. The guide I use to determine whether an experience will be helpful is to ask these questions of myself: "Why am I doing this? How am I going to use it?" Also I liken my life to the climbing of a tree. I may want to experience the exhilaration of creeping out on some limbs and even swinging from the branches, but I do not want to go so far out on weak branches that I fall and risk injury. And in my more vulnerable times staying in near the trunk and the large, sturdy branches is the best course of action for the time.

Powerless

In an ironic way Stage Six people have come full circle to the point of needing very little tangible power. The external power no longer matters, and the internal power has been transformed. Like Stage One people, Sixes seldom strive to get ahead; instead, they show almost an apathy for improving their own lot. There are some major differences to be sure, but on the surface Sixes sometimes appear to be uninterested in doing many things they should be doing for themselves. They are more interested in moving other people forward or in furthering principles in life.

When asked about their life purpose Sixes would probably reply that life *is* purpose. Just living from day to day brings purpose. Each day reveals new people to serve, new roads to travel, old friendships to nurture. They make no lists of things to do or career goals to meet. Living, for them, is giving and the rest works itself out. This can mean that Sixes are terribly committed to living out certain ideas, philosophies, or causes, but they live them from day to day without talking about them.

From this perspective it is easy to see why the lives of Sixes seem to become simpler rather than more complex. They can reduce their possessions and their lifestyles to the simplest of essentials because the richness of life emerges from within. They know that life can be such a game, anyway. For many, the game proceeds in this manner: The more you earn the more you want. The more you have, the harder it is to manage it and the more concerned you are about losing it. The more worried you are, the more stress you have and the more you cling to the external symbols. Think about this scenario: Suppose you were able to pay off your home mortgage and invest enough money to live frugally on the interest, which would rise with inflation. Would you be satisfied with that secure but small income that offers you the choice of working or not working or changing your type of work? Not many would, I'm afraid.

One wonderful person comes to mind as an example of a deliberately chosen lifestyle of simplicity. During all his years as a college teacher, Cal gave of his time and most of the money he earned from teaching to students or causes or traveling experiences with others. He had a habit of keeping money available in certain drawers in his desk so students he knew well and who were poor could help themselves without having to ask him. He financed trips for students to see special games, he bought new suits for their graduation, and so on. He never asked for or expected any of the money to be returned. In addition he simply befriended students whom he liked or who needed befriending. He talked with them, played games, taught them, laughed with them, traveled with them, and gave generously of himself. At the age of fifty he started having what was to be a series of heart attacks and had to retire early from teaching at age fifty-seven. His pension and social security are hardly enough to sustain him, even though his needs are minimal. He is sustained, however, by his friends to whom he had been so generous. One provides him with two round trips to the east coast, another brings him to the midwest. One family orders the *New York Times* for him. Another makes sure his clothes are in good repair. Some just send checks. What does he say to all this? "Oh, my gracious, my goodness! How could an old man be so lucky?"

Quiet in Service

Sixes may be found in any occupation. Their work for pay is usually secondary to their primary work, which is some form of serving or helping others to achieve a purpose, whether it be running a co-op, harvesting a crop, nursing a neighbor, listening to a person in pain, or visiting a child. Their paid work could also be their service, if it works out that way. Their service may even be to remain alert to every person they meet to make sure they are available for whatever needs to be said or done with each one. They tend to operate on a day-to-day basis, without much care or worry for tomorrow. That ability to put aside worry and anxiety is an unusual characteristic in anyone. Because Sixes have come to terms with their fears (for the most part) and because they understand their life mission or purpose in service, they find very little to be anxious about. And it gives them much more energy to use on other things. One Stage Six person I met has lived with cancer for six years and has a philosophy of life that goes something like this: "I live each day and each event as it comes, knowing that in each situation I have something to give and something to learn. When I got cancer I looked back over my life and decided I liked most of it, hated some of it. I resolved to live out my remaining years doing the things that have the most meaning for me. I changed my area of nursing from surgical to working in a hospice, and I lead grief groups in our church in the evenings. It's ironic, but in facing death, I feel alive again."

Sixes are usually not found in large or bureaucratic organizations. In fact, it would probably not be wise for managers to encourage Stage Six behavior in the organization, with the exception of a few "odd balls." Stage Six people operate better when they can influence an organization from an outside, independent stance. Most organizations cannot tolerate

Stage Six behavior; they don't know what to do with Sixes. Since Sixes are not motivated by the regular things and want to find meaning through their service, they tend to operate independently and live quite simply and well, blending their work with their lives. And that could be doing just about anything. It's not the exact work they do but the kind of effect it allows them to have on others that counts. The distinguishing characteristic is that their work does not feed them or build their egos, nor do they have much attachment to it. Their real energy and stamina comes from a transcendent source and flows through them to others, no matter what the setting.

This chapter is strange to write. I feel at times that I should have left it out, because to talk about Stage Six almost demeans or destroys it. In fact, one of the reasons it is so difficult to describe Sixes in detail is that they don't talk about themselves or name themselves as such. For, as I said earlier, anyone who tells you he or she is a guru, a master, a wisdom figure, or a spiritual guide *isn't*. The very nature of self-enhancing roles or relationships is anathema to Sixes. They may know very clearly inside that they are in the role of spiritual guide or counselor to others, but it is a nonverbal acknowledgment. They may even warn others to be careful in describing the relationship to others, for a following could develop that may force them to be the center of attention.

Clergy can be most threatened by Stage Six people because these professionals may fear that their role in people's lives will be usurped. They may strive to be a Stage Six person, yet many of them will never make it because they are afraid to accept their own humanness. And one of the allurements of their profession is allowing themselves to be put on pedestals by others. Sixes may or may not be involved with organized religion, but certainly they associate with a supportive community of spiritual people.

Sixes can be unknown or well known, as with every other stage, but they are more difficult to spot. This is because there are so few of them and also because of their quietness about their activities. If you think about the Six part of you, it is the part that fewest people see, that comes forth in the brief moments when you feel connected to the universe: experiencing a miracle, watching a flower open, healing a friend, experiencing deep, empowering love, creating a poem. During those moments nothing else is really of consequence. Sixes live a large part of their lives in that state of mind. No wonder they are alienated from the vast majority of people who totally misunderstand them!

In fact, to be at Stage Six means to be often misunderstood and even unappreciated by others. But Sixes are not trying to impress or change others, so they just accept these things with grace and a sense of aloneness yet connectedness. One of the main reasons there is no danger of the world's becoming overrun with these "strange" Sixes is that it takes too much commitment to move to Stage Six. It requires giving up a great many of the things that are most valuable to most of us. It reminds me of the rich young ruler who asked Jesus what he must do to be saved. "Give everything you have to the poor and follow me," replied Jesus. The wealthy man went away very disappointed. We all seem to want more, yet we are not willing to give up in order to receive more on a different plane. We're too afraid of the void that occurs once we give up something. What if the void is not filled? We are afraid to risk the chance of nothingness, so we go on searching for an easier route. A life of service sounds boring to some because they assume it must lack excitement, challenge, and recognition. Peace of mind even sounds dull. A life of service can be very exciting or very quiet—usually both. But excitement does not motivate Sixes. They would live a life of service no matter what it brought. So you see, Stage Six is not for everyone.

Ethical

Another distinguishing characteristic of Sixes is their code of ethics. They understand and even incorporate the inevitable evils of the world into their vision because they are realistic, but they abhor acts and events that deliberately harm other people. On many occasions they must say or do things that may bring sadness or anger temporarily, but they always trust the long-term effects of their actions or at least are aware of them. They cannot participate in events or situations in which people are plotted against or deliberately sacrificed for the greed or ego of another. On the other hand, they would die for a just cause. That's why they are sometimes so unpopular. They simply call it the way they see it. Their sense of right does not mean doing what will benefit them but what will be best in the long run for all people involved. They have integrity and a sense of moral justice, which goes beyond the law at times.

Ethical behavior is a quality that comes from an intent to be just, not from an intent to legislate another's values or morals. Sixes do not expect people to believe as they do, but to have thought through the issues and come to their *own* conclusions. Sixes generally make decisions or recommendations because they are the just things to do. At times this may even mean a loss for them or an admission of being wrong or uninformed. They can admit mistakes and do not usually let false pride get in the way of the truth—even if it is painful. Since they see the larger picture, they can make decisions based on long-term justice rather than on the expedient action. For example, let's say a Stage Six person is asked to consult on a situation in which two groups in an organization obviously need to merge. The leaders of both groups would be very appropriate leaders overall, but one of the candidates is overly confident, while the other is more insecure. It seems pretty clear to most people that the confident person will get the job. The consultant to the situation knows both of the people quite well and thinks through the situation carefully. Then she suggests that the more insecure-appearing of the two be selected, because he would learn more about himself in the new job than the one who is overly confident. Since long-term development of people is a key objective of hers (and of the department), it follows that the confident candidate would learn more about himself and life by having the experience of being passed over once. The Stage Six consultant simply takes an intuitive, commonsense and morally sound approach in the situation, and she is confident that it will turn out well in the long run. And she will not talk about the recommendation to other colleagues. The mystique of morality grows too when it is not always explained. Moral people have fewer regrets in life because they do not need to hash over or become defensive for their actions. They ask questions before making choices, such as, Whom will it hurt? How could it turn out to everyone's advantage? How will this decision affect the more important things in life, in the world?

Sixes are the kind of people whose advice rings in the back of our minds over the years. We can always count on them to be fair, not to always agree with us. And their advice may seem unusual, like telling us to forgive our enemies or to not defend ourselves or to let go or to give others what they've stolen from us. Hard advice, which we usually find a way to avoid following. But when difficult situations arise, we recall their voice and then the choice is whether to heed it or not. Gandhi gave advice to a raging Hindu man whose son had been killed by a Muslim. When the man asked how he could be set free from the hatred, Gandhi answered, "Find a Muslim boy your son's age whose family has been killed. Raise the boy to be a man, and raise him to be a Muslim."

On the Universal Plane

Stage Six people are children of the universe. They have a larger understanding of the world and the universe than most people. The pain and joy of the entire cosmos is like that of their family. It's easy to see why they are mostly against war, since there is no enemy who is different from us. Some of the Vietnam veterans speak profoundly of the difficulty of facing the enemy in Vietnam, who turned out to be villagers—men, women, and children. It was much more complicated, they said, than tanks fighting tanks, and rows of soldiers attacking each other head on. Sixes understand that war will never cease because humans will always be competing for power, but their understanding transcends the use of force to feel superior over another, to revenge past deeds, or to compete for world power positions.

Sixes also understand the depths of pain and even feel others' pain acutely, though not always directly. A story describes this idea. A very old man lived in a small town in the mountains of Austria. One day he got a message from a friend in the next town, ten miles away, requesting that he come see him right away for he was in terrible shock over the illness of his son. The old man hobbled through the mountains to his friend's home only to be astonished by his friend's response. "I am so glad you're here, but how did you know that I was in such a terrible state?"

"Something inside told me that I should come see you, and I got here as soon as I could," the old man said to his friend.

"It is amazing to me that you are here, but I don't understand how you knew. Let's go and talk over a good, long meal."

The old man stayed three days with his old friend until his son was over the worst of the illness. Then he trudged back over the mountains to his home.

A year later, the old man once again received a message from his friend, this time with the urgent words, "I'm dying, please come." The old man hurried over the long road to his friend's home only to find him in the local hospital with a heart attack.

"How wonderful to see you, my friend. I am very ill and I thought I would never see you again. But how did you know that I was ill?"

"I got another message from inside like the last one. It seemed urgent so I hurried right over to see how I could be useful to you."

"This is indeed confusing to me because I don't know how you knew I was ill when I didn't tell you. Anyway, I'm glad you're here again. You do know the times I need you most, my friend."

Years later, when the old man died, his family and friends were going through his meager belongings and they came upon a very interesting journal that the old man had kept for the last forty years of his life. His friend's son happened to be among the company as they were lovingly reading excerpts from the journal of this wise old man. One of the entries stated at the beginning of the day, "Deep meditation, voice of Peter, son is ill, I need you, come." The friend's son was overwhelmed by the message. He asked to read the excerpt from the next year, around the time of his father's heart attack. The same sort of entry appeared. "Morning meditation, voice of Peter, I'm dying. Come soon." He wept with joy over the sensitivity of the wise old man for his friend. No wonder there were no letters or calls!

It's better not to ask Sixes how things happen; it's better to just trust them that things happen. They understand it all on a plane different from the one on which we operate daily. And most of us haven't even scratched the surface of the other levels in which we could operate. To penetrate that surface takes a deep connection with the spiritual universe and requires long periods of discipline and quiet listening.

Wisdom figures find themselves alone in many different ways. They are not part of the establishment or the tradition of orthodoxy. Wise people speak and live the truths we all wish we were capable of living. They are at the margin of life but in its center. They are the question-askers, who explore larger visions with no thought of its effect on their position or power. They can function persistently in the presence of power, but their role is to challenge, to enlarge the vision, to give wisdom, to provide a basis for good choices in others. They are the souls of the universe. They have made peace with themselves and can function peacefully with the world.

Let's Meet Some People at Stage Six

The only way I can describe Stage Six people is to include brief quotes about the ways in which they have affected the lives of others. It would be too easy to misunderstand them if I described their behavior in case examples. They appear so simple that their complexity is lost in external behavior.

> "I've never known anyone who cares so much or so genuinely for other people. She is always seeing to it that others' needs are met, sometimes at the expense of her own. It seems she carries this deep, exuding love with her all the time, and she is not a martyr."

> "I know my mom and dad respect him a great deal and go to him for advice, but I think he's wacko."

> "He is the deepest, wisest person I know. I always go to him for his judgment, and he never fails to amaze me. He makes me reason and struggle through my questions so I come out with an acceptable answer, yet he only listens and asks a few questions."

> "I think this guy is just washed up. He got passed over several years ago, and now he's rationalized it so he can live with himself. He says he loves what he's doing now more than ever, but I don't understand how he can. He's not moving. I can't figure out why he's so darn calm and serene all the time."

> "I can't comprehend what makes her tick. She's just very closely connected with a deep well within her out of which perceptive wisdom swells. She provides vision for my life, gentle, unassuming, powerful."

> "She is so committed to this cause, she lives and breathes it, yet I don't think of her as the leader. She moves the cause along with invisible forces."

> "For his sake, I'm glad he's off on his own now. He should have left this organization long ago. He's too real, too perceptive, too threatening to the others. He doesn't try to be at all, it's just that

he's so right on, it scares people. He asks questions that stymie us all."

"I'm totally confused by her. She has her own wavelength in life, and it's not the one society lives on. So I tell her what I want from my career and she smiles saying something to the effect that this is indeed where I'm headed but not the final destination. Now how can she know that? But she's usually been right."

"Every time I'm around him I get nervous. He's so deliberate, so quiet, so intensely interested in me. I just feel like squirming, or I talk a lot more or faster. After about a half hour, though, his presence seems to calm me and I relax. I wonder what it would be like to live that way?"

SUMMARY OF STAGE SIX
power by gestalt

SYMBOL

DESCRIPTION

wisdom

souls of the earth

CHARACTERISTICS
comfortable with paradox
unafraid of death
powerless
quiet in service
ethical
on the universal plane

CRISIS OF MOVEMENT
humanness

WHAT HOLDS PEOPLE BACK?
human constraints

Another Stage?

I have a strong suspicion that there is a Stage Seven in this model of personal power. I have deliberately chosen not to describe the stage, probably because I had enough trouble describing people at Stage Six. My sense is that it would be called something like Power by Transcendence and that the crisis to overcome in order to reach it would be the crisis of being human.

Chapter 7

Leadership and Power

True Leadership

One of the two premises of this chapter is this: *People can be leaders at any stage of personal power, but they cannot be TRUE leaders until they reach Stage Four—Power by Reflection.* Leadership is always tied closely to the idea of followership, and people can motivate and guide followers at any stage of power, but true leadership is a term reserved for those who have experienced the crisis of integrity—people in Stages Four, Five, or Six.

What is integrity and the crisis of integrity? It is interesting to note that integrity and integrate (the latter meaning "make whole, complete; to unify") are from the Latin adjective *integer,* which means "whole, complete in itself." Integrity, a noun, has two similar meanings, each one beginning with "the quality of being." That alone suggests that integrity is not a momentary feeling, an act to play. It is a way of being. Integrity is "a quality or state of being of sound moral principle, honest, sincere, upright"; it is also "a quality of being complete, whole, sound, unimpaired." This does not mean to me totally perfect, but rather that we care and ask about the difference between right and wrong in dealings with people and organizations and take stands on issues that have been worked out inside. It means not lying, even if we may be served well as a result. It means saying what we genuinely feel and think, not what others want us to feel and think. It means not always having our own way, but being able to compromise when appropriate. It means accepting our whole self and feeling all right about the parts that are not so sterling, accepting being human and imperfect, which may be what it really means to be complete. It means being worthy of trust and respect even from people who disagree with us.

149

The requirement of an integrity crisis for true leadership does not mean that people in Stages One through Three lack integrity. It simply means that as they resolve crises in their work and lives the issue of integrity is not the major one they face. And they have not had a battle over the integrity issue yet. They think of their decisions in other ways, more linked to the structure or the norms of the organization. For example, each might say, "The norm around here is so strong that I would be ostracized if I didn't conform," or "I'm only doing what the stockholders demand," or "They who have the gold make the rules," or "Once I get to a higher position of power, I'll change the way things are done," or "I can't be myself here, but those are the breaks." People at Stage Three will undoubtedly bristle when I say they generally aren't true leaders, for their goal is to hold positions of authority so as to ultimately gain their own goals, sometimes at the expense of others. I'm not saying that people in positions of authority cannot be true leaders but only that the position or status is no guarantee of true leadership. The quality of the person is what determines true leadership, not whether he or she is in a position of authority.

 . One other question may arise as true leadership is discussed: If it takes getting to Stage Four to be a true leader, are all Stage Four, Five, and Six people potential leaders? Probably not, or at least not in the ways we currently think of people as leaders, i.e., those in positions of power in organizations and elected officials. Fours, Fives, and Sixes do not actively pursue positions of power for their own sake and may even shy away from them if the norm of the position is Stage Three behavior. They tend to lead by moving with, through, or behind others and do not gravitate toward the glory. Some of them would flatly decline the offer to lead because it is not part of their life purpose, or they would agree to be in a position of power reluctantly, only because they see the long-term changes that are possible.

The question of whether elected officials can be true leaders is especially interesting. A group of emerging community leaders were discussing this very issue with a group of elected officials. Someone noted that it is especially hard for elected officials at any level to be true leaders because there are so many pressures on them from constituents who threaten to defeat them if they do not support their point of view. Also elected officials feel they are principally reactors to crises, the needs of people, and to issues that already have support, rather than originators of new, creative, or venturesome ideas. The group concluded that leaders in fact may operate best from outside the political establishment, influencing and advising those in elected positions.

The question has also been raised as to whether managers are leaders. Dr. Robert Terry, director of a leadership program, makes the distinction between management and leadership: Management makes the system hum, attends to facts, motivates others, completes projects in a timely fashion, controls budgets, connects systems, sets goals, and builds teams. Leadership, on the other hand, sees the larger context, looks for quality relationships with followers, holds dialogues, and thinks of ethical considerations. These are useful distinctions, but I think there is some danger in saying that someone is either part of leadership or management. I think it would be more useful to say that management tasks may not necessarily lend themselves to leadership but that the quality of the person in the management role makes all the difference. Managers can be leaders depending on how they view themselves, others, and the world, and at which stage of personal power they reside.

James M. Burns has written a provocative book called *Leadership*, in which he cites two types of leaders: transactional and transforming. Transactional leadership means one person contacting others to exchange valued things, whether economic, political, or psychological. Examples are votes, goods, money, hospitality. No enduring purpose holds the parties together beyond the transaction. Transforming leadership means one or more persons engaging with others to raise one another to higher levels of motivation and morality. Transforming leadership is moral in that it raises both the leader and the led to new levels of human conduct through inspiring, uplifting, exhorting, preaching. Transforming leaders are involved with the led. Their purposes fuse and they feel a mutual support (pp. 19-20). Burns says the crucial variable is purpose. Leaders inspire followers to act for certain goals that represent values and motivations, wants and needs, the aspirations and expectations of both leaders and followers (p. 19). Comparing Burns' description with the stages of personal power, leaders at Stages Two and Three would be transactional leaders, and leaders at Stages Four, Five, and Six would be transforming types.

To reiterate, true leadership is a term reserved for those who, as leaders, understand and consistently operate with integrity and thereby acquire the respect of others. I strongly advocate that we redefine leadership in broader terms and that we each think more seriously about what it means to lead in our own lives. We need to redefine those qualities we are expecting from our leaders, both in organizations and in elected office. Perhaps instead of choosing from among the candidates who run for office, we should collect our Stage Four, Five, and Six people (thoughtful, egoless, wise) and choose among them for our leaders. Those who want it the least could be our first choice! Perhaps in organizations we could work harder to develop our people more personally and deeply rather than rewarding them for short-term skill-oriented performance.

Leadership and Our World

Some of you reading this may be asking yourselves at this point, "So what? What difference does it make to have Stage Four or Five leaders as opposed to having good old Stage Twos and Threes who are really motivated to get out there and win? Haven't we gotten along all right with the range of people we've had in the past? Look at how successful we've been. We're the most powerful nation in the world!" People who ask these kinds of questions illustrate clearly what part of the problem with our "leadership" has been. A majority of our leaders, both in elected and organizational positions of power, are not true leaders who operate consistently with integrity. They are predominantly Stage Three leaders whose major goal is their own success.

Thus, my second premise: *In order to survive into the next century, we must go beyond our traditional definitions of power and leadership (Stage Three—Symbols) and develop or encourage leaders who operate at higher stages (Stages Four and Five—Reflection and Purpose).* We tend to think of ourselves as against others in the world, as the most this or the least that. We gauge our success by whether we are the biggest, strongest, or best. These are all Stage Three concepts and a Stage Three way of thinking in a world that is rapidly becoming an international and interdependent neighborhood. Buckminster Fuller has said that nations are obsolete. He meant we are already inextricably linked to the larger world and we can't think of ourselves as separate any more. Just as in the time of the thirteen colonies when we had to become the United States, we are now over one hundred countries that must become a whole nation of sorts in order to thrive or even survive over the long term on our planet. And that won't be easy. Already we see that prices in the Middle East profoundly affect us, that war or natural disaster elsewhere often affects us, that our elections and economy affect others, and that nuclear war will affect us all. With the threat of nuclear destruction so close to our consciousness these years, we will have a far greater chance of survival if we have people representing us on all fronts—business, education, religion, politics, athletics, arts—who are Stage Four or beyond. Let me list for you the major characteristics of *TRUE* leaders.

True leaders: follow: a vision, a purpose, an ideal.

True leaders: allow for win-win, not just win-lose.

True leaders: empower others, not themselves.

True leaders: have balance in life, between work, community, and family.

True leaders: can be vulnerable and reflective.

True leaders: treat women, men, and minorities as equals.

True leaders: ask why, not how.

True leaders: have a spiritual connection to power within and beyond.

True leaders: see the bottom line as a means to a larger organizational purpose, not an end in itself.

True leaders: live with integrity as their hallmark.

We are at a turning point in our nation's and in the world's development, and it will take wise and visionary leaders to keep us from moral and financial bankruptcy. We need leaders in this century who will look at power and beyond and who can make a careful, long-range guess at our collective future without solely considering the good of one country or group of countries and their success; who will find it more important to serve than to win; who will not subscribe to the premise that anything goes as long as you don't get caught. Where are the lone, prophetic voices? Where are the people whose lives operate on the basis of principles, on thoughtful and clear values that uphold justice and fairness? Why do we find it so difficult to elect and live with unglamorous candidates who speak their conscience rather than what is expedient? How can we truly be of service to people in the world if we are solely intent upon winning the worldwide race for power? Now is the time for understanding, not naiveté or fear tactics. Now is the time for humility. Now is the time for bridge building. Now is the time for diplomacy.

We are full of material possessions but impoverished in leadership. Inner poverty produces a drive to have and to get that is not satisfying. The real hunger in the U.S. is for integrity and intimacy. We must go beyond the competitive view, experience our own crisis of integrity as a country, and begin being a true leader and role model to the rest of the world. We must take the risk to operate at Stage Four, being more honest and less self-serving, less greedy, and thereby encourage others to operate on higher principles as well—again, not naively, but with foresight. We may have to think differently about our role in the world. We may even have to give up a few of our symbols. I cannot prescribe exact actions, because that subject is far too complex, but only reiterate that integrity is a quality of being based on moral principles. It can be developed and it can make the difference. In fact, it may be the only thing that makes any difference.

Suppose we hypothesize that the traditional forms and definitions of leadership are not sufficient for our coming age and that we need to reconceptualize leadership. Suppose we think of leaders as those who would empower other people, create and give away things and ideas long-term and short-term, collaborate on solutions to problems, put integrity before expediency, develop others' capabilities, be self-aware and self-accepting, non-judgmental, and wise? Then grandmothers, artists, writers, poets, musicians, ministers, teachers, counselors, and secretaries could be more influential leaders. We would see different forms of leadership such as idea leadership, moral leadership, aesthetic leadership, and caring leadership as opposed to leadership based on ego, political, material, and financial criteria.

Suppose leadership really means striving for wisdom, as described in our ancient books and ideals. Suppose we really could depend on others to make decisions that were not self-serving but just. How would our management systems be different? our planning and implementing? our service to customers and clients?

Suppose we viewed the world as our neighborhood and all people as our brothers and sisters. How would we make decisions and work out conflicts? Suppose that the good of all was our chief basis for deliberation on worldwide policy, not just the good of the governed. Wouldn't our pettiness decrease?

What would happen if we all thought seriously about our life purpose and acted in congruence with it? What if we could remove our egos from the middle of our daily discourse and act on the basis of broader ideas? What if we had leaders who really knew and accepted themselves, who would be comfortable with the ramifications? What if all people had a connection with their own source of spirituality and lived accordingly? What if we were not afraid of death?

What if a condition of our emerging leadership consisted of having to choose two people who were younger than we to mentor along the way and to school in the arts of true leadership, as we would be learning from our mentors? What if we had a cultural tradition of true leadership that we could pass down verbally and behaviorally from generation to generation like our American Indian friends? What if we really cared about the future of our world and our leadership?

What if we rewarded people for being innovative, for taking risks, for empowering others, for trusting themselves, for encouraging the continuing personal search, for instituting alternatives for dead-ended people, for working out differences? *What if inner power were just as important as outer power?*

What if males and females were acknowledged for their own personal gifts and not as sex roles? What if minorities were acknowledged for their own capabilities and not as ethnic group members? What if people could go openly to each other to express their fears, concerns, and desires with no fear of reprisal? What if females and males could be free to use both their feminine and masculine traits when appropriate? What if age were revered?

Fritjof Capra, the eminent physicist, writes inspiringly in *The Turning Point* about the qualities and characteristics of what he calls the rising culture in our world. He describes the types of principles and beliefs upon which we have operated for the last several hundred years and argues convincingly that we are at a turning point. The rising culture he describes requires a new type of leadership, one that accepts a systems (everything is interrelated and integrated) view of life that is self-organizing and self-renewing. Leaders look at the world in terms of relationships and integration, not splintered pieces. Economic supremacy will no longer obtain as the predominant goal of national policy (pp. 266, 393, 417).

Leadership at Each Stage of Personal Power

Let's look more carefully at each stage's primary way of guiding or leading people. These differences show why there are varying levels of effectiveness among the different styles. Basically, leaders at each of the stages are like followers at each of the stages. The style of the person comes out in his or her leadership behavior.

Stage One Leadership:
Guiding others by domination or force

At Stage One people who lead generally use domination or force of some kind to get people to obey. They threaten others or use physical force to produce results. They operate on the basis of inspiring fear in others largely because they feel powerless and insecure themselves. They know of no other way and they are so afraid themselves that they cover it with authoritarian or even tyrannical behavior. Many times the motivation of the leader is bitterness or revenge due to having been treated in the way they are now treating others. People respond to this form of leadership only because they are fearful, unorganized, and powerless as well. Their only goal is to survive and to escape more physical or emotional abuse.

In organizations, this kind of leader requires blind obedience from followers. There can be few questions raised because this form of leadership is easily threatened and will punish whoever does not obey. The military dictatorship is perhaps the most obvious stereotypical example of this form of leadership. There must be obedience and

HAGBERG'S MODEL OF LEADERSHIP AND POWER

Leads by force.
Inspires fear.

1

Leads by
being . . .
wise.
Inspires inner peace.

6

Leads by seduction,
deals.
Inspires dependency.

2

Leadership and Personal Power

Leads by
empowering others.
Inspires love and
service.

5

3

Leads by personal
persuasion.
Inspires a winning
attitude.

4

Leads by modeling
integrity.
Inspires hope.

subservience of one's will to the leader. This is to ensure that all directions are followed in times of danger.

One of the most obvious reasons why this authoritarian form of leadership does not work effectively in the long run is that people rebel under such strict control. Many people do not like to be so closely governed and they resent the use of force to maintain order. Military coups led by young army officers are good examples of what happens when leaders are excessively authoritarian.

Here are some examples of the ways in which Stage One leaders think:

"I can't afford to let everyone do what they want to do. The whole place would be in chaos. People basically need to have structure and order. They are more secure that way."

"I don't care what you think and I don't care how you feel, boy, just *do* what I say."

"If you don't improve, I'll have to find something else or some-place else for you to work."

"I don't pay you to come up with alternatives. I pay you to get the job done, and done right."

Stage Two Leadership:
Guiding others by seduction or making deals

Stage Two leaders are much more subtle than Stage Ones. They would be reluctant to threaten the person directly, but instead they set up a barter situation, or they seduce people in other ways. They agree to give something to the follower in exchange for something else, usually behavior, votes, or tangible items. For instance, a boss might agree to let something else slide or do a favor for his secretary if she agrees to spend more time and energy on his pet project. The favor might be less tangible too, like giving recognition, approval, or just attention to the person if she follows the rules and remains a good employee. Or the behavior of the leader may be seductive in nature. The boss might grant special favors or good performance reviews if the employee gives personal sexual favors in return. The key to the exchange is that the employee is dependent, in need of security, either in position or relationship and is willing to enter into the bargain in order to obtain the necessary security. What is required of the employee is that they actually return the favor. Any crossing of this type of leader spells doom. They feel as if they've been found out or caught in a trap and they will either ignore the employee completely or they will become vindictive.

In addition to managers in organizations, the most obvious example of this type of arrangement is in politics, where the candidate promises a wide variety of things in order to capture the votes of the people who are dependent upon the candidate to do what is good for them. After the election, when circumstances inevitably change, the elected official must then strike some new bargains and persuade the electorate that the inevitable change in direction is to their liking. Eventually, when voters do not reelect them, they usually analyze the situation as one of bad timing or an uninformed electorate—rarely in terms of a breaking of the bargain on their part. They usually have more leadership and power when they are in the elected position, and most have much less when they are out of office.

The main reason this form of leadership is not as effective as some others is that people at this stage do not always keep their bargains and so lose the trust and confidence of the followers. If security or a better life cannot be guaranteed in the trade-off, the followers won't continue to participate in the bargain.

Here are some examples of Stage Two leaders' thinking:

"Say, I'm really feeling pressure from my boss to get this project done. Could you make this project a priority for the next two months? If you get any grief from anyone else, send them to me. I'll see that it is worth your while when raises are due."

"If you elect me I promise never to sign a bill that will raise your taxes."

"Why don't we go out for a long, quiet lunch somewhere just you and me, to talk it all over in a more relaxed atmosphere?"

"You know, I could really be much more supportive of you on the next promotion possibility if you were more solidly behind me and my ideas for this project."

Stage Three Leadership:
Guiding others by personal persuasion and charisma

Leadership at Stage Three is focused on success for those in the leader's group or on the leader's side but primarily the success of the leader. The leader uses personal persuasion or the power of personality, which is called charisma, to convince followers that they will share in all the success and glory if they follow the leader. The leader tries to instill in them a goal or image of success by pumping them up personally or by captivating their energy. They make others want to be part of the action so they can win and reap the rewards. They discuss tactics, teamwork, counterstrategies, and offenses as if they were pro athletes. Stage Threes believe that someone wins and someone loses, and they are out to instill a winning attitude in others. The stakes get increasingly higher, and the tactics get more complex, but the goal remains the same—win and get the trophy (status, money, title, glory).

Stage Three leaders will cajole, tease, embarrass, debate, or disarm people to get them to discuss the leaders' goals and then agree to share in them. Sometimes it is hard to turn them down. They give compelling reasons for doing what they propose to do. The glamour and the results they promise represent those symbols that so many people are taught to want in their lives. About the only sure way to get out from under the spell of Stage Three leaders is to get away from them completely.

In return for all the success they are willing to share Stage Threes ask for loyalty. Sticking with the team no matter what the circumstances is expected. When the going gets rough and the risks are great, Stage Three leaders need to know that the team will go on, despite injuries or setbacks. Those who sign on make a real commitment.

Prime examples of Stage Three leadership are corporate or organizational ladder-climbing people. To get to the top of a Stage Three organization one must learn to be a Stage Three leader par excellence. So one mimics the behavior of all the leaders who are farther along, hoping to inherit their formula for success.

Stage Three is the most prominent form of leadership in organizations, followed closely by Stage Two. Stage Three leaders are the most driven and outwardly successful of all of the stages. The major reason why Stage Three leadership ceases to be effective over time is that Stage

Three leaders wrongly assume that everyone else is satisfied by the same forms of success that they are. They think they can inspire everyone if they can just talk to them and share their goals with them. But not everyone shares the idea of success, and soon some begin to ask deeper questions. Also the odds catch up with Stage Three leaders and they lose a few times, thus shaking the confidence of their loyal followers.

Examples of Stage Three leaders' thinking:

"We have so much talent in this team, there is no way we can fail. I'll see to that."

"I am absolutely sold on this idea. We are both going to look so good when it's over, they'll be asking us to run the whole company."

"Give me three reasons why it can't be done, and I'll give you twenty reasons why it can."

"The only trouble with us is we need a bigger challenge. Give us a chance and we'll show you what we can do."

Stage Four Leadership:
Guiding others by modeling integrity and generating trust

Stage Four leaders are mostly concerned with doing the "right" thing, the fair or just thing in the long run. They do not depend only on immediate results but on maintaining quality and effectiveness. They lead with integrity. They lead because they have become deserving of the trust that followers have in them, and they are honest with their followers, even if it is painful for them all. They not only share their leadership, they share in the joys and pain of their followers. Above all, their sense of rightness evolves out of the deepening inner resources of their souls, and they take care to be among the people—not separate or apart. Stage Four leaders are not afraid to learn from others and they don't have to be authoritarian.

They lead by inspiring hope in others and helping them see what qualities are evolving out of them and out of the group. They may help the group change direction because they can sense the necessity before the group can. They're not afraid to talk about the things people usually try to hide. The sense of direction in a Stage Four comes less from the established plan and more from the ongoing life of the total group. They truly give the group choices, rather than merely talking about it and then making the decisions themselves anyway. They are beginning to trust themselves and their inner resources more and that is why they are appearing more quietly confident. They can take ups and downs in stride more easily because their self-esteem is not so tied to their success. They can listen more effectively and do not have to take strong stands on every issue. Fours think more deeply about how they lead people; for instance, those who are truly effective may lead people who are at different stages in slightly different ways even though their overall style will predominate. For example, one might be participatory with one group by giving choices among a few options, and participatory with another group by leaving the decisions totally up to them.

In return for insightful leadership, Fours require consistency and honesty from their followers. They would rather have the truth now, and think of ways to solve the problems, than have to deal with a series of cover-ups later that only exacerbate the problem. Fours, in fact, can usually tell when someone is lying, and they often have to confront the behavior and try to rid the person of the fear of honesty.

There are no obvious or easily recognized examples of Stage Four leaders. They can be almost anywhere and are not only identified by their positions or status. The quality of the person is the distinguishing characteristic. Stage Fours are those people you meet on boards, in meetings, in social settings who inspire people to listen to them because they are not self-serving, but thoughtful, sensible, and honest. Stage Four and Five leaders are the most effective in the long run because they think more broadly and begin to take themselves out of the equation. They may not be rewarded for this behavior, however.

If Stage Four leaders are not effective, a reason may be that the organization highly values the norms of Stages Two and Three. Stage Four leadership will not be nurtured if all that matters are the symbols of success at the expense of less tangible rewards.

Examples of Stage Four leaders' ways of thinking are as follows:

"I happen to have a number of people reporting to me, and I am finding, through too many years of experience, that the best way to teach people how to manage others humanely and with respect is to treat them humanely and with respect. The big decisions we make around here are far less critical than the ways in which we treat people every day. All those days of treatment add up to the morale issues as much as the business decisions do. For example, when times are tough, as they are from time to time, it is much easier to share the dilemma with people and talk about alternatives that will usually cost them something, if all along the way management has shown care and respect for them as individuals. What do I mean by humane and respectful treatment? I mean talking to them frequently, keeping in touch with their issues, helping them find ways to solve problems, giving them ongoing, honest feedback about their performance and behavior, listening when they need me, giving them as much authority and responsibility as possible, resolving conflicts between us, recognizing their achievements, thanking them for good work, sharing their joys and sorrows, being open and vulnerable if need be. Whatever comes up I try to remember to ask myself what is really the right thing to do. Not how will I look better, or how can I punish them, or how can I get rid of them so I won't have to deal with them. Some days it is extremely difficult to model the right thing to do because I'm tired, bored, or frustrated. So I may just say that and deal with what I can, waiting until a later time to complete the rest. But they usually understand and let me have my bad days too."

"Each and every morning I remind myself why I am continuing to remain in public office; not for my ego, which is always a battle given the attention I get; not for only one issue or interest group; not for reelection. I have to continually remind myself that there need to be voices of reason, less partisan views of issues that must be dealt with wisely in order for us to reach any fruitful future. Some days I wonder whether I wouldn't be more successful as a voice of reason outside of elected office. Practically the only thing that keeps me going sometimes are my trusted friends and colleagues who also can see beyond the daily political rat race to a broader picture. I spend a great deal of time reflecting, reading, thinking, musing so I can't get caught up totally in details. This means I have

to have a superb staff whose competence and judgment I trust.
They are really extensions of me, and I could never handle public
life without them."

"I guess you could say I am a powerful person—or at least that I am
in a powerful position. I'm not sure exactly how I got here considering my strong views against our usual leadership. Perhaps they
thought I'd keep my mouth shut if I were one of them. At any rate,
my sole basis for taking this position was to influence positively the
climate for world peace and to get as many other people of
thoughtful, realistic peaceful persuasions involved as possible,
from all walks of life. I'm very clear that none of the other things
we do really matter if we are about to blow up the world with a
nuclear bomb. It's insane and someone has to speak up even if it's
not necessarily the best timing. I don't want to be driven from
office before I have time to act, but on the other hand I'll influence
from wherever I am. It has become my passion."

Stage Five Leadership:
Guiding others by empowering them

Stage Five leaders can best be described as servant leaders. They see
their main goal as empowering others to be more fully human and more
fully satisfied. To accomplish this, Fives strive to be of service to others,
to provide ideas, support, encouragement, and love so as to draw out of
people their best. Stage Five leaders have vision that goes way beyond
the individual and the organization. It is of larger significance, like love
or justice, or peace for all. They share their vision through their behavior
without talking about it because how they live out their vision matters to
them—not how they can enhance their own egos. Stage Five leaders are
convinced that the good of all followers is more important than the good
of leaders, and they behave accordingly. They give and give and give
selflessly, not begrudgingly. They do not expect rewards in return, except
those inner, intangible ones that result from seeing others more satisfied
and human.

As with Stage Four leaders, it is hard to identify obvious examples of
Stage Five leadership. One way is to identify how you feel when you're

around them. After you've been around a Stage Five leader you feel lifted up, encouraged, affirmed, not cajoled, threatened, or sold a bill of goods. You have more courage and more dignity. You feel more self-acceptance and even a sense of purpose. For these are the qualities that Stage Five leaders seem to draw out of followers. Often it is really hard to explain, but they get a sense from a Stage Five person of a non-critical, accepting nature. It frees followers to expose their fears and insecurities and then to slowly rise above them. A Stage Five leader inspires followers eventually to find love for others and a service of their own, no matter how insignificant it may appear to be. Service makes us feel worthwhile as if we matter to someone else, and thus to ourselves.

If Stage Five leaders are not effective, a reason may be that so many people are stuck at Stage Three, and they cannot consider or understand the simple principles of Stage Five leaders. They do not understand and thus they fear Stage Fives.

Here are a few examples of the thinking of Stage Five leaders:

"I've never thought of myself as a leader. I hate applying for positions, running for office, or being in charge of groups. I like to sit back and reflect on what is being said, then offer perspectives on the issues that perhaps haven't been considered yet. Often, to my surprise, the naive-sounding questions I ask turn out to jog the thinking of the group and they get into a pretty fruitful discussion. I have to be careful though, so that I don't call attention to myself too much or people start looking to me for the answers too. That's the worst thing that could happen. For one thing it's better for the group to find the answers and for another thing, I don't know the answers anyway."

"I have chosen or perhaps been given a mission to accomplish in my lifetime. I think about this mission as the guiding force for my life, and no matter what I'm doing, it seems to permeate my consciousness. Therefore my work has really slowly molded itself around my mission, which involves being of specific service to people in the world. I know it may sound far fetched but it is my guiding light. It evolved out of a really deep crisis in my life in which I realized I had nothing to live for. Slowly I have evolved,

and I have written and followed now for five years a set of principles, a credo, for my life and work. Everything I do must meet the
conditions of my credo, or I know it is not consistent with my
mission. It took me five years to think about and write my mission
and credo and now I am at great peace as a result."

"The most important thing I do in my life is to find ways to help
other people develop. In my job I see people come and go every day
because I am in such a busy, public place; my goal is to get to know
those who stay well enough that I can support, encourage, brighten
up, challenge, or touch them in some way. I can ask questions that
allow people to open up with me quite easily, so I just ask questions
that will make them think or will challenge their negative thinking.
I've had some people say, after they've known me just casually for
three years, that they really look forward to seeing me because I
seem to know exactly where they're at and I always say something
helpful. I know it may seem trivial, but I believe that's how people
change and get healthier."

Stage Six Leadership:
Guiding others by one's depth of wisdom

Stage Six leaders are rarely found because most Stage Six people have no
aspirations to leadership of any kind. They are so truly selfless that if
they were to emerge as leaders it would be simply as a result of genuinely
living their life purposes and acting on the wisdom that dwells so deeply
within. Their way of leading then emerges out of their deep wisdom and
insight into the issues of the entire cosmos. For that reason our world,
which is tied to much more narrow visions, rarely can appreciate or truly
encourage the emergence of Stage Six leadership.

This kind of leadership inspires in others that which comes from deep
within, namely inner peace. Stage Sixes leave people feeling that there is
no reason to fear or even to strive for things. Things just are and will be.
Survival is not even the major goal but living consistently with moral
principles and a connection to deep spiritual sources. Stage Sixes lead in
strange ways, perhaps through their art, their touch, their writing, their
eyes, their music, their visions.

Though full of inner peace, Stage Six leaders are somewhat uncomfortable for others to be around because of their total dedication to that which their wisdom guides. Their model behavior asks the same of others and calls them silently to look inward and find out what their real purposes are. They call others to be unafraid of losing anything or everything along the way. This makes many people uncomfortable, so they choose instead to remain in awe or fear of Stage Sixes.

If Stage Sixes are not effective, it's probably that they are not interested or that they are not acknowledged as leaders. Stage Sixes don't lead, they just live.

Here are a few examples of Stage Six leadership thinking:

"My art is a way for me to express the churning feelings I have about the present stage of our culture. I want people to see, to think, to feel the destiny that we are creating. I try to make the message loud and clear as well as subtle so that people will stop and think. I experience our culture in a certain way and this I create. I can only create from the experiences that have been given to me, yet all of our experiences are deeply rooted in the same underground universal stream. So if I touch inside myself deeply, I can touch others deeply as well. And I want to create a lasting idea, a creation that can speak after I move along, a chronicle of my own and perhaps the culture's transitions."

"I listen, I speak, I float, I wait for messages. I'm on a day-to-day adventure with life. If I'm tuned in, I have an unusual ability to understand the inner workings of other people, not analytically but intuitively. For instance, I'll be given a message from some source within to call a person, blurt out a certain thing, give someone a book, ask a question. Almost invariably, for a reason unknown to me, the action on my part hits some chord, and I often get very quizzical or relieved looks from others. I've been part of some miraculous changes in people's lives. I've given up trying to figure it out, take any credit for it, or even be surprised. Now I'm just careful to listen for the messages."

The table on the following page is a summary of how leaders lead at each stage of power.

Summary of Leadership and Power

They lead by:	They inspire:	They require:
1 Domination, force	Fear of being hurt	Blind obedience
2 Seduction, making deals	Dependence	Return of favor
3 Charisma, personal persuasion	A winning attitude	Loyalty, no matter what
4 Modeling integrity, generating trust	Hope for self and organization	Consistency, honesty
5 Empowering others, service to others	Love and service	Self-acceptance, purpose
6 Wisdom, a way of being	Inner peace	Anything/everything

Looking for Leadership in Myself and Others

In looking for leaders in organizations you don't necessarily start by looking at the people in the positions of status; you look, rather, for qualities of leadership in people and *then* encourage them to be leaders. The qualities are those that we have discussed in Stages Four, Five, and Six and here in this chapter. Those qualities will be revealed by leaders or potential leaders when they ask questions like the following:

What are the ethical or moral issues raised by this problem?

How will each party to this agreement be able to gain something long term as a result?

How could we encourage individuals in our area to operate at optimum levels of creativity?

Why don't we commit ourselves to giving more and see what happens as a result?

If we look at this from the point of view of what's the "right" thing to do, how would we approach it?

What if we redefine the way the rules are put into operation? or redefine the rules?

What if we stress quality first, then quantity?

If we redefine success to mean personal satisfaction or peace of mind (or something else), how would we motivate people differently?

What if we trusted people to be trustworthy?

How could we all share in the success?

What is our long-term vision in this area? How will that affect us?

Why don't you try it and let me know how it works?

Intuitively, what do you think is the best approach?

How could I be more helpful, useful to you?

How can we keep people feeling renewed? What do we have to change?

The first question you must ask yourself before plunging into any discussion of personal leadership development is "What kind of leader do I want to be?" If the answer to your question is Stage Two, then you would go about the task differently than if you answered the question with a Stage Four response. To complicate matters, the kind of leader you will become will depend more on the kind of person you are and your home stage of personal power than on any specific skills you will develop. Most higher stage leaders do not aspire to leadership anyway. They just see things that need to be done, feel strongly about a life purpose, or understand deeply how people need to be treated in order to thrive.

Many leadership courses or skills sessions teach such basic things as leading meetings and discussions, asking questions, setting up budgets, forming agendas, delegating responsibility, and organizing. These approaches are useful and necessary as beginning points, but most programs end there. They need to go beyond that to teach the most critical things like use of intuition, developing honesty, integrity, life purpose, vision, inspiration, and wisdom, the qualities that are necessary in higher stage leaders.

I would suggest that most of the development of personal leadership be a challenging of yourself to search for inner resources and find out what is most important and real and to continually seek inner peace and wisdom. Along the way there are a few miscellaneous suggestions for people who want to stimulate a leadership discussion or even a crisis in their own lives.

For one thing, I would strongly encourage discussion of the leadership and power issues in many different arenas—on the job, in professional groups, among executives. There are other models and books worth reading besides *Real Power* that will stimulate thinking on this topic as well: *The Turning Point* by Capra; *The Leader* by Maccoby; *New Rules* by Yankelovich; *The Aquarian Conspiracy* by Ferguson; *The Servant as Leader* by Greenleaf; *Leadership* by Burns. (See Bibliography.) Ask questions such as:

How do people think as different types of leaders?

What motivates different leaders?

Who are examples of good and poor leaders in history, and why?

What kind of a leader am I?

At what stage does my group function?

What style of leadership does my organization reward?

What would a Stage Four-Five environment look like?

If I want to be different how can I go about it?

What kind of support do I need from others?

How will I adjust to being different from others?

Another idea for discovering what leadership is or can be is this: Seriously and deeply question leaders with whom you come in contact, especially those you admire. Ask them questions that will allow them to reflect and questions that will give you insights into their thought processes, their values, their decision making, and their behavior. Go beyond the mundane questions and probe for what really makes them tick. Here are a few examples of these kinds of questions:

How do you manage to keep going personally amidst the pressures of your role in the community?

What are the ethical tugs and pulls that you feel from your position or your stand?

What policy issues do you see on the horizon in your area of expertise?

How do you find personal support and renewal in your life and work?

What do you see as your role in your organization?

What is your personal vision as a community leader?

What is leadership, in your view?

Can you live out your personal values or life purpose through your work? your role in the community? How?

If you could change the rules in your field, how would they be different?

How do you get things done?

What is your hope for the world in the next twenty-five years?

What is your view of the quality of the people who are presently in positions of power?

What have you done that you are most proud of?

On the more personal side, you might ask yourself whether or not you have experienced the crisis of integrity and whether you want to. The crisis you will go through in deciding whether to explore the area of inner principles, sincerity, wholeness is a complex one because it calls on inner resources, and it threatens abandonment by people who have been used to you the old way. It is a lonely process to extricate yourself from the way you're expected to be and to look at the way it is for you. This does not mean that you become disloyal to the organization and totally narcissistic, but it does mean that you sort out who you are from what others are. While on the outside you are competent, trusted, influential, and respected, on the inside you must be willing to take time to be alone and to think about yourself.

Another factor in the crisis that comes from inside is the nagging answer to the question "Why am I here?" That answer often is "I don't know for sure." And if I don't know, who does? Or how can I find out? The question seems somewhat more penetrating than the "Who am I and what are my strengths?" questions of previous stages. It's actually somewhat easier to live through Stages One through Three in organizations, learning the ropes and fitting into the prevailing scheme of things than it is to sort out your own rules, your principles, and your sincere personal style. Generally it causes deep inner unrest, and even in the most insightful people, a time of self-doubt and discomfort. Not that it's all bad by any means, only that the crisis of integrity is a different sort of quest and one that is not openly rewarded in most organizations, because by their very nature, they are competitive, numbers-oriented, short range in their thinking, and symbols dominated.

Men particularly will find the crisis of integrity a confusing one especially if an external event propels them into it. Most men have generally been so accustomed to striving for the rewards (or thinking they should) that they find few role models once they discover the symbols aren't enough. Men have not talked to each other much (or to women) about the inner life, for such talk, they believe, makes them appear weak or soft. And being weak or soft has been frowned upon. So they stuff their feelings deep down and buck up for the next round. Only recently have men begun to talk more about breaking out of their molds and reaching beyond to vaster, broader, more satisfying futures— attained through a personal struggle. Women, on the other hand, grapple with the integrity crisis differently, depending on what they have done in Stage Three. Women don't have a large number of role models either, but because they can intuitively sense what Stage Five is like they have some hope in getting there. Stage Three women who've taken it on with a vengeance will have similar experiences as Stage Three men in moving beyond the symbols. Women who've dropped out of the work force will still have to do battle with their aspirations and value conflicts and get enough recognition somewhere outside themselves to satisfy the Stage Three urges. Women who balance Stage Three and "do it without becoming it" can look forward more to Stage Four because they have been waiting for it with inner relief. They may even create the crisis that starts the search.

As an aside, people have asked me whether men and women lead differently. That is a complicated question to answer. From a power stage perspective, people at different stages lead differently. So a woman and a man may lead according to their personal qualities, and either could be a Stage Two, Three, Four, etc., leader. Some say they're eager for women to gain more leadership so the system will be different. They may be very disappointed if the women who gain power are stuck at Stage Three or Two. And at least for now, many of the women who have reached powerful or authoritative positions did so within a Stage Three-oriented system and therefore have portrayed largely Stage Three type leadership. Let's hope they do not have to remain Threes permanently in order to continue in these roles. My vision of women leaders, and leaders in general, is much broader than position power—as you have read in this chapter. So perhaps the future of Stage Four-Six leadership for both sexes is still largely to be realized.

My last suggestion is that if you sincerely want to lead the life of a searcher after wisdom and will risk finding out about the true leadership capacity within you, you would do well to have a guide who can help and support you along the way. Making changes is risky and scary, not something any of us takes lightly. This person can be a professional counselor, a friend, a family member, whoever you trust and respect to be a listener and sorter with you. It would be helpful if the person is someone you think has already experienced the crisis of integrity because they may be more patient and understanding. Since you are not sure what to expect, you should be able to trust the person to deal with you sincerely.

This personal assessment might mean a lot of new things for you. It may mean, for example, examining the rules or myths under which you are operating and creating a crisis in your life by embarking on a personal excursion on power. It may mean trying out some new ideas or behaviors or talking to people who you think exhibit the characteristics of stages you aspire to. It may mean letting go of symbols and external power and looking at yourself from the inside. It may mean transferring security from outside yourself to inside yourself. It may mean finding out what your life's purpose is. It may mean letting go, and having faith and hope.

In conclusion, here is one word of clarification to people who want to move to Stage Four or beyond: You can stimulate it to begin, but at the same time, if you are not ready to move (beginning to truly wonder about the long-lasting satisfaction and success of Stage Three) it will be hard to force it. The best way to stimulate it is to think deeply about it and talk it over with someone. Don't let the feelings pass and become deadened, or it may be a long time before they return again. These are the fertile moments in one's life.

One thing I know for sure: You cannot become a leader in the sense I describe without being keenly aware of yourself and willing to give up many of the traditional beliefs about power and leadership. You must at some point take a "leap of faith" toward the emerging model of what it means to truly lead and away from the need to be successful, famous, rich, in control, or powerful. The kind of leadership I am advocating arises out of the understanding of pain, the loss of innocence, the love of others, the larger purpose, the pursuit of wisdom, the humor of life. Ask yourself if you are willing to take the risk. If you are, turn to chapter eleven, "Beyond Ego and Gender: Leading From Your Soul."

True leadership begins with the willingness to be someone other than who the world wants you to be.

Chapter 8

Managing People at Various Stages

One of the most difficult tasks in the world is to manage people well. Long-time managers tell me that the business side of management, the part they thought would be ninety-five percent of the job when they first took on the challenge, is a "piece of cake" now, and takes up a far smaller percentage of the time than it did before. The human side of management, which is still an art and upon which almost all of the business side ultimately depends, is the more difficult of the two, taking far more time and energy, and, of course, constant attention. And most of the seasoned managers say that only a certain amount of the human side can be taught. The rest must be gleaned from experience on the job. Some get very good at it by learning with each experience, while other managers never do learn the art, no matter how much they study or how much experience they have.

Why is it so difficult a task for some to manage people and not for others? Or what are the characteristics of successful managers that make them different from poor managers? The latter question is much easier to answer, and has been answered to varying degrees by many management theories and consultants. Some of the theories agree; others contradict each other. Describing each of the various approaches is not the goal of this book, but it is useful to have an understanding of management theory and practice as a starting point when analyzing a good manager's style.

The first assumption in this chapter is that all organizations are made up of people at various stages of development or power and that no one management theory will accommodate them all equally well. People at different stages of power need to be motivated and managed in different ways. A manager who relies on one theory only will surely not meet the needs of a wide variety of people. Here is a case in which treating everyone the same is clearly not useful or productive. This does not mean giving special treatment to certain people or giving up on others because they don't fit. It means learning eventually as a manager how to read employees and choose, in addition to the most comfortable managing style, one or two other available styles with which to manage them. For instance, a highly participatory decision-making style with Stage One people is premature, because they lack necessary information about the organization to give input on decisions outside their own job. Structure and direction with encouragement and support are more appropriate until their confidence is strengthened. Too open a style may breed insecurity, confusion, or resentment at this stage. A manager's own most comfortable style may be participatory, but with Ones it would not be the most effective style. Eventually these insights come intuitively, but at first they may seem difficult.

The second assumption is mentioned less often in management circles: that managing bosses may be just as important, if not more important, than managing employees, and the dynamics are different because of the power relationship. Understanding the people they work for—at any power stage—can teach managers more about themselves and their inner dynamics than most other work experiences. Most people's complaints about their work have more to do with their bosses than with their co-workers or employees, yet most people are never taught the fine art of being managed. Before we get too much further into this topic, let's look at the ways in which managers proceed through the stages of power as they learn the steps in managing people effectively.

Stage One—Powerlessness

This stage corresponds to the feeling employees get down in the pit of their stomach when they learn they are about to become managers. Mostly they feel the excitement of being chosen, of a new challenge, but there is also a thinly veiled feeling of fear, of wondering if they can do it, if they know enough, if they have the right knowledge and connections to manage well. Usually this stage lasts just long enough for them to finish lunch, because they are off on the task of learning to manage.

HAGBERG'S MODEL OF MANAGING
AND PERSONAL POWER

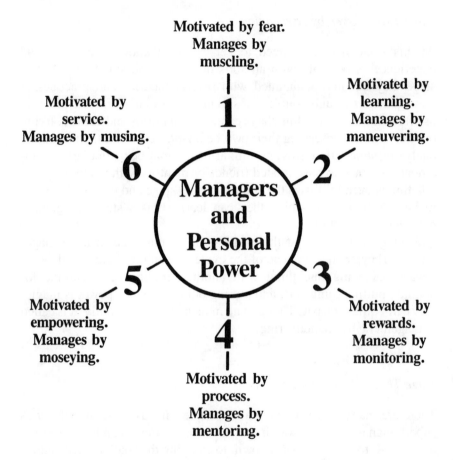

Motivated by fear.
Manages by
muscling.

1

Motivated by
learning.
Manages by
maneuvering.

Motivated by
service.
Manages by musing.

6

**Managers
and
Personal
Power**

2

5

3

Motivated by
empowering.
Manages by
moseying.

4

Motivated by
rewards.
Manages by
monitoring.

Motivated by
process.
Manages by
mentoring.

If they stay at this level in management they are likely to resort to threats and use of force to manage people, in an attempt to cover their own fears and inadequacies. It is called management by muscling.

Stage Two—Power by Association

At this stage managers need to get as much knowledge and broad experience as possible with all sorts of people and situations. At this stage they become acquainted with several theories and practices of management through courses, observing other managers who are seen as effective, understanding the organizational norms and culture, trying out new things, observing their own behavior, observing their boss and analyzing style differences and similarities. It may be particularly important at this stage to have trusted friends or mentors with whom they can talk things over, for this is the apprenticeship stage and they are bound to make mistakes from which they can learn. It is a stage for gaining confidence and skill.

Managers who stay at this stage seem to play "catch up management." They are never ahead of the cycle on planning, etc., so they are always balancing one thing with another, trading one deadline for another, putting things off, and putting out fires. Since power is magic, they can't quite grasp it. They end up maneuvering constantly. It is called management by maneuvering.

Stage Three—Power by Symbols

There are many motivations behind people's needs to be thought of as superb managers, from wanting to advance their own career, to wanting to be liked, to wanting to be known, to enjoying the challenge. Whatever the motive, Stage Three managers want to be good, and they want to be rewarded for it. Usually this means finding out which style of management is rewarded in the organization and then finding a way to be particularly good at that style. It means being observant and motivated enough to learn the prevailing management system and encouraging others to do so as well.

Managers at this stage constantly focus on results and rarely on process. They want the numbers to be right and the bottom line to reflect profit. This style is called management by monitoring.

Stage Four—Power by Reflection

After they have established their allegiance to the prevailing management style, it is time for managers to also establish their allegiance to the management styles that are most suitable to them and to the people they manage. This will make them even more effective, although they may not espouse as clearly the prevailing organizational style. To make this transition, they need to learn as much about themselves as possible from various sources, looking at both their strengths and weaknesses. They should try on different styles to see which ones fit best with their personality and values and then eventually settle into a most comfortable style for a base or home style. Then they should learn to accommodate the needs of people who work for them by having at their disposal one or two other styles. They can talk with other managers who are different from them but whom they consider competent, to find out how they manage different people. For example, if they operate with a tight rein, they should know which employees would be stifled by that and let them have more rope than others. They should observe both their employees and their bosses to discover at which stage of personal power they are, along with other characteristics (personality, motivations, values). Then they can decide by discussion, trial and error, analysis, intuition, which type of management approach these people work most effectively with and start using those alternative styles, especially on occasions in which managers want to see particular results or in conflict situations. They need not use a different style other than their own all the time, because the others would be able to tell if they do. The longer managers practice flexible management behavior with a consistent home style, the more intuitive its use will become and the sooner it will be incorporated automatically into their own style.

At this stage managers are also able to be mentors to other managers who are struggling with the conflicts of deciding which management theories and styles to study and to use. Stage Four managers look at process as opposed to content in their dealings with people. In fact, they do not feel that there is much that is more important than process. They increasingly take themselves out of the active management role and allow others to operate in their place. They are secure enough to teach others rather than doing it all themselves. They are managing by mentoring.

Stage Five—Power by Purpose

Managers at Stage Five should find an internal or external guide to lead them into the confidence of trusting their intuitive sense of management. At this stage, although they have an overall operating style, each person is seen as an individual to be treated differently and to be served. Good managers seek to understand each individual and empower them to develop and aspire to meet their inner potential. They mentor other managers in the art as well but by their role model, not through deliberate teaching. Managers at Stage Five seem to roam around and act more as catalysts and resource people, getting out of the way of their employees. They do not lead projects, they light the fires in others to encourage their projects. This kind of management is called management by moseying.

Stage Six—Power by Gestalt

Sixes get out of managing and into musing. They manage by musing.

How to Manage Employees and Bosses at All Stages of Power

The remainder of this chapter will be an outline and brief description of the ways in which people can effectively manage or be managed by others who are at different personal power stages. This discussion will be vastly oversimplified but will give impetus to a more thorough discussion within oneself and among manager colleagues as to the soundness of a more varied approach. A complicating factor will be the stage at which managers reading this identify themselves. A Stage Four manager, for instance, may manage a Stage Two person somewhat differently than a Stage Three manager would because of the Four's higher level of sensitivity, etc. These more subtle differences would have to be addressed individually since they are much more complex. For now, begin by just thinking about managing employees and bosses at each of the six different stages. Also employees who are at lower stages may have difficulty identifying higher stage managers because they do not understand their behavior. It does pose a problem for managing your boss. One suggestion would be to describe your boss's behavior to a person you think is at a higher stage and see what they think the stage of your boss is.

A simple rule of thumb in determining how to manage people at various stages may be that Stages One and Two respond more to structured or hierarchical management styles, Stages Three and Four to team approaches (Three to competitive teams, Four to participatory teams), and Fives and Sixes to laissez faire or informal management styles, if any. The real challenge, though, is to manage people at their home stage but also to encourage them to consider developing further. It means that in order to be effective, you should be moving to the highest stages too, so you can manage broader ranges of people at various stages.

Stage One: Powerlessness

Managing Employees at Stage One

1. Give encouragement and support. Build them up and encourage them to learn more skills and acquire more self-knowledge. Help them gain more information about their job.

2. Help them build a group and individual identity. Encourage a sense of identity by supporting group events and socializing informally.

3. Reward them concretely. Reward them with warranted verbal praise, salary increases, extra skill training, awards, recognition.

4. Provide structure and limits. Give direction and structure, guidance and concrete guidelines. Provide flexibility within guidelines but not ambiguity. Set and enforce limits on behavior, rules, policy. Help them learn to take responsibility for their behavior on basic work issues.

5. Be a strong, supportive role model, giving information about and access to new areas of learning and development. At times, this may mean almost taking on a parenting role, which is appropriate as long as this role does not foster dependency or condescension.

Examples of interaction might include:

"Please bring me all the data that I've circled on pages 3 and 5 by Friday afternoon."

"You did a very good job on the body of the manuscript. I found very few errors. I had the feeling you got tired when doing the tables in the appendix. Would you proof them and return them to me tomorrow, please?"

"I'd love to go out with the office staff for Carolyn's birthday. Thanks."

"I have some courses in mind that I want you to take this spring. They will give you much more information on how to accomplish your accounting tasks."

Managing Bosses at Stage One

1. Try never to work for a boss who is at Stage One.
2. Get another job.
3. If you are stuck with a Stage One boss, follow directions, mind your own business, and don't take anything personally.
4. Keep your fingers crossed. Your boss may retire soon.

Stage Two: Power by Association

Managing Employees at Stage Two

1. Give them information and experience. Let them try out as many new things, projects, skills on their jobs as possible. The more they try the more they learn, even if they are afraid.

2. Let them learn from mistakes. Mistakes are the best opportunities for learning. Encourage risk so you can help them gain learning from

both the successes and the failures. Help them learn to be competent and confident.

3. Encourage them to take responsibility for themselves on broader work issues, i.e., let them direct their own work and ask you for changes. Push them to open themselves to development, techniques and skills, as well as personal knowledge. Be available more to Stage Twos.

4. Confront them gently. Be more straightforward but still supportive, more direct but encourage discussion. Encourage them to bat ideas around with you and talk things through. Rein in only when necessary.

5. Encourage them to model the behavior of others. Look around for people who do things well and encourage employees to observe them and try out similar behavior. Use employees as examples of good behavior to others.

Examples of interaction:

"This is a new project for our department, and it will be a great learning experience for you. I know you can do it."

"Just go ahead on it. Check with me tomorrow if you have any questions. In a week we'll get together for a briefing."

"Let me give you some feedback on your behavior in the meeting this morning. You acted scared. Now, we're all afraid at times, but let's talk about effective ways to deal with fear so you won't be so exposed next time."

Managing Bosses at Stage Two

1. Cooperate and be helpful. If they strike a deal with you for favors, do it unless it is unethical or immoral. Encourage them to let you do extra work for them.

2. Ask for advice and bolster their confidence. They like you to be dependent on them. Find the area they know best and seek out their advice, encouraging their skill and expertise. Beware of becoming overly dependent on them because they may try to subtly keep you from developing further.

3. Don't threaten them. Encourage them, work hard, don't take credit, even if the work is yours, and never embarrass them in public.

4. Find someone else in the organization you can talk to who will keep your confidence. Talk to that person during stressful times. Plan your development with your boss using advice from the other person as well.

5. Hope that your boss continues to gain confidence and competence in the organization.

Stage Three: Power by Symbols

Managing Employees at Stage Three

1. Channel their energy into projects that will tap their strengths. Encourage them to build confidence, expertise, and depth in areas where they've been successful.

2. Teach them about the organization's culture and norms. Give them feedback and information on pitfalls, mistakes, traps, stumbling blocks. Let them work things out on their own. Get out of their way.

3. Give them regular and honest feedback. Let them know how they are perceived and why. Encourage and discourage particular behaviors. Discuss weaknesses with them. Ask questions of them and listen carefully.

4. Reward their competence tangibly while challenging their personal assumptions about success, thus creating dissonance. Provoke their thinking and be available when they start to question their assumptions.

5. Get them outside themselves, if possible. Include them in as much of your thinking and work as you are able to, without turning it over to them.

Examples of interaction:

"You are so good with budgets. Why don't you put together the first draft budget for the area this year?"

"Remember what you said to Tom this morning about the pricing? That was a real no-no. He shouldn't hear about it at all until we get the OK from Maxine. I failed to impress upon you the chain of command on pricing, I guess. Let's go over it."

"The reason you were passed over is that you are perceived by management as moving too fast and not getting seasoned well enough. Let's think about a development plan to remedy that in the next year."

"You have so much energy and drive. I think you would benefit from an extra project or two."

Managing Bosses at Stage Three

1. Work very hard. Don't compete with them but work hard to fulfill all the objectives of the job. Don't ask for help unless you really need it.

2. Make them look great. Focus on success. Be their shining star and cover for them if necessary. Don't ever cross them or go over their heads on anything. In other words, be good and have a winning attitude.

3. Know their rules and follow them as much as possible. Be a good member of their team. Admit mistakes and don't cover up. Know the games and rules so as not to be caught short. Talk about things in the office that show your interest in their ideas and values. Be appreciative of perks, promotions, favors they give you.

4. Work around the politics. Try to understand where your bosses are in the political scheme of things, but stay out of the middle of it so you can gather organization-wide information for them. Gain broader contacts so you can feed useful information to them in a nonthreatening way.

5. If their goals and values match yours, then hold tight! They may just move along and take you with them.

Stage Four: Power by Reputation

Managing Employees at Stage Four

1. Encourage self-direction in their work. Give them big enough projects and enough leverage to let them fly. Respect their style and self-acceptance by not forcing another style on them.

2. Expand their views and spheres of interest. Encourage them to broaden their views by involvement in the larger company, the community, the world.

3. Encourage their ideas and exploration. Let them have time to explore both within and without, the areas of creativity and ideas that will enhance their work. Listen to them, befriend them, learn from them. Watch for discouragement or self-doubt because of organizational pressure.

4. Educate them in mentoring, counseling, and true leadership ideas. Let them explore new relationships within the organization to allow their influence to be used and felt. If you are secure in yourself, involve them in managing the area you are responsible for, to the point of delegating much of your responsibility to them if you can.

Examples of interaction:

"You know what the parameters are. Just go to it and let's meet for lunch occasionally so I can keep abreast of your discoveries. We're all looking forward to the results."

"A Great Books seminar would be a wonderful development too for you at this juncture. Just be sure to take the time that is necessary to do it right."

"Don't let George get you down. He's wondering why he can't have the same type of project you do."

"I want you to serve on the company planning committee. You'd be a valuable resource and would learn a lot about the other divisions as well."

Managing Bosses at Stage Four

1. Use these bosses as mentors. Share with them, ask questions, test out ideas, observe them.

2. Be competent and develop your own style. Observe their styles but let them help you find your own style so you don't imitate them in a phony way. Always be honest with Stage Fours.

3. Learn the nonverbal, informal rules by which they operate. Watch and ask questions of them to fully understand their role in the organization. Let yourself live with confusion and unanswered questions as well. Be patient.

4. Keep in touch. Watch their long-term effectiveness. After you've moved along, stay involved with them and help them on projects or with information. Keep them as your colleagues.

5. Help them in their projects. If you can, catch the energy they have for moving worthwhile but difficult projects along. Let your own projects be second in pursuit of a goal that is important to them. You'll never learn so much. But watch, listen, observe, ask questions.

Stage Five: Power by Purpose

Managing Employees at Stage Five

1. Protect them. Keep them out of the reach of people who would attack them or their ideas unmercifully. They will not protect themselves, and their ideas are very useful to the organization.

2. Ask them for their insights on larger issues. Be sure to consult them on the major decisions you make because their ideas, questions, and visions will be broad and will challenge your thinking.

3. Don't leash them to rules. Let them operate as freely and openly as possible. Encourage their work and keep up with their progress. You may learn a lot from them. Let them develop their capabilities in the seemingly odd ways they choose.

4. Have long personal talks with them over lunch or after working hours. Learn all you can and capitalize on their role in your organization. Ask them how they would like to be rewarded.

Examples of interaction:
"I'd really like to know what you think about this new project idea. The numbers look good, but are the idea and direction sound?"

"You can work any hours you wish. Just keep me posted on progress and call with any questions."

"Would you sit in on this manager's meeting? Something's going on and I'm not sure what."

"You said something the other day that made me think long and hard. Can we chat about it over lunch?"

Managing Bosses at Stage Five

1. Thank your lucky stars. Long-term learning is near at hand with this kind of boss.

2. Don't get frustrated with their unwillingness or inability to play by the rules. Share your anxiety with them so they can teach you the art they know. Let them empower you and don't take this responsibility lightly. Try to find your own true purpose if you are ready.

3. Have other contacts in the organization so you can keep a realistic perspective on the way things function elsewhere.

4. Be careful not to exactly imitate them. Learn about yourself and accept yourself as separate, developing on your own path.

5. Watch and listen. Take risks. Absorb everything and ask the questions that perplex you.

Stage Six: Power by Gestalt

Managing Employees at Stage Six

1. Don't try to manage them at all.

2. Keep them in the organization if you can. You can learn from them and try to understand them.

Managing Bosses at Stage Six

1. Who are you kidding? Most people at Stage Six got out of "bossing" long ago. Become self-directed and hope for the best.

Chapter 9

Women and Power

Power is a women's issue, whether we like it or not. We are in transition and therefore confused as to what we will become. Women are the poorest of the poor in our country and, at the same time, are increasingly taking their places in the ranks of the wealthy and ruling classes. And there are thousands in between. Women have awakened and now are stretching.

Iris Sangiuliano writes insightfully about women's lives in her book *In Her Time*. She says that women's lives, in general, are not predictable, that they are based more on what happens in other people's lives and are awakened by crises and shocks, not by gradually evolving development. Traditionally, women have been late bloomers and often experience a new burst of energy, a second life in their forties or fifties, generally after children are launched. A forty-year-old former homemaker and community activist, now an association executive, told me that she feels like she's twenty-five in terms of her work, just launching into her career. Full-time career women may feel that their lives are a strange concoction, including some characteristics of women's traditional patterns and some characteristics of men's patterns, as described in Levinson's work *Seasons of a Man's Life*. He describes much more predictable stages in men's lives based on longitudinal studies of many men.

My own observation has shown that for working women, age thirty-five (plus or minus two) is an important decision-making time or a turning point. At thirty-five, women feel more compelled to pursue marriage or let it go, to decide whether to have more or any children. Careers have been or can still be launched and the commitment to career becomes more conscious. What was just a job is now a career. When women decide what they want out of life, they then begin to take themselves more seriously and to invest in themselves. They realize that there is a wider variety of possibilities for them. That is the point at which the personal power model takes on the most significance. And that's where the frustration and potential excitement begin.

In relation to the power model, women who choose full-time home-making are in a slightly different situation from those who work outside the home. If they are totally dependent on their spouses and children for their security and self-esteem, they will not become personally powerful. Personal power in our society is the combination of external and internal power. Unless a homemaker also reaches into the external world (the community, the neighborhood, the school) and establishes herself, she has no way to garner the external power that in combination with internal power is necessary to become personally powerful.

The Paradox for Women

In a provocative book entitled *Reinventing Womanhood*, Carolyn Heilbrun writes that women's movements have failed to maintain momentum in their achievements because of three factors:

1. The failure of women to bond
2. The failure of women to imagine themselves as autonomous
3. The failure of achieving women to resist . . . entering the
    male mainstream, thus becoming honorary men.

I interpret Heilbrun to mean by "bonding" that women don't stick together as closely as men do. There is an analogy that may fit here, derived from an old tradition on the east coast. It seems that crab pails do not have to be covered to prevent the crabs from escaping because when one of the crabs reaches the top of the pail, the others pull it back down in their attempts to escape too. This analogy fits some women. Not that men are always supportive of each other, but women have been known to be more outwardly unsupportive of their women colleagues, particularly in the last several years when women have begun to advance in organizations. A secretary will get promoted to an exempt job, and her old friends will snub her or may even try to do her in, rather than support her and hope to keep the relationship. Some would say that is due to women's not having played on teams as children and not knowing how to compete. Another reason may be that women see the resources as limited (money, jobs, manager's time) and want to get their share, like children wanting attention from mother but knowing it has to be divided among others. It may also be related to some of our messages that the only people worth bonding with are men. Men, we were told, will help us out if we are coy and seductive. Women, it was acknowledged, can be closer, more intimate friends with each other than most men can be, but we were led to believe that true intimacy is sexual and that is reserved generally for men. Sexual intimacy as a bonding force has not held up very well so there is even more confusion about whom we can trust. Women at Stages One and Two need to be able to bond particularly with other women to get support and self-esteem. At Stage Three they need each other more than ever to avoid being stuck in their masculine side. Sometimes the "right" men can help women at Stage Three by encouraging them to hold on to their feminine side. Women need to feel good about being women. They need to see other women as allies and partners. We need all the help we can get, and we must not be divided against each other if we are to make continuing progress.

Heilbrun's second point, of women not being able to see themselves as autonomous, seems like a paradox. We cannot bond together and we cannot stand alone. We have been taught that we need to rely on, even live through, a man. If we stand alone we are either so self-sufficient that we could not find anyone, or we are undesirable. It did not cross my mind, for instance, until I was involuntarily single after ten years of marriage, that being single could actually be challenging, satisfying, and mostly positive. And then it became psychologically difficult for me to remarry even though I wanted to, because I kept asking myself, "What will I have then that I don't have now?" The only answer in the end, after all other things were compared, was a husband and a commitment. Commitment is a very important thing to consider indeed, and the commitment that comes from a public ceremony is different from a private verbal one; but the thought process was very different than it had been the first time around. So I knew I could be successfully single. I knew that I had choices and that there would be joy and pain, loss and gain. Some women, though, get swallowed up in relationships or marriage and think nothing of leaving organizations or professions for the sake of them. It's as if they are living autonomously only until they are rescued by their prince. Ironically, these same behaviors we've been taught to nurture in ourselves—giving up our goals for theirs, being taken care of, being a helpmate and selfless mother—are those that cause some men to lose touch with and respect for us. I am not suggesting that women should always work, but that they not sacrifice themselves totally for husbands and children without some self-nurturing activities that keep them growing as well.

Women need to learn how to be autonomous, to practice the art of being alone and self-sufficient within a community of others, friends, family, and coworkers. This could include making financial decisions, traveling alone, having a private room of one's own, living alone, running a business, leading an organization, having one's own name. It means keeping part of you as an individual identity, no matter what your life circumstances may be, yet doing so in a context of community. Women at Stages One and Two particularly have to be able to become autonomous in order to have a healthy self-image and a life of their own. Once a woman has learned to be autonomous, both her work relationships and her intimate relationships are usually healthier.

Thirdly, Heilbrun says achieving women cannot resist becoming honorary men by entering the male mainstream. She sees these women as dependent on men professionally, not supportive of other women, seeking social status through men, being feminine but giving up womanhood (p. 29). We call them Queen Bees. I see a new breed of achieving women—those who have perhaps gone one step further. They have risen in organizations to Stage Three with all the right degrees and moves, and they think that the way to get ahead is to play the games and compete just like the "boys" do. They sacrifice their feminine side and act like men, in language, dress, and everything. It may, in fact, work for a while and bring the same rewards that men seem to be getting—money, status, success, position, control. But sooner or later the word gets out. The behavior she thought would buy acceptance is now labeled aggressive. She's called a tigress, a "tough broad," and, worst of all, a castrating female. The pendulum has swung too far, and she is losing out because she is understandably out of her element and not being herself. The irony here is that she is once again dependent on men—their style, their dress, their games, their acceptance—to provide her with the self-esteem that she can get only from being herself. And the result is anger at herself, anger at others, and anger at men for deceiving her into thinking it would work. I am not suggesting that women not take on their masculine side. On the contrary: Women must take on their masculine side in order to move through Stage Three successfully. But they must not let the pendulum swing too far for too long. Women can be strong, self-sufficient, analytic, decisive and still be women who love, care, nurture, and feel. A woman gubernatorial candidate stated that women can be loving and tough, can wield power and have a gentle touch. Women can be good wives, mothers, and sisters, and still ask for positions on boards and ballots without a contradiction.

Heilbrun says it even more strongly: "If I imagine myself (woman has always asked) whole, active, a self, will I not cease, in some profound way, to be a woman? The answer must be: imagine, and the old idea of womanhood be damned" (p. 34). She suggests that women "while not denying to themselves the male lessons of achievement . . . recognize the importance of taking these examples to themselves *as women,* supporting other women, identifying with them, and imaging the achievement of women generally."

Stage Three women will have difficulty moving beyond it if they stay in the masculine too long. They need to move to the position of being themselves, at once masculine and feminine and individual. They need to ask the broader and deeper questions like "What are my real strengths, weaknesses, interests, and values? What do I really want out of life and work? How can I be respected and competent and still be true to myself?" It involves finding out who you are rather than who you thought you should be in order to get ahead or prove yourself. It is more authentic and successful in the long run.

Masculine-Feminine

I've been alluding to masculine-feminine dichotomies in this chapter and throughout the book. It's time to discuss more fully what I mean by this language, since it is useful as well as irritating at times. At least two books about women, *The Coming Matriarchy* by Elizabeth Nickles and

Women's Reality by Anne Wilson Schaef, have referred to male systems or types (Alpha) and female systems and types (Beta). The two are distinctly different and we all know that the male system dominates. Women (including myself) can easily slip into the male versus female debate, asking which system is better. Some suggest that if the predominant system were only female things would be better for everyone. I think that is much too simple and perhaps even naive. Organizations are less than effective whenever any one system dominates because the whole picture is not represented. Although I agree that the masculine system predominates, I have some questions to raise about separations along male-female lines.

We get into difficulty when we categorize all men like "this" and all women like "that," because all men and women are not like all other men and women. For example, I know several successful men who have the ability to show behavior that is loving, nurturing, feeling oriented, yet they will never be female and they are not considered feminine. On the other hand, there are many men who clearly and distinctly fit all the stereotypes of the masculine—macho, emotionally tight, strong, fearless—who are not accepted in the system. I also know many women who exhibit strong masculine traits who are not successful in the system, and I know as many feminine women who are very successful in their work. So masculinity or femininity alone does not determine success. And learning the male system does not mean success either in the long run. Both masculinity and femininity have negative as well as positive aspects. So how do we work this out and find ways to work together amidst all this confusion?

One answer to the confusion is for both men and women to develop the ability to use either masculine or feminine behavior depending on what is the most appropriate for the situation. This concept of behavior flexibility is described by the term "androgyny." Androgyny is the harmonious coexistence of masculinity and femininity within the same individual (June Singer, Jungian analyst). Men and women always have been and always will be different. I applaud that. What I will call flexibility means that men can be masculine and at appropriate times can draw upon their feminine behavior; it also means women can be feminine, and at appropriate times draw upon their masculine behavior. This is obviously ideal behavior I am suggesting, for none of us would ever be totally balanced. But it gives greater ranges of behavior for those who want that. The following analogy explains this well: Each of us is born with our very own watercolor paint set containing all the colors of the rainbow. The warm colors (yellows, reds, oranges) are our feminine colors, and the cool colors (blues, greens, purples) are our masculine colors. Some people have limited themselves to using only one side of their paint set, only cool (masculine) or only warm (feminine) colors. Others use only bold colors or only muted colors. Androgynous or flexible people use all the colors in their paint set and even mix the colors as needed. This means that if the picture they are painting has in it a bold red building, they can paint that accurately. They can also paint the muted shades of gray-green in the building next to it. They may *prefer* one or the other, but they can still paint a full, representative picture. In organizations and families, flexible (androgynous) people use all their emotions; they can nurture others, make tough decisions, use their intuition, disagree openly, do kind things for others, and be strong. The key is that they know what the appropriate behavior is for the given situation and they use it. Then if they have shifted from their most comfortable "color" in order to respond, they can move back to paint where they are comfortable once again. It means men can cry and women can shout. And it means crying may not necessarily be seen as reflecting weakness, but as evincing feeling and wisdom, and shouting may not be seen as evidence of aggressiveness but as rising to the occasion. As I said, this is the ideal direction in which we must continue to move to develop together and work successfully in organizations.

I am concerned that the management and leadership potential in women will be stifled if they are not able to achieve this balance and if men do not appreciate it in themselves. Effective mangement theory can support a flexible way of relating without sacrificing the bottom line. *The Art of Japanese Management* states that women in middle management have a greater capacity for interdependence than the men for whom they work. It is threatening for men to exchange dependencies because it goes against the culture, threatens sex role differences, is seen as a sexual come-on or an invitation to take care of women. Women's most important contribution may be to role model the forms of interdependence that some men need to learn. Research shows that having minorities and women in organizations makes for better managed companies (pp. 128-129).

I firmly believe that women will be a key factor in helping to move organizational leadership from Stages Three and Four to Stage Five (Power by Purpose). But in order to do that women will have to stay in the system and work through Stages Three and Four without becoming honorary men, and they will need support from men to do that. Men will have to be willing to learn from as well as teach women. They will both have to help the management and organizational norms change slowly from within to bring about flexibility, a use of both masculine and feminine, without losing either. In the future I see organizations that have been predominantly Alpha (masculine) in the past now seeing the usefulness of incorporating some Beta (feminine) styles, as a result of competent, strong, and feminine women who have not become Alpha along the way.

Betty Friedan sums up the current scene forcefully in an excerpt from her book *Second Stage*. "We have to break through our own feminist mystique now and move into the second stage—no longer against, but with men. . . . We have to free ourselves from male power traps, understand the limits of women's power as a separate interest group and grasp the possibility of generating a new kind of power, which was the real promise for the women's movement" (*New York Times Magazine*, July 5, 1981, p. 14).

Emerging Women

To talk about women as a category these days is difficult because there are so many more categories of women. We are not largely homemakers, nor all married, nor all in nearly the same income brackets, as we used to be. Sangiuliano writes mostly about women who raised children and then launched another career, whereas now many more women launch careers and then decide about children. Three groups of women are rapidly emerging in our society, who I think will be very involved in different ways in the leadership and power issues of the next decade.

Ambitious Career Women: On the Seam

The first group are those ambitious career women who were born in the period from the mid-thirties to the early fifties, who are between the old and the new worlds of women in organizations, and who are not living the traditional homemaker lifestyle. A friend of mine described them as being "on the seam" between the old and the new. They have had more options than their mothers in education and opportunity, and they grew up as the forerunners of today's opportunities. They were the "front line" in a lot of ways. They are super achievers and are quite successful in their careers—sometimes even more successful (position, salary) than their husbands. Nickles, in *The Coming Matriarchy,* calls these women pacesetters and describes them as strong, independent, educated, goal directed, determined, self-confident, career oriented. Many of these women are single or married with no children. They simply do not have strong domestic ties.

Another part of this group has decided to do both—and achieve superwoman status all the way around. This puts enormous pressures on them both at home and work, and they feel they can opt out of *neither.* If this were ten years hence, they might hire live-in help, but being on the seam means they want the old *and* new at once and at the same level. They don't want to give up their career success and they don't want to change their view of what a good wife and mother should be. None of us has the energy or stamina to carry both roles at a super level and surely not the amount these women need to once again lead the way by creating options that will relieve the pressure on them. This may be the time for men to do more than ponder their role as parent, to take action in a more concrete way (as many have), to really share the childrearing and home-making. Lack of action on the part of men may lead to burned out women. A somewhat alarming option for many professional women who have had children in their mid or late thirties is to leave their organizations altogether. I understand why this occurs because several women have told me that some organizations will not bend an inch to accommodate family responsibilities and neither will some spouses. It is sad that these women feel this is their only option at this point and it would not be their choice. A study by General Mills on work, stress, and the family cited the fact that 51% of executive women said they would prefer to work less than full time. It seems time to look at organizational structures and policies to see whether they will cause organizations to lose good people because of inflexibility.

Young Pacesetters

The second group of women emerging these days are the young pacesetters in their twenties, who have all the qualities of the older pacesetters except that they are not on the seam. They have not had to fight for what they want (yet), nor do they feel much discrimination. They simply do not have the history of their older female colleagues. All education and graduate programs are open to them, and their male peers are more like brothers than potential spouses. They make a better starting salary than many women who've been working ten years. They have almost no conception of what it's like to be poor or displaced or dependent or rebuffed by society. They are young "whippersnappers," as the saying goes. They are starting out, in fact, more even with men for the first time in history—capable, intelligent, educated, determined, motivated, and knowing no bounds.

But do they identify with other women? And what will happen to them in the next decade as they watch their older female colleagues struggle with being on the seam? Will they become more balanced, more flexible, more feminine? Or will they take the male world on and become honorary men? I think the saving grace for these women will be that which is inherent in most, if not all women: the need for balance and for loving, caring relationships. Many of these women will face, sooner or later, the idea that "life is too short" to be lonely and unapproachable, albeit successful and intelligent. Another saving grace is this: According to Nickles, these women are motivated more by self-actualization and income than by traditional forms of power. So people at higher stages should be able to influence them by modeling androgynous behavior.

Women in Poverty

The third group is the growing number of women in our society who are in poverty. In fact, some writers now call poverty a female issue. These women in poverty are those who are uneducated and unskilled, usually single heads of households. They are malcontent and lack self-esteem, feeling trapped by the system in which they once believed. They are in a vicious circle, not knowing how to break out. At the same time, they usually do not take responsibility for themselves even when given it, perhaps because they don't believe anything will change. The chapter on powerlessness describes them quite well. The concern I have is that the first two groups are moving far out of touch with the third group and are not helping it. In the past more women could identify with "women's issues." Now it seems there are distinctly different issues for different groups of women; there is some danger that women leaders may increasingly become the enemy. Unless higher stage women continue to identify with what it means to be a woman in the best sense—to be giving, supportive, long-range thinking, intuitive, nurturing, thoughtful—and unless lower stage women learn to develop their other side—the assertive, self-promoting, directed, goal oriented side—women will continue to grow farther and farther apart. Women need to understand that they are part of an entire community of women. They have a responsibility to themselves to pay attention to the entire community, if things are truly to improve for all women. Some would argue that men are really trying to split women into groups to keep them apart—a new way to maintain control.

Women and the Power Model in Organizations

In the introduction to this book, I pointed out which stages were feminine, which were masculine, and which stages organizations reward most. Let's refresh our memories.

Stages Two and Five appear to be more feminine.

Stages Three and Four appear to be more masculine.

Stages Two, Three, and Four are most often rewarded in organizations.

HAGBERG'S MODEL OF PERSONAL POWER

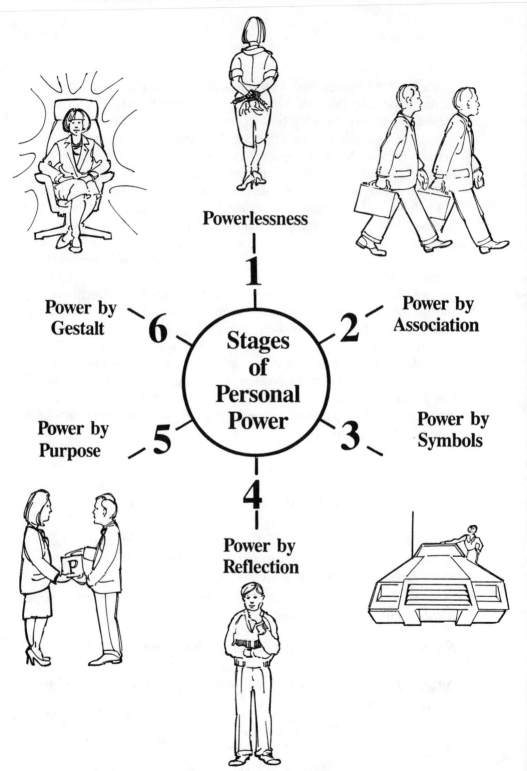

Powerlessness

Power by Gestalt — 6

Power by Association — 2

Stages of Personal Power

Power by Purpose — 5

Power by Symbols — 3

Power by Reflection — 4

It appears from this information that women's stages are generally the least personally powerful and the least rewarded in the organization or too advanced to be recognized. I affectionately call Stage Five the light at the end of the tunnel for women. My reasoning is that those qualities of Stage Five (having purpose, giving power away, using intuition, empowering and developing others, being stable, seeing visions beyond oneself) are the qualities that are inherently more flexible, using both feminine and masculine. In fact, men have to take on their feminine side in order to move from Stage Three to Stage Four and then learn to balance both at Stage Five. So, if women in organizations can prove themselves capable of working and competing with men at Stage Three without succumbing, and if they can become better acquainted with their own style and competence through Stage Four, they can come into their own, be rewarded for their most comfortable way of being (while still using all the colors in their paint sets) at Stage Five. And they can then be the role models for men in the organization who want to move beyond their tightly prescribed masculine roles. Women and men leaders at Stage Four and Five will lead us more effectively into the next century.

In an over-simplified summary, the power model operates in the following manner for women:

Stage One—Powerlessness

Women at this stage are powerless and dependent on others (some women, but mostly men) for almost everything, even though many of them live alone or with children. Men are our bosses, our teachers, our partners, even our knights in shining armor. We can feel secure as a result but we can also feel like children. Some of us, in fact, don't like ourselves and may even allow ourselves to be used, physically, emotionally, or intellectually, in order to obtain love or attention. To move to the next stage, we need to learn who we are, what we can do, what our worth is, and get support for ourselves, preferably from other women. This may be the hardest stage for women to break out of because of the cultural pressures on us to depend on and wait for others.

Stage Two—Power by Association

We learn that we are individuals and that we have skills and abilities. We

look to role models or mentors (bosses or others) whom we can work for
or emulate. We get to know the culture of the organization, which
sometimes frightens us and at other times gives us energy and exhilaration. We are striving for the credentials that will make us acceptable to
others. We make mistakes. But we need to learn, especially from our
mistakes. To move, we need to take more responsibility for ourselves,
volunteer for assignments, go out on a limb, push ourselves, get degrees
or credentials, set goals, take risks. At the end of this stage, we need to
take on the masculine side of ourselves, those behaviors that may not
come naturally and that may make us uncomfortable. This is a major
turning point for women and difficult to do. To keep from getting
overwhelmed women could ask themselves "What's the worst thing that
can possibly happen?" If we can prepare for that and then see ourselves
surviving it, we can continue to move toward our goals. Movement out of
Stage Two doesn't have to entail a promotion in the organization. Much
development can occur inside of us as well as in the community or in
professional associations.

Stage Three—Power by Symbols

This is our most uncomfortable stage and the most dangerous. We enter
the masculine side of ourselves and the organization, becoming responsible, competitive, political, game-playing, self-proving, and energetic.
The rewards are alluring—money, success, prestige, moving up. If we
buy in totally, we lose our womanhood. If we don't buy in at all, we're
not accepted or respected. We can become bitter and discouraged and
drop out, or we can recognize and understand Stage Three as temporary
and necessary to the future stages. We need to be *in* Stage Three but not *of*
Stage Three. We can get support from others who understand, avoid
getting trapped in games, ask a lot of good questions, take our bumps in
stride, not resort to tantrums, and be straight and clear about our
feelings. To move we need to become more reflective about who we are
and what it is we truly want. Can we be more our real selves now within
the organization? Second, we can try our leadership skills outside the
organization, like professional organizations or community boards, thus
giving us practice if and when we take on more inside the organization.
We need to learn more about the scope of the organization and be clear

about our strengths and limitations, fitting into that scope, not trying to do everything and burning ourselves out in our prime. Third, we need to stay closely connected to supportive women and men at all levels, those who are below us in the organization, those who are our peers, and those who are our role models and mentors. It is important to maintain contact with other women because at this stage we can too easily believe we can do it alone or that we do not need the feminine. We need to gain visibility but within our own areas of strength. One way to do this is to get involved more widely in the organization on committees or projects, always doing a very competent job for other people and making them look good.

Stage Four—Power by Reflection

At this stage we can increasingly take on our own personal style because we have proven that we understand but do not necessarily always play the game. We can take more risks and broaden our activities in the organization and in the community because we have a base of support. We're trusted, perhaps because we trust ourselves. And we trust others, delegating much to them or sharing with them. We are finding our sense of integrity, what we truly stand for as opposed to what others want us to be. We should avoid becoming haughty, self-sufficient people who think we've made it. This could be a hollow victory if abrupt changes occur in the management of the organization. Coalitions are even more important to develop now so we don't get caught in tricky Stage Three games. Our confidence should be much broader in the organization now as well because we have wider spheres of influence. Most important, we need to remember that our energy no longer goes toward our own personal gain, but toward helping others to gain what they need. Our focus must shift, or we will get stuck in reflection at Stage Four.

To move we need to reaffirm the feminine in us, the true nature of us as women, no matter where we are in the organization—manager, secretary, supervisor, director, clerk, engineer, president, or chair of the board. We are beginning to take on the other form of power, power for others. We need to be reflective, to assess our deepest values, to look at larger visions, to take a deep breath, to launch, and possibly observe a whole new world for ourselves. We need to let go. . . .

Stage Five—Power by Purpose

Stage Five women are in the most comfortable stage of all for them, although it is decidedly less secure than Stage One. We are able to channel energy to others in the organization, give things away, delegate more, be role models for men, but only as we fully accept ourselves and the struggles we face in organizations that reward Twos, Threes, and Fours. We will feel at home and free ourselves but out of sync with many other people. They may misread our motivations. We know our life purposes, our inner aims, and goals. And these things go beyond us, our egos, our reputations, the organization. But particularly, our thinking goes beyond our egos. We draw our strength from a source beyond ourselves. Stage Five women do not calculate where a decision will get them, but how it will affect others and whether it is the best for all in the long run. In fact, they involve a lot of others in their decisions, teaching and learning as they go. We trust ourselves and our judgment, and we are not aroused by promises or threats of money, titles, or power plays. We are part of a much larger life plan in which our work, our efforts now take their proper part. We involve ourselves in the larger world, in visions for the organization or professional groups. We mentor men, we nurture others, without knowing where it will lead, and without having to. We may have gotten pretty far in the organizational sense, or we may not have, but we like ourselves, accept ourselves and the respect we get from others for our competence and integrity. To move we need to relax.

Stage Six—Power by Gestalt

Stage Six is a wonder to behold in women. We are personally purposeful but in a quiet sort of way, integrated and calm because life is best when we try the least. We have internal calm and external respect based on the painful and joyous experiences of life that have formed us. We see paradox and we love it, because we know too much to believe otherwise. We have nothing to prove, no one to impress, and our community is the world. We care not for titles or even for glory. We're victorious because we're human and can fully admit it. Our behavior is truly our own and the masculine/feminine dichotomies seem to have slipped away somewhere a long way back. We say what we think, and it is usually wise because we are not trying to be wise anymore. We are at peace with ourselves. We may believe strongly in causes or questions or ideas and work valiantly for them, but our identity is not tied up in the ends, only the means. No one fights us for control because we have voluntarily given up control to others and our need for self-control long ago. Now we just are. To move, we need to enter into another level of reality.

Women and Leadership

Many women are natural leaders. We just don't think we are because we don't tend to lead in the traditional Stage Three ways that are so accepted. So we lack confidence in our ability to guide others, particularly men. I would strongly encourage women to read carefully the chapter on leadership and power, and take note of the behaviors and styles of leadership at each stage. Women can learn much from men about leadership at Stage Three, but to go beyond it to true leadership, they must learn from each other, from themselves, and from the few role models, both male and female, who are at those higher stages. The worst thing women could do is to accept the fact that leadership can be only the way we observe it currently. Women, being less constricted by role and expectations at this point in time, have the potential to go beyond the familiar territory, to be models for others of the way true leaders (Stage Four and beyond) behave. It will be challenging but also frustrating. For example, one woman manager told me that she likes to motivate her employees by mostly praising them and fueling their energy, then asking them to critique themselves. She feels this style is successful in the long run but takes longer and requires more patience. She gives them responsibility and then has to teach them how to use it day after day. Her male boss tells her she's not tough enough, that she should critique and criticize her people because only then will they really learn to toe the line. She has tried that but she comes across as a phony, and her people resent the feedback. She is trying to get people to be more self-reflective and responsible, but her boss wants short-term results.

Women in organizations are beginning to come together to discuss among themselves what power and leadership mean in their organizations. This is a wonderful first step in breaking down the barriers that separate women from each other and encourage competition. At one such meeting of women managers, the following questions were used to stimulate discussion of the power stages and leadership:

1. Which stage of personal power do you identify with most in your work?
2. What are the predominant values in your organization? In other words, what is the corporate culture? What power stage is valued the most?
3. How do you move from Stage Two (Association) to Stage Three (Symbols) in your organization (degrees, experience, contacts, risk taking, competence, right place-right time, confidence, mentor, networks)?
4. How could one keep from becoming an "honorary man" in the most masculine of the stages, Stage Three?
5. How would a Stage Four style differ from a Stage Three style in your organization in the following areas?
     competition
     planning
     relationships
     career goals
6. What would a Stage Four-Five culture look like? Describe it in your department, in your job. Get a firm image in your mind.
7. How would you act like a Stage Four-Five person in a predominately Stage Two-Three world?
8. What can you as individual members and as a group do to help, support, encourage, and empower yourself and other members of your group?
9. What are two characteristics of leaders at each stage of power?
10. How does a true leader act in your organization?
11. How can you develop your own leadership qualities?

I strongly encourage women to meet together, preferably with some higher stage women present, to discuss their own feelings about leadership honestly and sincerely and to discourage women from becoming honorary men in organizations. The future leadership of America is being formed through the values and behaviors that are being learned right now; if women are the hope for a different kind of leadership, they must begin to develop further now.

Chapter 10

Men and Power

Men and power have been, in most cultures, synonymous from the beginning of recorded history. As children, wherever we turned the power of the family, neighborhood, community, state, and country was in the hands of men. Or if they didn't possess it, they certainly desired it, and they moved with great speed and deliberateness to gain it. I do not mean to say there were not women of such mind; but we have witnessed mostly men pursue power throughout history, and they continue to do so today. What do they work so hard to obtain and retain? Why do they want it so much? Why are they so afraid if someone else gets more? What dilemmas does it bring them? What are the stages of power that tend to represent men more than others?

Men in our culture—particularly white men—are in the middle of a deep dilemma. They are the most externally powerful group of people in the world; they know the formula for success; they are privy to the old boys' club; they have all the advantage of strength and skill; they make a lot more money than women; they have visibility. At the same time many of them feel trapped in their role, with very few other options in life, having to compete forever to get to the glorified top, and are very unhappy. The dilemma is that they can't figure out *why* they're unhappy. They have or are headed for all the things that society has promised men who do well. Yet something is wrong, and they're unclear about what it is. And no one feels sorry for them because, after all, they're on top and they should be happy. So characteristically they twist and turn, and about the time of mid-life show forth their deep-seated dilemma by leaving their wives, losing their jobs, moving away, becoming twenty-five again, getting ill, being miserable, or dying.

The problem is that the dream they all thought they had bought into freely is a myth. They are in much more tightly prescribed boxes than most women are, and they don't know how to get out. The prescription for men is to get education or skills to land a job at twenty, work with few breaks until age sixty-five, and then die within five years. They look at the dream, the right position with all the responsibility and authority and power, the right salary, the right home in the right place, the right spouse, and the right kids. And somewhere along the way they discover (or more accurately try to hide the fact) that they either do not really want or cannot really achieve the dream that the family, their peers, the community, and they themselves had fostered for them. So they feel like failures because they are not perfect. And that is the first big part of the myth. It says that perfection is desirable and that men surely can attain it because of all their opportunities. The second and equally big part of the myth says that being perfect means being all the "successful" things in our culture and that ultimately these successes bring satisfaction or happiness or something good.

So most men who face this dilemma just take a peek at it and find it too awesome to investigate. They close off the part of themselves that is beginning to ask questions, the part that is getting suffocated in the narrow box, and they plod along complaining of something wrong in the organization or of their inability to change because they're too invested already. To look at the unknown and to sort out and unravel the long-term myths with which they have learned to operate is just too frightening and confusing. Also the culture prescribes men's behavior and emotions. They are to be characteristically strong and not to show emotion. Looking at the dilemma and the myths would force them to look at their real selves, their inner life, perhaps even to feel some new emotions, and that is very new and frightening.

It is one thing for me to explain to men that external power is not enough and that men in our culture may have to move beyond the traditional expectations they have of themselves; it is quite another thing to be a man in the position of wondering whether, in considering another way of being, he will lose all he has gained, or lose what it means, in his mind, to be a male. For most men, to be male is to be powerful, to have the success and symbols of external power. And that power is synonymous with men; it seems that power was and is in fact a way to describe men, and to consider taking it away from them is in fact to ask them to give up their primary identity and search for another. As we all know, any change is difficult. It implies giving up something, a difficult task even for the strongest. Let's examine how the quest for external power in men became so entrenched and what power means to men.

The pursuit of power, and therefore control, is something men are all taught from their earliest days as boys. This gets played out in competition with siblings, fights on the block, in sports, and in school. The message is clearly that if they are the best at whatever they do they will be respected and in turn will have power and control over others. They hear this message throughout their youth and adult lives, and it continues to haunt them until they die. The irony of it all is that the things they have managed to master, control, or accumulate do little to give them the satisfaction that they were told to expect. We all know of people who are the best at what they do but still find themselves unsatisfied with life. These people have been accumulating things that they were told would bring them much satisfaction and peace. And they found that these things did in fact bring them satisfaction but not all that they had hoped for. More important, the attainment of these goals tended to bring satisfaction for only short periods of time. Therefore, it became necessary to continue to reach for more in hopes they would get back the feelings of accomplishment, satisfaction, and in turn power and control. The cycle resembles addiction to drugs, alcohol, relationships, etc. And we all know the result of such addiction.

By acquiring power men seek the assurance that they are in control and will continue to be so in their own lives and in the lives of their loved ones. They want assurances that they will be able to determine their fate and most important that they will avoid pain from outside forces. They understand intellectually that this is impossible because they see people of all socioeconomic levels experiencing pain and anguish regardless of their station in life. And yet they still work hard to get more power and control so everything will be all right. At the base of this is their fundamental fear of not being important, cared for, and useful to others. These emotional needs far outweigh their intellectual understanding of their folly. *So the pursuit of power is in fact the pursuit of themselves as worthwhile human beings.* They, in fact, feel it is their responsibility to prove to the world that they are worthwhile human beings. This can also turn them against those who are not able to "pull themselves up by their boot straps" and cause them to treat others as less worthy, the basis of prejudice of all sorts. They believe that the more they can own, the higher they can climb, the more money they can make, the more powerful they are. They want this external power badly because without it they think they will not be accepted and respected, and therefore they will be nothing. Again, the focus is obviously on the externals without any reference to internal factors.

The origin of man's quest for power is found in the identification of the family as the most important organizational group in any society. Traditionally, man is described as the head of the family with primary responsibility for providing and protecting it from outside forces. All other members of the family group are given areas of responsibility only if they as members are in support of the family growth and protection and, more importantly, if they are in support of the man who is charged with being the leader and the person ultimately in control. If a man is in this role or aspires to it then he must begin early to prepare himself for it: get a degree, maybe two or three, get a good job, work hard to move up the organization to a higher position, get a bigger office, higher title. All of this puts him in a better position to be the leader of the family unit. Sadly, even if he does get to this high level and salary, he will not be guaranteed health, happiness, or peace of mind, but he will have a big house, office, and fat checkbook.

The point in all of this is that the culture calls men to find and accumulate power so they can accomplish their role with the family. But in the meantime, the family has changed. Only seven percent of households are rated as the traditional form, with father the working head and mother and children at home. Over fifteen percent of the households are headed by women. This makes the pursuit of these goals by men even less possible, and in fact the pursuit of this power "for the benefit of the family" may be one of the major contributors to the family's destruction. Their drive for the pursuit of more power—defined as more things—so they can carry out their responsibilities to take care of the family may be one of the major reasons men work so hard to accumulate more power and in fact the major reason they often end up with so little satisfaction or happiness. This is a good example of Stage Three behavior.

If men were to focus more on finding their own sense of inner peace and balance, they would ultimately be contributing more to the strength of the family. To move from Stage Three men must learn to think of power without control and of empowering others as a superior way of collectively gaining more for everyone concerned.

Emerging Groups of Men

While the opening scenario of this chapter applies to white men in our culture, in general it does not take into account some important groups of men who are not experiencing the myths and the dilemmas in the same ways. These three groups have either not bought into the myth of control and power, have tried to avoid it, are struggling with a different form of it, or have overcome it.

Gentle Men

The first of these groups is the one that was mentioned in Chapter Two, those men we will call the sixties males, those who are, as a book title suggests, "too gentle to live among wolves." They do not express and adhere to the values of the predominant culture of males, and they do not fit into the prevailing organizational structure or display its symbols. They feel out of the mainstream and more than a little lonely at times. Their formative years were lived during the Vietnam era and the women's movement. They do not accept the macho image of themselves as males. On the other hand, they are quite aware of and sensitive to the feminine side of themselves. It's as if they developed the feminine side before or in place of the masculine because macho looked like the only male alternative, and they didn't want that. It appears they are in Stage Two because they see no way to be Stage Three in our society and not be competitive or macho—almost the reverse problem of the men in Three who can't imagine moving to Four and looking at themselves reflectively.

In the May 1982 issue of *New Age* poet Robert Bly describes the problem for these sixties males, saying that while they are more thoughtful and gentle than most men, they are not more free. He says they are unhappy even though they're ecologically superior to their fathers and sympathetic to the harmony of the universe. This is because they have little energy in them. They are life-preserving but not life-giving. Bly uses a Grimms fairy tale to illustrate the process these men need to go through to once again regain their balance. It speaks of making contact with Iron John, a wildman, who lives in the bottom of a water hole. He is not the macho man but the "deep masculine," the primitive, instinctive male, who is under water. The key to understanding and releasing the Iron John within all men lies with their mothers, or more succinctly, it consists of letting go of their mothers. This is a slow, painful task, done with other men, Bly insists, and results in "an energy of forceful action undertaken, not without compassion, but with resolve" (pp. 31-35).

These men have been disserved, in a sense, because they are unaware of a third option—of going beyond the traditional masculine and their own feminine to a more seasoned, strong but sensitive masculine side. The women in their lives have reinforced their gentle side by rewarding them for it. These women have generally been strong, energetic women, mother-figures, in whose presence these men have not allowed themselves to develop. "Getting in touch with the wildman means religious life for a man in the broadest sense of the phrase," says Bly. And their energy needs to be revitalized. They need to "make a connection in their psyches to their kala energy—which is just another way to describe the wildman at the bottom of the pond. If they don't, they won't survive" (p. 51).

My sense of this process in terms of the power model is that this group of men need to define Stage Three for themselves in their own masculine terms, not in the terms of the fifties macho male under which we still operate. They need to define the characteristics of themselves and their wildness and then behave in their new masculinity—as true men. Only then will they be able to go on to see the integration of their newly found masculine with their feminine and respect them both, a task not unlike that for women who are moving into Stage Four. The role models for this growth in men are just beginning to emerge.

Minority Male Professionals

Another group of men who are emerging as a vibrant force in our culture, but until recently have not been sufficiently recognized or given credit for their accomplishments in our culture, are minority males, especially Blacks and Hispanics. They are slowly finding their way among the conflicting values and cultural pressures of organizations and grappling with the issues of not only what it means to be a man in our culture but, more important, what it means to be a person of color. Some interesting issues come to the fore when one thinks about minorities and personal power in our culture. I am referring to professional minority males, men who have achieved some prominence through education, skill, and organizational experience and who have acquired positions of some responsibility as a result. I am limiting comments to this group because in achieving a status in the academic, organizational, or political world, they have a sense of the kinds of success that most men aspire to.

The issue, in a word, is confusion. They are caught between the male-dominated values of the organization (and the frustration of trying to be like white men to be accepted) on the one hand, and on the other hand, their own values, norms, and culture, many of which they are proud of and want to maintain. The question is, how much do they buy into the dominant culture in order to be accepted, powerful, and successful? Once black became beautiful, for instance, it was not as necessary to be white to be taken seriously, and with that increase in self-confidence came the possibility of becoming more equal. Becoming more equal unfortunately (for women and minorities) usually means becoming more like the majority, the powerful, thereby possibly losing what it means to be different. Being assimilated, we sometimes call it. So do they learn to play the game the same way, or do they develop their own rules? Will they be any happier, more satisfied when they become part of the system and take on the responsibility for it? Aren't they too still defining themselves according to white men's definitions by relating their success to white male standards? Many are asking the question at this time, "Who are we, anyway? And what do we want to be?"

These are challenging questions and challenging times. This group of men has more potential perhaps than most other groups to help men change the way they do things. History reveals that those who have been governed by others and have gained power do not necessarily act in a more human way, nor more democratically than the way in which they were governed, unless the emerging leaders are thoughtful and wise. Professional minority males have the opportunity to be different types of leaders, just as women have that potential. It depends on the kind of people they develop into and whether they become just like the system from which they are emerging. They can be personally powerful without becoming Stage Three precisely because they are men in our culture who have had a different way of viewing the world. They understand not being on top but still having self-worth and valuing things other than wealth and fame. They can show white men that just because men are in the organization does not mean they all want external power, whereas women can't do that for men in the same way. Minorities can show white men that differences between men are widespread and that there are other ways to be and still be masculine. They can be one form of new model for the future, if white men can get over their deep-seated fear and insecurity, which causes them to behave paternalistically or hatefully towards minorities.

By describing professional minority men as a hopeful emerging group I do not mean to overlook the doleful situation confronting most minority men (and women) in our culture. On the whole, minority men have the highest rate of just about everything: unemployment, discrimination, health problems, crime, educational failure. The situation for most is still appalling, yet the emerging professional minority leaders who do not forget their own roots and their identity are a hope for the future.

Integrated Males

A small but growing number of men have done battle with the crises of integrity and ego (the major struggles on the way to inner power) and are emerging, not as new men but as whole men. They do not have to measure themselves by the traditional symbols of power because their worth comes from the inside. It doesn't matter what positions they hold because they know their life purpose goes beyond their work. They do not feel they are weak because they are sensitive and alive to their feelings, yet they do not hide behind their feelings either. They have a full range of behaviors at their disposal, firmness and resolve as well as compassion and caring. They use the behavior that is appropriate for the time. They have passed perhaps the biggest hurdle in their lives: finding out and being who they are rather than who they thought they had to be.

They have grappled with the myths of men's lives and accepted themselves with all their shadows instead of attempting to be perfect. They are real. They are thoughtful. They are becoming wise.

The lingering dilemma for them is to become comfortable with another way to be in our culture. Giving up the glory and would-be success for an uncharted alternative is frightening and unpredictable as well as exciting. They ask, "If our leaders, our 'big men,' are not just those in positions of power, then how will I emerge as a leader in the new model? What does it mean to not be the head of a group and to still lead? What if I am in a leadership position but see it as enabling others rather than myself? Or what if I just want to be, to read and talk and touch people and ask questions and love and not take on any more responsibility? What role is there for this whole me? I'm not sure what the road is to this place I'm on my way to. Perhaps I'm carving my own road!" The most important step was stepping out before they knew what the future would hold. That was the risky adventure for each one of them.

Whole men know many of the questions, but they do not have to have the answers. They are confused at times but find that not having to know is part of the delight too. Many of these men credit women at some point along the way for being instrumental or even critical to their continued growth. Many women who trust their intuition and deep wisdom can encourage men to explore more deeply the new ways to be beyond Stage Three. A few other men who crossed the threshold can also be very instrumental in showing men that there is life after symbols. But in the end, the process of movement is a solitary one. Whole men will tell you that it is a lonely, long, continuous struggle to uncover the long-capped feelings, let go of the myths, believe in another way even though it's not always apparent, and give up power and control for peace of mind. Ironically, another kind of power—inner power, which is so much stronger—is the result, but it is definitely not clear to Stage Three men that anything is beyond where they are. To think so would be heresy to the male club.

The integrated males can risk more than ever because they have principles that cannot fail. They can make surprising moves in their lives because they are not afraid of losing. There is very little to lose anyway. Life is an adventure, a peaceful, empowering walk on one's own real path. As Thoreau says, "dwell as near as possible to the channel in which your life flows."

Critical Issues

If men are to go beyond the stage at which the myth is complete (Stage Three) and emerge into something else, they must face or reconcile several critical issues. For each man it may be a different issue or the struggle may be different, but nevertheless there will be no movement if there is no integrity crisis. For many men there will be no crisis because there is no desire or need to move. Some men have bought so strongly into the myth of male as powerful and in control that they are hardened. Others are stuck at Stage Three because it has replaced their own sense of self-worth. Others have closed off their feelings thoroughly because of the fear of facing painful memories or the fear of getting hurt.

We need men and women in families, organizations, governments who lead out of personal power not position power. To do that, the crisis of integrity that is encountered between Stages Three and Four must be faced; to do that, some of the following issues must be addressed.

Self-Worth/Security

Unfortunately, many men view themselves as worth something only to the extent that they make a continuous and rising wage and get promoted to new positions along the way. They know they are good people because they do well at work. And the better they do the more secure they feel. The more secure they feel, the greater the price they pay because they depend on the ongoing security and benefits resulting from their work. The term "golden handcuffs" is descriptive of the reason people can't leave or even consider changing what they're doing on the job.

Until self-worth and security can be generated from *within,* no matter what job, health status, or position one holds, there is no true self-worth and security. Self-worth disappears the minute any of the safety elements are taken away. The sad thing about men and retirement is that many men identify so strongly with their work that they die within a few years after they cease to work. As the adage goes, "If you are what you do, then when you don't you aren't." If there is no interest or identity within oneself or outside of work, the gap that retirement brings is too wide to bridge.

So the issue here is getting self-worth from inside. But this is not an easy task. It involves soul searching, self-knowledge, and self-acceptance. It is a daily practice of accepting the bad with the good and believing in the worth of one's creation, not the worth of one's work or place in society. It is a practice in humility but also one of forgiveness of self and thankfulness for self. It is a slow and constant task, often brought on by unexpected loss of one of the security props one was holding on to. However or whenever it happens, the lasting effects are known. The basic question for testing self-worth is this: If all I have was to be taken away and all I had left was my core (without home, family, work, identity), would I still be a worthwhile person? If the answer is yes, in behavior and in feelings, then one's self-worth is indeed emanating from the inside. If the answer is no, then those things that one does, has, or controls are the means to self-worth. Changing that is a long, slow process, which only begins when one admits that self-worth is important and that one is willing to risk uncovering all the layers that separate the real worthwhile person from the current facade.

Vulnerability

This is a word that most men do not even like to hear, for all its connotations seem negative. To them, being vulnerable means to not be in control, to be weak, to let someone else have the advantage. In fact those things are true about vulnerability. But that's precisely the advantage. Men can never learn how to not be in control without being in control, especially emotionally, which is the finest kind of vulnerability. Yet I've never seen men squirm and struggle more than when they are emotionally vulnerable. It's easier to lose on the gridiron or the battlefield than to break down and admit to emotional needs and fears.

Yet men do have deep and strong emotional needs and fears. The more aware they are of them, the sooner they can understand the role these underlying feelings have in their behavior and in their lives. Two elements seem to be necessary in order to be vulnerable. Both are difficult to accept. One is that one cannot be vulnerable alone. Being vulnerable means to be in danger of being wounded or open to attack. The fear in being deliberately vulnerable with other persons is that they will get you when you are down. They will attack your weak spot and hurt you. Although this is indeed possible, in every case I've known exactly the opposite occurs. People respond to honest vulnerability with sympathy, love, or with their own vulnerability in return. And the relationship usually becomes closer or stronger as a result.

The second element in vulnerability for men is even more difficult to achieve. They must give up the myths and the constricting boxes they have been living in. To do that requires discussing and understanding what it means to be in the boxes and what it means to accept the myths and to leave them. It means fear, anger, disappointment, loss of meaning, loss of love, loss of prestige, loss of pride, abandonment. Whatever the constraints are, they have to be put out on the table, to be exposed for what they are and what they mean. That is vulnerability.

The Meaning of Strength

To be strong in the culture of men is to be the one who is always responsible and can be counted on. The strong one never flinches, never cries, never buckles, shows appropriate kindness but never compassion. The strong one is impregnable and indestructible. Those descriptions sound like a stone fortress, certainly not a human being. But then, some would say, men are not raised to be human beings, they're raised to be strong. Men in fact get robbed of half of the experience of life if they accept this is the only way to be. Being vulnerable and in need of love and care is a comforting experience, that of going back to childhood with the memory of a parent who indeed knew how to care for and nurture the "little part" of each of us. Before we could grow up we all needed to learn to be small and some of us cannot accept the fact that a small child is still in all of us that wants to be loved. Some of us did not get that nurturing as a child and have never been able to admit or accept it. Yet we need it desperately. So the cover-up continues.

To always be strong means to lose sight of the humanness of us all, the part that needs someone else's arm, loves someone else's warmth and touch, secretly craves the times when we don't have to be in charge. To be human means to be in charge sometimes, to not be so strong at other times, and to be weak once in a while too. There is nothing honorable in people who pride themselves in not shedding a tear over a close friend's or family member's death. It is a denial of perfectly understandable and acceptable feelings. To deny them is to stash them away and be haunted by them in the future.

Men need to redefine male strength as the ability to be human and responsible but also to feel and to be able to accept love, care, and nurturing from others. True strength comes from deep within, tempered by experience and fueled by a wide range of emotions.

Leadership

Men need to seriously rethink the form of leadership they have been perpetrating on the family, the community, the organization, and the world. It has not been of sufficient integrity to enable us to live together peacefully, and it threatens to destroy us. People in this country do not trust power because they say it is always self-serving. That is why people always want a balance in power, even if they dislike one side or the other. The American people increasingly mistrust the organizations that are dominated by personalities or can be led by a single person. That describes Stage Three leadership precisely, and until self-service is not a major motivator of power, we will not have integrity in our political and organizational leadership.

So the whole or integrated men, the minority professional males, and the higher stage women may be our major hope in redefining what leadership is and how it behaves in practice. They may begin soon to be the models for the transforming, empowering leadership we will require for moving into the next century. The chapter on leadership describes how people at each stage lead, and it stresses the concept of integrity as the key factor necessary for the emergence of true leadership.

Since most men in our culture are still scrambling for Stage Three, it leaves a lot of work undone. But since men have hold of the reins in our culture, I'd suspect the leadership revolution will go on among them, with those whole men and professional minorities moving themselves surreptitiously around in organizations, acting differently than the Threes, but remaining strong and competent in the organization. Slowly they will move to Stage Five behavior, not by any mandate but by the process of their own development, until the norms eventually begin to change. It will take men working with men, aided and abetted by women who have gotten beyond Three, to make any changes in the future. There are no tricks, no techniques, no magic clues to making organizational leadership change. It takes individuals changing themselves and then acting differently wherever they are, treating people differently, asking different questions, questioning policies, working unceasingly on issues, seeing a vision, and acting in everyone's best interest. It means becoming a Stage Four or Five individual and living accordingly. It means being alive, not being detached, being sensitive to self yet putting more energy into empowering others, working to serve, not living to work. It is a transformed individual who transforms others, and together they transform organizations and countries. Nothing happens that is not thought of by someone and agreed upon by others. And the most profound ways of changing others is the personal touch.

Men Moving Beyond Stage Three

There are various ways for men to become unsettled at Stage Three. Sometimes an outside event catapults them into thinking things over. At other times, the satisfaction they thought they'd feel when success arrived as a result of being a provider, of having a good position, or of acquiring the necessary possessions just wasn't enough. Somehow they were still disappointed, in themselves or in the things they'd accumulated. The material things didn't continue to bring the kind of acceptance that they'd been seeking. The next step for them is to try by some means to understand what is blocking them from the peace and satisfaction they want in life. Many possibilities are available, but it is important they understand the process and not get absorbed in it, only to find out that they are being seduced by the process and not by the change. Whatever process they use to confront the move beyond Stage Three, whether counseling, reading, listening, or writing, the real process begins in earnest when they stand face-to-face with themselves. That usually requires a personal guide with much patience and wisdom. One example of the way in which men choose to make changes is to go to a personal counselor, a trained person who can talk out the situation and help them gain insights. Let's explore the path that many men take.

It is a logical path because it is difficult to be objective or insightful enough to see oneself as others can. One of the first things many Stage Three men discover in counseling is that they are insensitive—insensitive to the needs or feelings of an individual, of a group, or of an organization. So they work first on becoming more sensitive, more aware of their behavior, more in touch with their feelings. They are understanding more about themselves and slowly letting their feminine side emerge as a legitimate part of themselves.

Many men leave counseling at this point, assuring themselves that if they are just nicer and more aware of others they will be accepted and loved and satisfied. But frequently they discover that this too falls short of the satisfaction they now so desperately want. With the next step they return to counseling, thoroughly discouraged, only to find that the real search now, at the next deeper layer, is the search for themselves, for the self that goes beyond masculine or feminine to the core of one's being. In this search they find out that they are many things and that real satisfaction comes from standing face-to-face with themselves, accepting themselves, and then going outside themselves to the needs of others from a deeper base.

Males and the Stages of Personal Power

There are certain stages of personal power that men identify with more than women do. These stages on the model are Stages Three and Four. Men move quickly through Stage One and usually stop off only temporarily at Stage Two on the way to Stage Three. Here is a brief description of the ways men behave at each stage of power.

Stage One

Most men quickly move out of Stage One due to their position in society and in organizations. However, there are still large groups of men in our culture and in the world who are powerless compared to other groups of men. Minorities, disabled, prison inmates, the poor, the aged, and the chemically dependent are some of the less powerful groups. Men who are seen as powerless are those men who are emasculated, who are not in control of their lives or the lives of others, or who are barely able to be in control due to poverty, lack of education, discrimination, or illness. They are not able to perform the functions they have expected of themselves and are dependent on someone or something else for their survival.

Stage Two

Men at Stage Two are usually just passing through the stage on their way to the next. They are finding their way, learning the ropes in the world and getting ready to take it on. They often see this time as their warmup period, preparation time during school, or their apprenticeship. Once they've paid their dues, they can go on to where the real action is.

Another type of Stage Two male is the one described by the section on gentle men. They are stuck at Two because they are pseudoinnocent and passive. They think lofty thoughts and care about the right things, but they bring no energy to the world. They were enervated by growing up during the Vietnam war and the women's movement and they got no further. They ceased to grow, to develop, and to confront their masculine side, and now it's too scary to do so.

Stage Three

This is the spot on the model where most men think they ought to be or wish they were—their dream-come-true stage. It includes the right symbols and the formula for achieving them; if one is successful the American Dream of happiness and satisfaction will follow. To be at Stage Three is to be "powerful" and in control, to be the ultimate that men in our culture are supposed to be. The only thing that is better is to be more of the same for more rewards at a higher level.

Stage Four

For many men, moving into Stage Four is definitely the most difficult of

all transitions, even though they increasingly desire this stage. Stage
Four requires an inner journey, a deeper questioning, while at the same
time maintaining the outward competent facade. It means being reflective and honest, willing to let go of some of the symbols that have for so
long dominated men's lives. It is scary and new. The crisis is one of
integrity: each man must find out who he is instead of who others want
him to be. Men must explore their feminine side before they can proceed
through Stage Four. The qualities of self-reflection, of finding one's own
style as different from the organization, of learning to use one's intuition
make many men feel as if they're losing whatever had made them strong
in the first place. It is a deep and often a frustrating dilemma, but always
alters the way in which men live henceforth.

Stage Five

The crisis to overcome in moving to Stage Five is one of ego. This is a
different type of task altogether, because no one warned men that after
searching to build up their egos and self-esteem they would then be asked
to give them up. How can anyone justify being a king of the culture and
not have all the ego gratification that goes along with it? It's hard to
voluntarily give up something that has provided so much security for so
long. And letting go of ego goes hand in hand with finding one's life
purpose, that which one lives for. For men to give up control of their lives
to a purpose in life larger than themselves is a monumental task,
especially when they may not have had such experiences before. Women
intuitively understand Stage Five because they know how love works,
and they've been taught that love goes way beyond oneself. To have love
is to give it away. Men who truly understand what all of this means and
live it usually find it necessary to have a guide because it is so easy to slip
back into controlling themselves and others. They feel so out of the
mainstream of men that to be comfortable with the inner peace and
vision of Stage Fives almost requires them to look weak, weird, not
strongly motivated, not on the cutting edge. It takes real courage to be a
Stage Five male in our culture, but it also signifies potential wisdom as
well as leadership.

Stage Six

Men at Stage Six are sages. They are so at home with the universe that they have no need to be in anyone's way with a right answer or even a right question. They just *are*, at Stage Six. There is a wonderful peace about them and a sense of purpose that reaches out of the organization and into the world. They are wise and they have a glint in their eye.

Chapter 11

Beyond Ego and Gender:
Leading From Your Soul

Ultimately we have just one moral duty: to reclaim large areas of peace in ourselves, more and more peace, and to reflect it towards others. And the more peace there is in us, the more peace there will also be in our troubled world.

Etty Hillesum, holocaust victim, *An Interrupted Life*.

Leadership is a journey. It is not a trip, with an identifiable destination and triptiks to keep you on the right road. A journey unfolds gradually. It meanders. You stop and start, take side roads, get bogged down. You meet travel companions and sometimes stay with friends for a while. A journey is not predictable, even though there may be an end goal. On a journey, the process of getting there is part of the overall goal.

So it is with leadership. The end point of leadership is not just the position of power we reach, but the continual change and deepening we experience that makes a difference in our lives, our work, our world. Our leadership journeys are only at *midpoint* when we have achieved a position of power.

The second half of the leadership journey comes once we pass age thirty-five; it is then that we have the opportunity to lead from our souls. We find few role models and not much written on this type of leadership. Soul leadership begins to emerge when we find our existing leadership style less rewarding, less satisfying than it was; when we must either shift to the inner leadership journey or recycle to an earlier leadership style which is more comfortable and predictable.

The leadership journey is a matter of the soul and that is where the energy and the focus have to be. As Etty Hillesum writes in the introductory quote, this is more about inner courage and peace than it is about strategic planning. It is not about skill development, it is about facing fear, letting go of control, gaining self-worth and inner strength, finding inner freedom and moral passion—the things you learn only after you think you know it all. This journey takes you to your core, including your dark core (shame, fear of abandonment, rage), wherein lies the raw power of transformation. It is not an easy journey, and the goal is not to be successful in the traditional sense; it is to be faithful to the journey itself. The only requirement is courage.

I am describing a different kind of leadership than we are accustomed to. Leading from your soul involves things like meaning, passion, calling, courage, wholeness, vulnerability, spirituality, community. It does not represent the traditional forms of leadership and it goes beyond the newer feminist forms, intriguing as they are. This leadership, which I call soul leadership, transcends both masculine and feminine forms, reaching to another level, in which we connect with our souls, our cores, our essence.

Why is it necessary to have leaders who lead from their souls, people who can operate from a place of inner power? Because the future requires leaders who do not operate out of fear or ego gratification, who do not revert to traditional authoritarian styles when things get tough, who do not have to prove their worth by supplying the answers. To requote Rob Harvey of Herman Miller, from the introduction to this book,

> Leadership always comes back to the issue of character, of deep foundational values. In the current reformation this country is experiencing, and the instability we are feeling, you cannot lead by forcing compliance. It simply doesn't work. The rate of change is too high to be managed from the top down. In order to lead, one must engage followers. You will not find followers without caring, connecting and creating. Would you follow someone who did not care about you, connect with you, or did not wish to create a new reality? Mere compliance today is a recipe for disaster. As leaders, or would-be leaders, we must be vulnerable. None of us has arrived. We must recognize our own voyage. We can only lead effectively by enabling others to maximize their contribution. We are all on the journey together, accomplishing things that none of us could accomplish alone.

How do we recognize people who lead from their souls and how do we know when we are leading from our souls? Answer the following questions to discover for yourself.

1. Who, other than your parents, made you feel worthwhile before you were twenty? How did he or she do that? How did you react? How did it affect you in the long term? That person was leading from his or her soul. When you make someone else feel worthwhile you are leading from your soul.

2. Do you ever hear a little voice speaking inside you? You're not sure where it comes from but it tugs at you, asks you to go in a different direction, say something you wouldn't ordinarily say, or stop what you're doing. Listen to that voice of wisdom. What is it saying to you now? If you can distinguish that voice from your ego, it will take you to your soul.

3. What was the moment of keenest insight in your life? How did it happen? What was the result? Recapture that experience as an example of soul leadership behavior.

4. Which of your personal behaviors hurt or scare you or other people? Do you know these behaviors intimately, so that you can choose not to do them but to learn from them? These behaviors, if left unchecked, will block you from leading from your soul.

People you and I know who lead from their souls have some of these characteristics in common:

- They know intimately what it means to be part of or create community.
- They do not depend on themselves for the vision of the organization.
- They can give power away without feeling a loss of self.
- They are peace-filled in crises as well as in calm times. And during crises, they do not revert to authoritarian or avoidance behaviors.
- They are connected intimately to a Higher Power.
- They do not project their pain or addiction on others.
- They do not burn out or succumb to stress.
- They practice integrity, reflection, and collaboration.
- They have a strong sense of humor and creativity.
- They are courageous.
- Above all, they are life giving.

We are all capable of leading from our souls. We were made to do it that way in the first place. When we begin to lead from our souls, we feel as if we are coming home, coming to the place in which we were meant to be, even though it usually means living counter to the culture. But inside, it is a wonderful and relieving feeling.

Getting to that place in which we lead from our souls requires a giant leap of faith. The whole world tells us to lead in another way, the way the books tell us to lead, the way the people in positions of power do it. It tells us to be in charge. It defines leadership as vision, mission, engaging others to meet goals, confidence, career climbing, strong ego, program planning, long range strategies. And for the first half of our leadership journey this style of leadership works, and works well.

But in the second half of our leadership journey, roughly after we reach the age of thirty-five, being in charge doesn't work anymore. It helps us prosper but it will never transform organizations. To transform organizations we need to transform ourselves. We have to become whole. And that is a profoundly spiritual journey requiring courage.

It requires a leap of faith to lead from our souls. It requires courage: a conscious reflective decision to act on life-giving principles, despite the consequences, even if they threaten our priorities or existence. Think about this. Courage is not spontaneous or instinctive, like heroism, or a learned skill, like bravery. How do we get courage, and where does it lead us? Courage is what we develop on this journey to soul leadership. It takes us into new territory. It allows us to go beyond what we were capable of saying and doing before. We go to our depths and find our heights, and in our lives we emerge as wise leaders. The journey of leadership I have been discussing is depicted in this rather convoluted-looking model.

In this model, the first half of the leadership journey is represented by an outward and then upward line. Moving out in early leadership ventures requires risk. Then you build on those experiences, develop skills and move up in leadership. This part of the journey parallels power stages one and two. The peak of the journey, at the top of the cycle, coincides with stage three.

The second half, the phase of soul leadership, is more of an inward, downward, and then onward journey, depicted by the second half of the chart and described in stages four, five, and six. The moving in phase, the downward and inward journey, requires courage, and the transformation happens in the swirl of lines that looks like a collapsed web. That's what it feels like when we are in the thick of change. Next we experience the inevitable, onward journey that rekindles our spark in a totally new way and results in a calling. Moving beyond requires grace, which is unconditional love from a sacred source inside and outside yourself.

Leadership Development Cycle

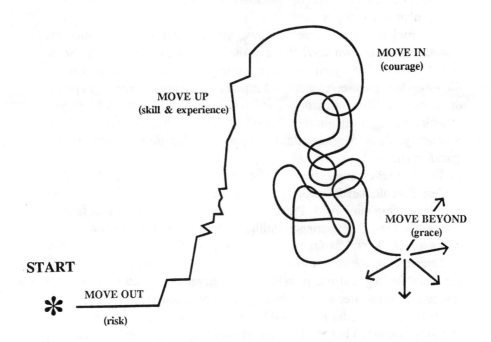

Unfortunately, no seminar or workshop program can move you quickly to this next place on your journey. It can only introduce you to the concepts and let you try on a few. The journey takes a long time, generally several years, and requires immense soul searching. The work of this inner development requires that your foundations shake, jarring you into a new way of thinking. It is not easy work and cannot be done quickly. Remember, courage is a decision.

Developing Soul Leadership

What follows is my long-term process for developing people who lead from their souls. It is based on the behaviors and practices of people in all walks of life who live and work from their souls. As you read it, you may agree with the principles and think you are well on your way. I applaud you. Keep going. My experience tells me that you must genuinely engage in two-thirds of these activities before they make a life-changing difference, and that a few, like embracing shadows and taking spirituality seriously, are absolutely necessary.

This soul leadership process allows you to enter into transformation gradually in your own way, either in the order listed or randomly. Some aspects of your life—your work life, your community life, or your home life—may lend themselves more to this process than others. Since we operate differently in different parts of our lives, it may be wise to pick one part in which to begin this journey. Then, as you continue to develop on the journey, you can integrate additional parts of your life gradually into the transformation.

The first seven suggestions are intended to get you started, since they are less difficult than the second set. These are : 1. Be accountable. 2. Assess your leadership journey. 3. Practice vulnerability. 4. Play without feeding your addictions. 5. Experience solitude regularly. 6. Try one new artistic endeavor. 7. Travel as far from home as possible.

The next six are more difficult. They ask you to enter into a covenant for inner healing and life transformation. Enter into them seriously and reverently. These are: 8. Take your spirituality seriously. 9. Find a mentor at the fringe. 10. Find peace and intimacy in your relationships without avoiding conflict. 11. Embrace your shadows and childhood wounds. 12. Discover your passion. 13. Accept your calling.

1. Be Accountable

The first myth to shed about soul leadership is that you can do it alone. Perhaps the most humbling thing you will learn on this journey is that you need help. Many power leaders are loners, very much in control and independent. Most people—leaders and otherwise—are not used to talking about personal issues with people and can easily deceive themselves. However, soul leaders never isolate themselves or operate in a vacuum. A critical foundation for all the other soul experiences is accountability. So this is an appropriate place to begin the inward journey.

The second myth to shed is that you are in charge. The soul leadership process is not about taking charge. It is about letting go. Part of letting go is letting others into the process with you, to keep you honest and to support you. You need to be regularly accountable to another person or to a group in order to do this soul work. I recommend meeting every two to four weeks with a counselor or mentor who is beyond you on the journey, or with a small group with wise people in it. If you don't have these people, the process will eventually be aborted, because ego will be leading ego.

Meet regularly and start keeping a personal journal on your experiences and their effects on you. A journal is simply a notebook you write in, a safe, private place to record your thoughts, feelings, reactions, and questions. This reinforces your experiences and helps you reflect more deeply on them. This leadership development process is profound, not programmatic. It has whole life consequences, not merely quarterly or annual results.

You may also choose to engage in specific group experiences over a shorter period of time to take on burning topics. One group of people from several different cultures started an isms group, simply to look at all the ways in which they live out their prejudices. They learned that they had more isms than they thought, and they became more aware of them in everyday life. They also learned that each of them had a characteristic that was on someone else's list of isms in some form. It was an enlightening insight. Each of them committed to making specific changes and reporting on her progress to the group.

A group of men call themselves Talking Heads. They meet for breakfast every month to talk over what is going on in their lives and how that affects their families and the community. They ask for feedback from the other members and bring in articles and ideas that they want to discuss or question.

Vaclav Havel, playwright, dissident, and former president of Czechoslovakia, described the process of accountability for soul leaders well when he spoke before the U.S. Congress.

> We still don't know how to put morality ahead of politics, science and economics. We are still incapable of understanding that the only genuine backbone of all our actions—if they are to be moral—is responsibility. Responsibility to something higher than my family, my country, my firm, my success. Responsibility to the order of Being, where all our actions are indelibly recorded and where, and only where, they will be properly judged.
>
> Consciousness precedes being, and not the other way around. For

this reason, the salvation of this human world lies nowhere else than in the human heart, in the human power to reflect, in human meekness and in human responsibility. Without a global revolution in the sphere of human consciousness, nothing will change for the better in the sphere of our being as humans, and the catastrophe toward which this world is headed—be it ecological, social, demographic or a general breakdown of civilization—will be unavoidable.

Another great thinker and wisdom figure, Eleanor Roosevelt, summed up the process and results of moving to true leadership when she said,

Somewhere along the line of development, we discover what we really are and then we make our real decision for which we are responsible. Make that decision primarily for yourself, because you can never really have anyone else's life, not even your child's. The influence you have is through your own life and what you become yourself.

2. Assess Your Leadership Journey

Create a leadership journey chronicle by looking back over your life to the events, experiences, behaviors, and people who were integral to your leadership development to date. Write these events, experiences, and people on a sheet of paper in any way that makes sense to you, by influence, event, or chronology. Take a while to reflect on this, because more experiences will emerge as you allow them into your consciousness. Ask yourself these questions:

1. How did you develop as a leader before the age of twenty?
2. What have been your leadership turning points, both negative and positive?
3. How do you describe yourself as a leader now?

After establishing where you are and how you got there, ask yourself the following questions and answer as honestly as possible in your journal.

1. What was the most important question you asked yourself about leadership and about life ten years ago? What is the most important question you ask yourself today?
2. What do you consider success?

3. What gives you your identity as a person? As a leader?

4. What are you most proud of? Most sorry about?

5. What is the energy or passion that drives your life?

6. When were you most vulnerable? What happened?

7. When do you experience powerlessness in your life? How does it feel?

8. When have you practiced soul leadership? What was it like for you? For others?

9. What's become clear to you?

10. What beliefs about power do your current leadership behaviors reflect?

Share your answers with your accountability group or person. If you really want a dose of reality, summarize your leadership self-portrait and give copies to one or two people with whom you've had adversarial relationships, asking for their feedback. Explain to them that you are assessing your leadership and that their ideas would be helpful to you. Their views won't reflect all of reality, any more than yours do, but you might use their feedback later on in the process, when you get to the section on embracing your shadow.

At this point you need to read about leaders who operated at a soul level. Biographies are best. Read about Anwar Sadat, Mother Theresa, Ghandi, and Martin Luther King for starters. Read leadership books if you like, but choose carefully. In *Leadership*, James McGregor Burns describes transformational leaders well. The ethics and morality chapters of John Gardner's *On Leadership* are inspiring. The chapter titled Inside-Out from Stephen Covey's *Seven Habits of Highly Effective People* cites the character principles that have been missing from the leadership ethic since World War II. And in *Managing as a Performing Art*, Peter Vaill writes well about whole people working collectively, reflectively, and spiritually smarter.

The best writing I have seen on the topic of soul leadership is a pamphlet by Parker Palmer published by Servant Leadership Press called *Leading From Within: Reflections on Spirituality and Leadership*, in which he describes the responsibility leaders have to be in touch with their own inner monsters so they know clearly how they can damage people if they are not in touch.

More important than reading, though, is interviewing several people you think are soul leaders. Ask how they got there, how they think about themselves, what they do to stay grounded in times of stress, what they consider worth doing. Ask them some of the questions you asked yourself in your leadership journey assessment.

After you have read books and interviewed these people ask yourself what success is for a soul leader and what might it be for you.

It is important to take this assessment process to its next inevitable incarnation. It must be manifested by your behavior in the real world. Try one new behavior at work or at home to push yourself into a new place as a leader. Here's an example from an executive who has worked on soul leadership.

Diversity was a goal of Helen's organization. She could have hired a diversity manager to develop or fix things, but she decided to try a new approach. She chose two of her best, most open and alive managers to join this project with her. Together they made it their goal to learn as much about ethnic differences as possible. The three got together regularly, read and talked candidly, and attended seminars. They found out about their overt and hidden racism. They also found out that they had all been discriminated against in some way and could therefore identify with other people's pain to some extent. They asked each other to hold them accountable for their behavior and review it regularly.

The result was that they constructed their department as a community, not as a group of individuals. They began talking and acting as a community, using each other to learn, grow, and help solve issues, not just to satisfy diversity goals. They began hiring more people of color, disabled people, and retarded people, making the environment conducive to differences and talking about different ways of approaching issues and ways of life.

What evolved was a new culture that valued differences as ways to attain community and to be more effective. Fears, problems, and conflicts were addressed without retribution. The community has slowly coalesced, and even during hard times, they work better together than ever before. Turnover is at an all-time low and other managers want to know how they did it.

If you are an especially high achiever, here is a sure way to challenge yourself and your leadership journey. Find two or three young people in your organization whose skills, style, or personalities draw you. Work with them as a mentor until they are *better* than you at the same work. I did not say as good or competent as you, but better. This will bring you into unchartered territory. Record your observations of and feelings about this experience in your journal and talk with your accountability people about your reactions.

3. Practice Vulnerability

In order to be a soul leader, you need to develop vulnerability. Vulnerability means knowing yourself first and then being willing to disclose who you are to others. It requires you to be self-aware and willing to admit your fears, joys, and sadness to yourself and others, even if it puts you at risk. Vulnerability is refreshing and generates trust in others. This is because you have to be secure and self-trusting in order to be vulnerable. Max De Pree, chairman of Herman Miller, said the two top qualities he looks for in leaders are integrity and vulnerability.

Let's start with a simple experiment to see how readily you take to being vulnerable. For the next few weeks, observe and record honestly what you laugh at each day. At the end of that time, ask yourself why you thought each incident or joke was funny. Who got hurt or diminished as a result of the humor? Why? Do you feel defensive when asked to look at your humor? How did you feel when you acknowledged what is funny for you?

Even a cursory examination of humor shows that we laugh mostly at things that put other people down or embarrass them. The topics are wide ranging: sex, mothers-in-law, politics, current events, ethnic groups, women, senior citizens, abuse, personality quirks. I am sobered when I look at what makes me laugh. The more one laughs at others in demeaning ways, the more it points out one's own insecurities. We frequently cover our fear, anger, or hurt with diversionary humor.

Try instead to learn to laugh at yourself, not in a put-down way, but by looking at the funny, ironic, eccentric things in your own behavior and seeing the humor in them. It helps the process of not taking yourself so seriously. My philosophy of life is "if you don't learn how to laugh at yourself sooner or later, someone else will." If you can laugh at yourself—and not in a demeaning way—it helps your vulnerability.

When I was a child, a small plane crashed into my elementary school playground. No one was hurt, but the incident is marked indelibly in my mind. I have told the story so many times that my family can fill in the sentences for me. Now when I say, "Did I ever tell you about the plane that crashed in my school playground?" they all smile and say, "No, Janet.

Why don't you tell us about it.'' I say, ''Well, just one more time.''

Reflect on how it feels to be gentle with yourself and others by laughing at shared foibles. Write about this in your journal. Observe how other people react to self-observant humor.

Another way to be aware of vulnerability is to accept your body with all of its idiosyncrasies and weaknesses. We are a culture that values physical perfection. Yet none of us measures up, really. Try seeing your body not as an adversary or a training machine, but as a message center which is trying to talk to you, alert you to what is healthy or dangerous, teach you to slow down or let go.

For one year, listen to your body instead of talking to it, swearing at it, or cramming it into uncomfortable things. Listen to aches and pains as messages. What is your body asking, saying, or shouting? Eat when you are hungry, and eat what your body asks for. Listen to what your body tells you about your sexuality, your interests, desires, attitudes.

Draw an outline of a body on a sheet of paper and mark with a heart the places you like and with an X the places you don't like. Ask yourself why you like or dislike each part. When did you stop liking the unliked parts? If you want to go deeper, write to the parts you like and dislike, allowing them to answer you back.

If you want to work more on vulnerability, skip to the section on embracing your shadows and childhood wounds.

4. Play Without Feeding Your Addictions

Most high achieving leaders think they know how to play because they engage in competitive, adventurous, or physically strenuous exercise. Our culture encourages these activities as a way to balance a stressful work schedule. I would suggest that these activities be called stress reduction techniques but not be confused with the concept of play. Most of them inadvertently feed people's addictions, especially the work addiction, and do not relieve long-term stress, which leaves deep scars on the psyche.

Before I discuss play, list on paper the activities you have done in the last six months for recreation, exercise, play. (Do not list things you would like to do but never get around to.)

Play is a concept many of us left behind as children, but playing without feeding your work or other addictions, helps you understand soul leadership behavior. Consider these as the primary characteristics of play and see what activities come to mind for you. Which of your regular activities have these characteristics? Which don't? Why?

- Activities that leave your body, mind, and spirit rested and refreshed, even though you may get physically tired.
- Activities in which you do not have to win or be expert to feel good about yourself.
- Activities that stimulate your creativity.
- Activities that take your mind completely off your work and problems.
- Activities that increase your appreciation of others, of nature, of relationships.
- Activities in which you laugh freely and do not feel angry, tight, or ashamed afterward.
- Activities that do not require you to travel long distances.
- Activities in which you do not have to prove yourself or be in charge.
- Activities that do not require a large investment of money or exhaustive maintenance.
- Activities that bring you closer to who you were as a child.
- Activities that feed your soul.

Ask yourself if the activities you listed meet at least half of these criteria. Some probably do, and some won't. Try substituting one new play idea for one of your current ones. You may have to expand your concept of play to include things you previously would have rejected. Or you may consider doing your current recreation in a different way. Don't expect people to applaud you when you change. Most people are moving too fast to notice. You can applaud yourself. My list of play activities includes doing jigsaw puzzles, playing golf according to Hagberg's Rules (I'll explain that later), riding roller coasters, reading in my hammock, walking, driving on curvy roads, watching murder mysteries on TV, drawing, reading mail order catalogues, browsing in card shops, parasailing, and watching college basketball.

In my family, golf is an important activity. My father-in-law was the son of the head groundskeeper of a large metropolitan golf course. He plays exceptionally well. His handicap has been eight for most of his adult life. My husband and two stepsons also play well. So naturally I play too. It is our family sport, and it is competitive. Tempers flare when things do not go well. I finally figured out that although I love golf and can hold my own with these men around the greens, it was not fun or relaxing to always be competing, betting, or asking for scores.

I decided to play my own golf game. First I read the book *Inner Golf* and practiced the principles until I was playing a relaxed inner game. I forgave the golf god who gives only three good shots a round, and rewards each shot with either direction or distance, never with both. Then I decided to enjoy the weather and nature, since they are major reasons I like golf. Lastly I decided to scrap the official rules and make my own rules, Hagberg's rules. If I don't like the lie of my ball, I improve it. If I don't like the length of the hole, I shorten it. When I am tired and we come to a long par five, I use what I affectionately call the 150-yard mark rule. I drop my ball at the 150-yard mark and play from there.

Then I have the ball redemption rule. If I hit a ball into the woods and I can't find it, but I find another ball instead, I have redeemed a ball from oblivion and I move it to the edge of the fairway without counting a stroke. If I find two balls, I subtract a stroke. I began enjoying golf so much that I made a decision that almost started a riot. I quit keeping score. It was like I had committed a mortal sin. I told my family I wasn't playing against them but for me. I now keep letter scores: W for wonderful holes, S for scenic holes, G for one great shot. We now have official rules and Hagberg's rules. My philosophy of golf is, "It doesn't matter." Not only do I enjoy it immensely, my game is more relaxed and consistent.

5. Experience Solitude Regularly

The world is afraid of being alone lest it face itself. Yet no amount of frenetic activity, or even strategic planning, can bring you to the inner journey of your soul. You must set aside time and space to be alone and let the pace, noise, and activity of your external life quiet down. At first this may be frightening. What will you do with your time? What if you are bored? The point is not to find things to fill the space but to ask how being busy got to be your identity, how what you do, not who you are, came to determine your worth.

One place to start being by yourself is to go on a retreat or weekend workshop in which there are activities and quiet time, so you can get used to being alone. Some people find, as I did, that when they first take time to be alone all they can do is sleep, even in the middle of the day. They are experiencing soul fatigue, a result of being on the merry-go-round of work too long without stopping.

A good solitary activity is walking by yourself in your neighborhood, without thinking about work or problems. Listen to the birds. Observe the flowers, grass, trees. Smell the fragrances. Watch the seasons change as you travel that same path every week for a year. Stop running and start walking. It is a great metaphor for life, even though it may frighten you to think you are slowing down. It will stimulate all kinds of internal dialogue. Listen for your wise inner voice, that little voice that tugs at you, gives you courage to ask for what you want, tells you to stop, or turn around, or call someone on a particular day.

Find a place for solitude in your home as well as away from home. It can be a den, kitchen, office, bed, or even bathroom as long as it is a place where you can go to be alone, to be with your inner thoughts, feelings, voices. Let others know that when you ask to be alone there, you are not to be interrupted. It is a haven. It is your place to get grounded. My quiet place is my bed, in which I have a great pillow backrest. My husband calls it my throne.

After practicing ways to be alone, try setting aside at least three hours every week to be alone. Even extroverts need time to themselves, especially after age thirty-five. One woman who works and has small children regularly schedules child-care on Wednesday nights and does relaxing things for a few hours that evening. Her only rule is she can't work at the office or do household tasks that evening.

When you are alone, observe how your body reacts, how you feel, what comes up in your mind, what you read. Observe which books, ideas, or people emerge in your life. Listen to your inner wisdom, even if it flies in the face of reason. Follow its direction and be thankful you have not drowned out the inner voice. If you have, wait and be quiet. It will come.

You may want to try this sobering exercise after you have practiced solitude for a while: Have an inner dialogue with your own death. Think and write about what it will be like. Where will it be and with whom? What do you want to say to family and friends before you die? And what would you want to be said about you at your funeral? Write down how you would sum up your life. What would you want to do before you die that you haven't already done?

You may get in touch with some of your core feelings, fears, dreads, joys, memories. Many people are afraid of solitude for that very reason. And solitude reminds us of the quieting of our bodies and souls, which feels like the beginning of death. The truth is that if we can't begin to approach our death, emotionally or physically, we will always be afraid of life.

6. Try One New Artistic Endeavor

A whole new world speaks to you when you tap into your creative side and listen to it or look at it. It operates on a different wavelength and takes you to places you have never been before. Creativity is latent within all of us. Creativity is wide ranging, not limited to painting or writing. Expand your views of creativity to cooking, conversation, letter writing, gardening, music, dancing, designing, wit. Add your own ideas.

It is valid to cultivate creative activities you already engage in, but the chances are you do them with a vengeance or at a high level of competence already, as most achievers are prone to do. To really experience this process of soul leadership, start fresh on a new artistic endeavor as a fledgling, a newcomer. Take a class in something you have never tried before but which interests you. You will get in touch with your fear of making mistakes, your need for approval, your drive to be the best or quickest. Stay with those experiences and let yourself learn naturally, asking the questions your child inside would ask, not just the ones about getting it right.

Creativity does not call you to achieve. It calls you to go deeper, to plumb your depths, to find your voice, to express your truth. It will exasperate you, but it will bring you closer to who you really are. That I promise you. Before you begin any artistic activity, stop and ask of it what *it* would like you to experience today. Ask the wood where you should begin, ask the paper what it wants from you, ask the garden where it wants assistance. It may sound strange, but it needs to be strange to get your attention away from racing to the place you think you need to begin. After a while it becomes second nature to be more in relationship with your art rather than be in charge of your art.

Art can feed you, touch you, and inform you at times of distress in ways nothing else can. It can get through the defenses and fears by going in the back door when the front door is heavily guarded. I experienced this vividly when I was in a deep personal abyss. I went to my drawing teacher to tell her I couldn't draw any more. I was too distraught. She asked why. I told her about how dark and dank the abyss was, and how alone I felt. She said gently, "Draw what you see on the walls of the abyss." "Right." I said sarcastically, "I can't even see the walls."

She said, "Just wait. You will."

So I waited. In a few weeks an image came to me from a book I happened to be reading. It was of a powerful ancient woman figure, full of wrathful energy and resolve. It was a scary image, but I began drawing it. Over the months of drawing it, I felt power and energy returning to me. But it was a different kind of power than I had felt before. It was the calm power that comes from facing the darkness. The darkness was becoming the light. And slowly I began to emerge from the abyss.

7. Travel as Far from Home as Possible for as Long as Possible

Get away from what is familiar and safe for you. You may want to start by moving into a different place in your organization, a different board in the community, or another person's culture. But put yourself in a place where you are the oddball, the token, the stranger. Women and minorities have known what this is like all their lives, so this is most important for white males, who are rarely in the minority or disenfranchised. If you are uncomfortable in the new arena, you have found the potential for learning. If you are still comfortable or people are treating you deferentially, you are not far enough away from home.

When you feel uncomfortable, try not to write off the experience by projecting blame, stupidity, or lack of sophistication on those around you. We usually do this to cover our fear and insecurity and to reject what the experience has to teach us. It keeps us arrogant. Instead, feel your ignorance, inadequacy, fear, anticipation, and floundering. Ask for assistance.

Then up the ante on yourself and go to another ethnic culture outside the comfort of your work place, or outside your own country. Don't go primarily as a spectator, teacher, vacationer, consultant, or anthropologist. Go as a student, even if you use one of those distancing roles as a way to get to the culture. Think about what it would be like if you had grown up in this culture. Get inside the culture. Taste it, smell it, touch it, ask for help, speak the language as best you can. Take down your own strong defenses. Be a child again. Cast aside prior assumptions. Leave your take-charge attitudes at home. How would you be without your title, salary, or privilege? Who would you be?

Take these experiences back home with you and apply the attitudes and learning you gained from outside your culture to inside your culture. You will find yourself a more receptive and wiser person. Observe the differences. Write about these experiences in your journal and share them with your accountability person.

Here is an example of a professional who traveled to Central America to interview people as part of an academic project and instead experienced a transformation. He writes:

> Doing the interviews made me aware of how much my power depended on my title, position and capability to communicate, none of which "fit" for three months. I felt frustrated, angry, powerless, dependent on my oldest son, who is fluent in Spanish and in the culture. He was the one who was respected. And out of our travels and travails grew an entirely new relationship, a friendship. Even now, four years later, tears come as I write about it.
>
> On that same trip I gained a whole new appreciation for my father, who at the age of twelve came to a strange land and strange language, with no return ticket to a home of comfort and security. Others in Europe were dependent on him to make a living and send for them: a mother, sister, and brother. I am sad because Dad is gone and I can't tell him how much I respect him now that I have a better understanding of who he was and what he had been through and what he had accomplished. I still wish I could ask his forgiveness for judging him so harshly because he wasn't a "modern" American.

Soul Leadership Process: Phase Two

These next six suggestions will engage you even more deeply in the process of soul leadership. They are not to be taken lightly nor to be engaged in frivolously. They ask a commitment, a covenant for inner healing, leading to transformed leadership. Stop and ask yourself how you have changed by engaging in the previous activities. Are you ready, and do you have the support around you, to take further steps?

8. Take Your Spirituality Seriously

It is risky to talk about spirituality in a secular publication, but the simple truth is, you cannot be a soul leader without it. To be a soul leader, you must change your focus from leading to being led. And this cannot happen without an ever-deepening spiritual base. Many powerful leaders write off spirituality or denigrate it, calling it soft, weak, or inappropriate. Nothing could be farther from the truth. Their attitude is a sign that they are deeply afraid of the power it actually has.

Unless the spiritual undergirding of your life is closely attended to after the age of thirty-five, your leadership may become rigid, in danger of atrophy. If you nurture your spiritual life and allow yourself to be led, new levels of intuitive, inspired, creative, and courageous leadership will emerge, unique to your life calling.

Most leaders who have had a profound effect on the conscience of our world have a deep spiritual base, because they know that one cannot do such courageous things on one's own. As a result of their spirituality and courage, soul leaders call us to think differently about the things we worship, take for granted, or even deny. Consider how these recent leaders made us rethink things: Dag Hammarskjold, Mother Theresa, Vaclav Havel, Elie Wiesel, Martin Luther King, Jr, Anwar Sadat, Rosa Parks, Gandhi. But you do not need to be famous to have a profound effect on someone. What is essential is that you let your spirituality guide your life, your response to deep crises, and the way you live out your calling. Leaders become aware through their life crises what their spiritual calling really is about.

In *Managing as a Performing Art*, Peter Vaill says:

> To work spiritually smarter is to pay more attention to one's own spiritual qualities, feelings, insights, and yearnings. It is to reach more deeply into oneself for that which is unquestionably authentic. It is to attune oneself to those truths one considers timeless and unassailable, the deepest principles one knows.

I will go even farther than that and say that spirituality is our response to the Holy, whoever or however we name it, and the life changes that result from our response. Faith is a dynamic process of gaining intimacy with the Holy or our Higher Power. Belief systems and religious dogma are not central to gaining intimacy with the Holy, although they can be part of the process. In other words, you can be spiritual without being religious, or you can be religious without being spiritual, or you can be both.

The central struggle in becoming intimate with the Holy is understanding what gets in the way of that intimacy, what separates you from closeness. And that struggle takes you to your core issues: what you worship, where your pain is, and where the healing will take place.

Henri Nouwen, a prolific writer and a priest, says it well when he describes the dilemma religious leaders have with power. His words have a very familiar ring in the corporate world as well.

> Maybe power offers an easy substitute for the hard task of love. It seems easier to be God than to love God, easier to control people than to love people, easier to own life than to love life. (*In the Name of Jesus*.)

How do you gain more intimacy with the Holy? What kinds of things deepen your spiritual base? A simple answer is, you get intimate with your Higher Power in much the same ways that you get intimate with friends: you spend time together, talk and listen, work through conflict, share crises, make yourself vulnerable, give and receive love, laugh and play.

Moving spirituality from a nice concept to a reality in your life requires involvement in personal spiritual disciplines. There is no substitute, no short cut. These spiritual disciplines vary depending on a person's background and form of spirituality. It also presupposes a relationship with a higher power as part of spirituality. Disciplines include being in nature, meditating, writing, doing dream work, listening, reading, studying, praying, journaling, enjoying music, visualizing, discerning.

In *Principled Centered Leadership*, Stephen Covey offers an approach which is used in many spiritual traditions. He suggests that daily reflective study of Scripture is "the single most important and powerful discipline in life because it points our lives, like a compass, to 'true north'—our divine destiny."

Some people encourage their spirituality in a professional relationship called spiritual direction. This is a relationship in which a trained person walks with another on his or her spiritual journey, listening to his or her inner voice, making observations, asking questions. It is not dogmatic or rigid, and the experience can move a person to a deeper level of intimacy with the Holy, adding an element of accountability which is healthy as you go through transitions. If you enter into such a relationship, be sure you are comfortable with the person, that they are qualified, and that they honor your form of spirituality.

Several issues emerge for people as they seek out intimacy with their Higher Power. Images of the Holy are one and childhood religious experiences, good and bad, are another. Exploring these issues can lead to astonishing insights and healing of childhood hurts. Use these questions as starters to begin your spiritual deepening:

What do you want your spirituality to give you?

What is your image of the Holy and how has it changed if at all, since you were a child?

Where do you experience deep awe and joy in your life?

What are the truths you believe in most deeply?

How has your parents' spirituality affected your own?

How did your early religious experiences, or lack thereof, affect your life?

How do you defend against spiritual intimacy?

What does your heart want?

For what in life do you have the most passion?

Why do good people suffer?

How can you tell the difference between your voice and that of your Higher Power?

How is the Holy involved in your pain?

What are you called to do with your life? Why you?

What happens when you take your spiritual life seriously and do inner spiritual work? You will feel unconditionally loved by your Higher Power, perhaps for the first time. You will slowly gain feelings of deep self-worth. You will begin to see the truth about your life. You will face your fears. Your character will begin to be changed, refined, rekindled. You will find yourself feeling less anxious, more courageous, more willing to live out principles that are life-giving. Inner peace will allow you to tolerate pain without chaos. Gifts of the spirit of life will emerge.

Anwar Sadat learned about intimacy with God when he spent eighteen months in solitary confinement in Cell 54 of a Cairo prison, awaiting trail for assassinating a traitor. He says in his autobiography that he learned

the most important things in his life there. He found self-knowledge in a
deep sense, going to his very center. He found out what he could and could
not accept in life. He found a relationship with a "God who created us
and cannot be evil in any sense." He goes on to say,

> My relations with the entire universe began to be reshaped, and love
> became the fountainhead of all my actions and feelings. Armed with
> faith and perfect peace of mind, I have never been shaken by the
> turbulent events, both private and public, through which I have lived.

Sadat was acquitted and resumed public life, a changed man. Later in
his life, he shocked the entire Middle East by going to Jerusalem to make
a peace gesture toward Israel.

If you want your life to be transformed, to experience profound levels
of leadership, begin by spending your best thirty to sixty minutes of the
day alone with your Higher Power, and then write about it and talk to
someone else about it. Do this in whatever way is best for you, by being
quiet, reading, writing, listening, or walking. The activity needs to be
solitary, and it needs to be done for the rest of your life. Gandhi set aside
one day each week for this. You will deepen, your soul leadership will
slowly emerge, and you will be awed by what intimacy with the Source
can do.

9. Find a Mentor at the Fringe

In our culture, there are lots of people in the mainstream. These are the
people most of us interact with every day. On weekends, we see more of
them, only in different activities. If we live in suburbs, we see almost
exclusively mainstream people.

But there are also people on the fringes of our society. Our society is
increasingly set up so there is no physical meeting of the mainstream and
the fringe, and especially no contact between the wealthy and the poor.
Guarded communities are deliberately designed to keep out anyone who
does not have permission to be there. We isolate ourselves to feel more
secure, when in fact it makes us more frightened.

Let me make an outlandish suggestion. Let someone on the fringe of
our society be your mentor for at least a year. Let him or her teach you
more about yourself than you ever knew before. Who are the people on

the fringe? They are the people who you think are as different from you as you can imagine. They may be the homeless, the retarded, people over eighty, battered women, people in prison, gang members, children, people of other ethnic groups, drug dealers, prostitutes.

How do you let one of them be your mentor? How do you do that? Find a way to engage personally and regularly with one fringe person or a group of fringe people you are not related to. You may have to be clever to find a way. You may find you can work through an already established organization or activity. Ask your network to help you. You may have to begin this relationship by trying to help the person, alleviate some problem, or give him or her something. That's the way a lot of people start, and fringe people are used to it. They can see it coming. You may lose some money, or get conned, or get angry that the person doesn't appreciate your efforts. If this happens, it's an opportunity to learn if you stay in there and don't leave.

Eventually you will get to the point of admitting failure. This is where the real learning and mentoring begins. Just be with the person in his or her real life, listen, get to know him or her. Get on his or her bus and ride it for a long time, without having to help or save the person. Be with your mentor in his or her pain. It is holy to just stand with a brother or sister in pain. You will eventually tap into something inside yourself that totally resonates with that person's pain, feels compassion, feels familiarity, feels love, because love is what it is all about.

Then you can look at your own homelessness, your own inner prisons, your own retardation, your own battering in a new and more compassionate way. Your mentor will bring you to *your* fringe issues, and you will live differently in the world. You have been found out and you are still okay. You are on your way to a new wisdom. Stay with your mentor long enough and you may even be led to making a dent in the world's pain.

Some good examples of this concept have come out of Hollywood, of all places. The movie *The Fisher King* chronicles the story of the homeless man, Perry, played by Robin Williams, as he struggles with his inner demons, portrayed graphically by a flaming horse and rider. His friend Jack, played by Jeff Bridges, thinks he could change Perry's life by giving him money and finding him a new girlfriend. Paradoxically Jack finds out instead about his own kind of homelessness. Perry teaches him, in a very strange and round-about way, what friendship and love are all about.

Three other superb Hollywood examples of the fringe mentor concept are *Rainman*, *Dances with Wolves*, and *Children of a Lesser God*.

10. Find Peace and Intimacy in Your Relationships Without Avoiding Conflict

This step in the soul leadership process is about intimacy. Many people go through their entire lives without intimacy, even though they may have good friends, live with other people, or marry. Intimacy is based on vulnerability and trust with another person. In an intimate relationship, caring, conflict and differences can be dealt with openly and without retribution. In primary relationships, intimacy also includes sexuality. The ability to be appropriately intimate with other people is a primary quality of soul leaders in organizations.

Single people sometimes think it is more difficult to work on intimacy or to expect it because of the lack of everyday continuity in their relationships. Yet it is just as important for singles to develop intimate, committed relationships and to work through the process of commitment and conflict as it is for married people. We all need intimacy in order to survive and thrive.

The process of developing intimacy is similar in all relationships. It involves knowing who you are and what baggage you bring to the relationship, being vulnerable and open, having appropriate boundaries, knowing how to nurture both yourself and the other person, knowing what baggage the other person brings, working through conflict, and respecting your differences. It sounds simple until you try it.

I want to focus on committed relationships because they are riddled with myths and unreal expectations. Most people find that, contrary to what they thought, they have to work at their committed relationships in order to get their basic needs met. It doesn't just work automatically. And for that reason, marriage and committed relationships have been, for most people, both their heaven and hell. Instead of focusing on our marriages, we focus on work or children because we get more recognition and gratification there. We cover well and achieve a lot as a result. If we are succeeding externally, then we have something to be proud of. The greater our insecurity, the higher our need to achieve.

If we ignore our relationships, however, they will rise up eventually to remind us, just as our bodies do. Committed relationships are the most obvious but also the hardest place to admit and take care of our real needs, because in these relationships we have the most potential to be loved and to be rejected. Wherever there is a potential for emotional and physical intimacy, there is also a potential for rejection. So our committed relationships store within themselves all our unspoken fears and insecurities.

If there is love in a relationship, even a little bit of love, and if there is resolve, then working on your issues is possible. Doing this calls forth an inner courage that you may never have tapped, even in years of a conflict-ridden career. It is the inner courage that comes from facing fear, conflict, shame, and abandonment head on and finding that not only do you survive, you are stronger, individually and as a couple. You address who you are in this relationship and what you want. This can be done best with good therapy, and it may take years to accomplish. Sometimes during the process, your relationship has to sustain your love because your love would not sustain the relationship. But finding peace without avoiding conflict revolutionizes relationships.

Courage in facing couple and individual issues allows each person eventually to come as a whole self to the relationship and to allow the other to be a whole person too. Courage means not avoiding the conflict that is inevitable, but it also means dealing honestly with the conflict without projecting the anger inward (seeing oneself as victim or getting depressed) or outwardly (as abusing or blaming others.) Courage also means finding ways to take care of yourself instead of asking the other to do that for you. Then joy, freedom, and fun can also emerge more freely in the relationship.

If you take the time and garner the courage to find peace in your relationship, you will have taken a big step toward finding peace in your career, your community, and the world.

An organizational leader told me he was having an affair and was thinking seriously about a divorce. A friend challenged him, telling him an affair was a symptom of not facing the issues, of lack of courage. That got to him. He decided to face the issues. It shook up his marriage of twenty years. The inner work was difficult for both him and his wife. They nearly separated, and lived in different parts of the house at times. But with help, they resolved their trust issues and started over again. The most interesting result was he respected both himself and his wife more. He saw the effects of his new behavior in his organization too. He wasn't afraid to face conflict in the workplace any more. He could hear the truth and deal with it. The ripple effects among his staff are still going on.

11. Embrace Your Shadows and Childhood Wounds

Parker Palmer describes leaders as people who have the most potential for affecting other people's lives, either positively or negatively. Leading is an awesome responsibility. Most leadership programs have lots of skill building and self-assessment components. Rarely do they take us beyond the self-descriptive stage, however. Soul leadership requires us to be keenly aware of our shadow behavior, the negative affects we have on people because of our own denial.

For instance, we may subconsciously diminish others because we are afraid or have been diminished ourselves; we may overwork to cover our insecurity; we will dislike other people because they remind us of hidden things we dislike in ourselves. Nouwen says boldly, "The temptation to power is greatest when intimacy is a threat. . . . Many empire builders are people unable to give and receive love."

To embrace these shadows, we have to go down into them and face our demons. It is like riding monsters down into our own depths. The only way out of the depths is through them.

Parker Palmer, in *Leading from Within*, says,

Great leadership comes from people who've not only made the downward journey through violence and terror, who have touched the deep place where we are in community with each other, but who can help take other people to that place. That is what great leadership is all about.

Why would anyone want to go there? No one would. It is a call we receive, an inner yearning to touch our core, and to connect with community, compassion, and our ground of being.

Palmer goes on to say that leaders' shadows are usually composed of the following five issues. 1. Insecurity about their own identity and worth that is so deep they try to deprive other people of their worth. They reduce people to numbers, employees, patients. Who they are depends on what they do. 2. The belief that the universe is hostile and life is fundamentally a battleground. It is based on competition, which has at its base fear.

3. The belief that ultimate responsibility for everything rests with me. This leads to workaholic behavior, stress, and burnout. 4. Fear of the natural chaos of life. This leads to over-ordering and control. It destroys creativity. 5. The denial of death, which leads to fear of failure and hanging on to things that need to die.

Palmer maintains the key to working on these issues is to affirm our spirituality, which allows us to move through darkness to great leadership. Because of our strong egos, successful track records, and confidence, it is difficult, almost impossible for us to see our shadows, our negative projections. That's why they're called shadows, because they are behind us when we face the sun. How can we find out what our shadows are?

One simple but excruciating method is suggested by William Miller, in his book called *Making Friends with Your Shadow*. Try it with great care, because it may awaken your monsters. Think of the two or three people in your life or in the world who you really do not like or get along with. Get them firmly in mind. Then on the left-hand side of a sheet of paper, list all of their qualities that you do not like. You may need more than one sheet. Look over the list and choose those qualities that you find absolutely despicable. Write those in capital letters in a list on the right-hand side of your paper. The qualities written in capital letters are your shadow, the parts of yourself that you would rather not see. Compare them with the feedback you got on your leadership assessment from the one or two people you've had trouble with. Are there any similarities?

Another way to understand your shadows is to observe your children's behavior. They frequently live out the behavior that is hidden inside you. That's a sobering thought.

To make matters even worse, you are not to try to eliminate all those qualities from your life, but to embrace them and see what they want to teach you. By embracing them, I mean knowing them so intimately that you know what they mean in your life. You do not need to act them out, but to listen to them and let them teach you.

If this sounds difficult, it is because you are facing the place where your ego must be relinquished. Soul leaders must face that place to become great leaders. The inner journey is the key to interior freedom. Your shadows will lead you to your addictions and to your monsters, and they, in turn, will inevitably lead you to your childhood wounds, the wounds that were inflicted on you early and were incorporated into your self-image. They need to be discovered, grieved, understood, and healed for you to gain interior freedom.

I will use myself as an example here. I have to admit to being intellectually arrogant. I despise arrogance in others, so, of course, it is my shadow. Because I teach, I am especially arrogant in situations where I am the learner. I slowly came to realize that the flip side of arrogance is insecurity. Ouch. When I am arrogant, I am really insecure. *That* is what my arrogance is trying to teach me. So now when I feel my arrogance rising, I ask myself what I am afraid to learn. When I can answer that question, I embrace my shadow.

A more complex example involves abuse. A friend of mine abhors people who abuse others, physically or emotionally. How could she possibly be doing that herself? It took a life crisis and therapy for her to uncover the immense amount of self-abuse she was subjecting herself to. She was abandoned by her mother and left with her father when she was ten years old. As an adult, she never understood her fear of abandonment. She went to counseling because she was in a dating rut and she was sick of it. She dated men serially and always left the relationship when it was just starting to go well, or she chose men who would be emotionally unavailable so there was no risk of love. Her friends saw the pattern long before she was ready to.

Once she did face the monster of her fear, she slowly began to feel the powerful energy that comes from facing the truth. Out of her pain, sadness, and anger came a rebirth. Light shined in the darkness. Now she can more fully understand the abandoned orphan part of her and therefore give herself choices in every situation. She has a freedom she has never experienced before—an awesome inner power.

Now she can also ask herself what she really wants in a relationship. And she can see herself as worthy of being loved and not abandoned. It was a transforming experience. She stopped changing jobs every three years and asked herself whether she wanted to be such a driven, high-flying professional. She had been abandoning her work before it could abandon her. Now she is on her way to finding out what her calling in work is and how she can live it out both in the community and in her paid work.

Retrospectively, she sees that the darkness became a gift—a painful gift, as any reawakening experience is. Suffering or pain does not happen so that you can learn. It just happens. And it is excruciating. But if you stay with it for a while, live one day at a time, take care of yourself, let your spirituality be your guide, and reinforce your strength with good outside professional support, you will emerge as a whole person.

What you learn down among the monsters is how to befriend pain without shedding responsibility for self-care. You can confront your basic fear, which always stands in the way of courage. You can look death in the face and not cringe. Ironically, behind the dark shadow is your golden shadow—those qualities you admire and envy in others—just waiting to be embraced as well. By embracing your dark shadow, you free your golden shadow to emerge. By entering your own inner darkness you will find the light.

When you embrace your shadow, who you are as a leader will also be transformed. You will not be able to work the same way. Your rationalizations will be gone. Your projections will fade. Your self-incriminations will not stick. You will emerge as a whole person, embracing shadows and helping others to face their shadows as part of your work, whatever you are called to do.

12. Discover Your Passion.

In my twenty years of career counseling, I've learned a few nearly universal truths. One is this: Everyone wants to have meaning in their lives. They want to know that something they have done has made a difference, has touched someone else. They want to get up in the morning and look forward to something. They want to care about something and see how they can affect it positively.

Most people, even hard-working people, even leaders in positions of power, struggle with meaning. Going to work isn't enough; making money isn't enough; getting promoted isn't enough. Where and in what ways do people find meaning?

I think people find the deepest meaning when they find their passion. Oh, they are challenged and kept busy for years by other things, but once they know they can achieve, the old longing for meaning comes back again. And the higher people go in organizations, gaining success but no meaning, the lonelier and more alienated they become.

Passion is the relentless pursuit of those life-enhancing activities or experiences that give our souls meaning. Passion comes when we connect with the things, people, causes, issues that touch us at our deepest place.

We may not even be sure what it is about, we just know that we are inextricably drawn to these things. At other times we know why we are drawn and we are grateful.

Passion can occur on the job, as the focus of our work, or it can be part of our personal or volunteer lives. Whichever it is, it fuels our energy and gives the rest of our lives added meaning as well. Once we have found our passion, we feel a strange contradiction: On one hand, we could die today and life would have been worth it, and at the same time, we want to live forever to continue our connection to our passion. Passion is not easy work, nor is it always rewarding. That is not the point. Passion is the engagement of our soul with something beyond us, something that helps us put up with or fight against insurmountable odds, even at high risks, because it is all worth it.

People with passion are incredibly inventive and tenacious individuals. They go way beyond the call of duty and frequently either work on their passion without pay or give more of themselves than their pay warrants. And I do not equate passion with workaholism, in which people say they love their work so much they do it all the time. Workaholics are working to fill a vacuum, or to escape, not to connect with their souls.

When we hear examples of passion, we are usually inspired, because it taps into the part of us that longs for meaning. Passion can emerge from events that forged us early in our lives, or from a scene we view which taps into our own soul. If we were victims of racism or abuse, we may end up working on those issues; if we viewed the death of a child, we might work with sick children; if someone we love commits a crime, we may be drawn to crime prevention.

Passion can come from that same profound place in which our deepest pain or woundedness lives. The energy for working on both is the same. Many people who engage with their childhood or adult wounds are surprised to feel passion arising out of those ashes. They find energy they never knew they had, coming from a different, and not frenetic force.

The following are examples of people working on passion. You can name many of your own.

• Mary lost her eight-year-old son to leukemia. During her grieving process, she felt led to work with families of leukemia patients as a volunteer. She felt a strong sense of connection with the families and she gave tirelessly of her time and energy to journey with other families.

- A businessman became aware of the loss of hope and spirit in minority communities due to the loss of manufacturing jobs. It tapped a fear he felt for his own future. He set about the task of working with the city and the business community to create training programs for skilled jobs and new futures.

- A minister responding to the African famine initially visited Africa with gifts of food and money to build wells. He was so deeply touched by the spirit of the people he went back with teams of people every year and dedicated his life to furthering this work.

- A business manager felt so strongly about community in the workplace that she kept it as a goal in everything she managed. Her emotional abandonment in childhood made her especially sensitive to the issue. People asked to work in her department and they learned her philosophy, spreading it throughout the company as a result of her support.

- A mother grieved her daughter's death at the hands of a drunk driver. She turned her anger into action and created an organization to monitor, convict, and treat drunk drivers. It is called Mothers Against Drunk Driving, MADD.

- My own passion is speaking out against domestic violence with art, writing, and community awareness. This interest comes out of my own family journey and it fuels my energy. The main forms it has taken are an art exhibit, The Silent Witness Exhibit, honoring the twenty-seven women who were murdered in Minnesota in one year, and a book I co-authored on the exhibit's impact.

Passion is important, yet it can be driven by ego. If you want the credit and limelight for the work you do on your passion, if it is only *your* project, it is driven by ego. If you want your passion to be truly from your soul, you need to undergird it with spirituality that is rooted in humility and calling. That is why both spirituality and calling are included in this section of soul leadership.

13. Accept Your Calling

Once you have engaged your shadow, you are more able to see and accept your life's spiritual and vocational call. You have interior freedom. You have courage. You are more willing to let your Higher Power and your inner power entrust you with a life's work, no matter how small the task. And you are willing to use skills or abilities that are not your strong suit, because only then are you dependent on a Supreme Being as your mainstay. Remember the call from a Higher Power is to be faithful, not to be successful. Success appears in a different form than the one you are familiar with.

Understanding your call, whether it emerges out of your experience of darkness or out of your passion, is a life-long venture. It may or may not involve a change in your career, but it always involves a change in who you are and how you relate to others through touch, love, sacrificial living, or service. Calling involves more of you than your passion does, and feels more all-encompassing. It can be equated with your life's purpose. There is no workaholism or burnout when you live out your calling, because you are in intimate touch with the Holy and therefore can honor your limits. And your ego will be relieved not to have to prove itself any more.

Calling is different for each person, and it is designed especially for each person. It frequently goes against the grain of who you were. High achievers frequently find their calling in things that are not instantly successful, or they take a different pathway from the typical success-oriented ones. There may be little external reward to show for their effort. This is as it should be. The internal reward is enough. But our calling always relates to what our *hearts* really want. Our hearts remind us of who we are and whose we are, and they remind us why life is worth living.

The chairwoman of a corporation told me that her calling is to encourage honesty and true collaboration in the workplace. It has gone beyond passion. It is her work, her raison d'etre. In turn, she counts on honesty and collaboration on the hard issues, even during tough times. This is the way in which the workplace is transformed. She said,

> I didn't think it would work at first because I thought everyone would give it up easily on all our work when business took a downturn. One year during a long recession, the department heads came through with several ideas generated by their task teams working overtime. They actually sustained *me*. And we came through with flying colors.

I know a man whose life calling is to live peacefully, inside and out. He has to be diligent in his internal spiritual practices to do this, and his life stance is noticeably different from other people's. In his consulting practice, he is strong, creative, respected, and sought out for his wisdom. My own life purpose is so simple yet perplexing to me that I think I will never live into it. To appreciate it, you have to know me, my passion for angels, both figurative and literal, my love of winter, and my spiritual and vocational calling. My purpose is "Make angels in the snow and elsewhere."

I use the words "life calling" and "vocation" interchangeably, since the root meaning of vocation is "to call." In *Wishful Thinking*, Frederich Buechner says vocation is "where my deep gladness and the world's deep hunger meet." Because vocation is so individual and internal, it is difficult to cite examples. It can be complicated, like ending violence or reducing poverty, or simple, like being available, connecting with strangers, or empowering others. It doesn't matter what it is. What matters is that it is yours and that you are not doing it from the strength of your ego. Your calling will emerge as you continue on the journey to soul leadership. Remember this is a long-term process.

Soul Journey Results

It is impossible to predict how each person will experience the journey to soul leadership. That is why it is a journey, a process. The process is as important as the destination. In fact, the process may be the destination.

Etty Hillesum, who went voluntarily to a concentration camp to be with her friends and family, writes about her inner process in an intimate way in her journal, *An Interrupted Life*. I started this piece with her words and I want to end with them as a reminder to us all of what soul leadership is about.

> Ultimately we have just one moral duty: to reclaim large areas of peace in ourselves, more and more peace, and to reflect it towards others. And the more peace there is in us, the more peace there will also be in our troubled world.

I can attest to a few characteristics that emerge universally in people who've taken the inner journey I have described. They have peace even in chaos, they are clear and undiluted, they are compassionate, they are courageous, and they listen to their calling. Henri Nouwen describes them well in an uncommon view of maturity when he writes that maturity is "the ability and willingness to be led where you would rather not go."

Soul leaders will change the world.

SUMMARY OF THE SOUL LEADERSHIP
DEVELOPMENT PROCESS

Discipline	Behavior It Develops	Effects
Be accountable	Responsibility	Reduction of ego
Assess your leadership journey	Self-reflection	Insight
Practice vulnerability	Self-awareness	Honesty
Play without feeding addictions	Relaxation	Calmness
Experience solitude regularly	Intimacy with self	Clarity
Try one new artistic endeavor	Trust in self and in the process	Creativity
Travel as far from home as possible	Accepting differences and uniqueness	Appreciation of others
• •		
Take your spirituality seriously	Surrendering, letting go	Peace of mind
Find a mentor at the fringe	Humility	Healing
Find peace and intimacy in relationships without avoiding conflict	Courage	Intimacy
Embrace your shadows and childhood wounds	Facing fear	Interior freedom
Discover your passion	Self-connection	Going beyond self
Accept your calling	Faith	Wisdom

Appendix

The National Personal Power Survey

The purpose of this survey is to better understand how people view personal power from an organizational and an individual perspective. I want to know how you reacted and responded to the personal power model and the practical applications of the model.

You don't have to be at any particular power stage to answer this survey. I want as diverse responses as possible, so I can see how valid the model is for everyone. The more I can learn about you, the more I can understand and share with others in the future who have questions about power.

You may answer this survey anonymously. You don't need to sign it or give me your address. Just make a copy of the survey, answer the questions, and mail to the address that appears at the end of the survey.

All questions and answers are voluntary and individual responses will be kept confidential.

PART ONE

Answer the following questions briefly, or circle the appropriate response.

1. What is the title of your present position? (Or the last job you've held.)_____
2. How long have you worked in that position?
   _____ years
3. What two previous jobs have you held?
   1. _____ 2. _____

261

Place a number beside each of the following items according to the following scale:

1 = strongly agree
2 = agree
3 = neither agree nor disagree
4 = disagree
5 = strongly disagree

4. _____ Would you say you are still "learning the ropes" in your work?
5. _____ Do you feel you have few skills and little knowledge?
6. _____ Do you strive for things like titles, higher salary levels, a larger income?
7. _____ Are you considered a sage?
8. _____ Do you think beyond your current job and peers as your base of influence, i.e., community, professional, political arenas?
9. _____ Are you *un*impressed by organizational rewards: salary, status awards, bonus plans?
10. _____ Do you feel that competition is at the base of most work situations?
11. _____ Do you find risk-taking unthinkable?
12. _____ Have you consciously developed your own personalized style in work relationships that is different from what the organization expects?
13. _____ Do you try to emulate more powerful people, i.e., dress like them, be around them?
14. _____ Do you feel complete peace of mind?
15. _____ Do you care more about empowering other people than developing your own career?

16. On the following scale, indicate how personally powerful you think you are by circling a number.

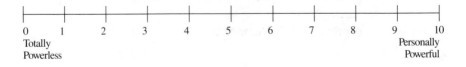

```
0    1    2    3    4    5    6    7    8    9    10
Totally                                      Personally
Powerless                                    Powerful
```

17. Before you read this book, how much knowledge did you have of power, power stages, and ways to use power?

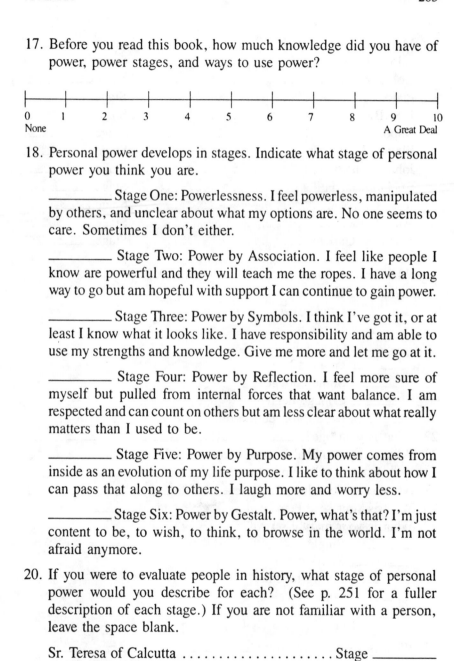

| 0 | 1 | 2 | 3 | 4 | 5 | 6 | 7 | 8 | 9 | 10 |

None   A Great Deal

18. Personal power develops in stages. Indicate what stage of personal power you think you are.

_____ Stage One: Powerlessness. I feel powerless, manipulated by others, and unclear about what my options are. No one seems to care. Sometimes I don't either.

_____ Stage Two: Power by Association. I feel like people I know are powerful and they will teach me the ropes. I have a long way to go but am hopeful with support I can continue to gain power.

_____ Stage Three: Power by Symbols. I think I've got it, or at least I know what it looks like. I have responsibility and am able to use my strengths and knowledge. Give me more and let me go at it.

_____ Stage Four: Power by Reflection. I feel more sure of myself but pulled from internal forces that want balance. I am respected and can count on others but am less clear about what really matters than I used to be.

_____ Stage Five: Power by Purpose. My power comes from inside as an evolution of my life purpose. I like to think about how I can pass that along to others. I laugh more and worry less.

_____ Stage Six: Power by Gestalt. Power, what's that? I'm just content to be, to wish, to think, to browse in the world. I'm not afraid anymore.

20. If you were to evaluate people in history, what stage of personal power would you describe for each? (See p. 251 for a fuller description of each stage.) If you are not familiar with a person, leave the space blank.

Sr. Teresa of Calcutta .... Stage _____
Richard Nixon .... Stage _____

Martin Luther King, Jr . . . . Stage _____
Adolf Hitler . . . . Stage _____
Golda Meier. . . . . Stage _____
Plato . . . . Stage _____
J. S. Bach . . . . Stage _____
Napoleon . . . . Stage _____
Eleanor Roosevelt . . . . Stage _____
John Kennedy . . . . Stage _____
Buckminster Fuller . . . . Stage _____
Jesus Christ . . . . Stage _____
Your mother . . . . Stage _____
Mahatma Gandhi . . . . Stage _____

21. What level of formal education do you have?
_____ None
_____ Grades 1-7
_____ Grade 8
_____ Grades 9-11
_____ Grade 12
_____ Some college
_____ College degree
_____ Grad./prof. education

22. What is your age?_____

23. What is your annual income before taxes?_____

24. Do you work full or part time?_____

25. Are you self-employed?_____

26. What is your sex? Female _____ Male _____

27. What is your marital status?
_____ Single
_____ Married
_____ Living together
_____ Separated
_____ Divorced
_____ Widowed

28. What is your ethnic origin?_____

PART TWO
Open-ended Questions

In this part of the survey, I am interested in your personal opinions on a number of questions. I suggest you answer these on a separate sheet of paper. I'd like to know how you think about power as it relates to various areas of your life. Answer these in as much detail as you can, or tape record and send them.

1. How would you define personal power?

2. What stage of personal power do you identify with the most and why (your "home" stage)?

3. How did you get to the stage you're at presently? Be specific.

4. What stage would you like to be (if different from present)? Why?

5. What power situations leave you most frustrated at work or at home? Why?

6. In which stage of power do you see your most intimate relationship? How do you feel about that?

7. At what power stage is your boss? How can you tell?

8. At what stage would you like him or her to be? Why?

FOR WOMEN:
9. As a woman, do you feel the pressure of taking on Stage Three behavior at work? How does it affect you?

10. What do you do/have you done to grapple with Stage Three people?

11. Is it possible for you to hold on to your feminine side (even though you take on your masculine, too) and be recognized, successful in your organization?

FOR MEN:
9. Do you feel pressure in your organization to achieve Stage Three as the ultimate stage? How does it affect you?

10. Do you see any sense in developing the "feminine" in you (caring, nurturing, sharing emotional intuitions)? Why or why not?

11. How would your organization respond to someone who was competent but chose to be different?

FOR ALL:

12. Do you know people who are at Stage Five or Six? Who are they (no names, just descriptions) and how can you tell?

13. Where do you think our nation's "leaders" generally are in the power stages? Where do you think they should be? Why?

14. Other ideas, insights, comments.

MAIL YOUR COMPLETED ANSWERS TO:
The National Personal Power Survey
c/o Janet O. Hagberg
7 Sheridan Ave. South
Minneapolis, Minnesota 55405

If you would like to know which stage of power you identify with most and how that affects you, send for a copy of the Personal Power Profile. It is a self-scoring instrument measuring your six stages of personal power.

Write: Personal Power Products
       1735 Evergreen Lane North
       Plymouth, Minnesota 55441-4102
       612/551-1708

Enclose $4.95 each plus $1.00 postage/handling for each.

Bibliography

Ambrose, Delores. *Leadership: The Journey Inward*. Dubuque, IA: Kendall/Hunt Publishers, 1991.

Becker, Ernest. *The Denial of Death*. New York: The Free Press, 1973.

Bly, Robert. *Iron John*. Reading, MA: Addison-Wesley, 1990.

_____. Interview with Keith Thompson, *New Age* magazine. May, 1982.

Bridges, William. *Transitions: Making Sense of Life's Changes*. Reading, MA: Addison-Wesley, 1980.

Burns, James McGregor. *Leadership*. New York: HarperCollins, 1982.

Capra, Fritjof. *The Turning Point*. New York: Simon & Schuster, 1982.

Cleveland, Harlan. *The Future Executive*. New York: Harper & Row, 1972.

Covey, Stephen. *Seven Habits of Highly Effective People*. New York: Simon & Schuster, 1989.

de Chardin, Pierre Teilhard. *Toward the Future*. New York: Harcourt, Brace, Jovanovich, 1973.

DePree, Max. *Leadership Is An Art*. New York: Doubleday, 1989.

Dluhy, Milan. *Changing the System: Political Advocacy for Disadvantaged Groups*. London: Sage Human Services Guide, No. 24, 1981.

Dyckman, Katherine, and Carroll, L. Patrick. *Inviting the Mystic, Supporting the Prophet*. New York: Paulist Press, 1981.

Ferguson, Marilyn. *The Aquarian Conspiracy*. Los Angeles: Tarcher, Inc., 1980.

Fiedler, Fred, Martin Cheners, and Linda Mahar. *Improving Leadership Effectiveness*. New York: John Wiley and Sons, 1977.

Frankl, Viktor. *Man's Search for Meaning*. New York: Washington Square Press, 1963.

Friedan, Betty. *Second Stage*. New York: Summit Books, 1981.

Fuller, Buckminster. *Critical Path*. New York: St. Martin's Press, 1981.

Gandhi, Mohandas K. *Gandhi: An Autobiography*. Boston: Beacon Press, 1951.

Gardner, John W. *Self-Renewal*. New York: Harper & Row, 1964.

_____. *On Leadership*. New York: Macmillan, 1990.

Gilligan, Carol. *In a Different Voice*. Cambridge, MA: Harvard University Press, 1982.

Goodman, Ellen. *Turning Points*. Garden City, NY: Doubleday, 1979.

Gould, Roger. *Transformations*. New York: Simon & Schuster, 1978.

Gray, Elizabeth. *Sacred Dimensions of Women's Experience*. Wellesley: Roundtable Press, 1988.

Greenleaf, Robert. *The Servant Is Leader*. Peterborough, NH: Windy Row Press, 1973.

————. *Servant Retrospect and Prospect*. Peterborough, NH: Windy Row Press, 1980.

Hagberg, Janet and Richard Leider. *The Inventurers*, rev. ed. Reading, MA: Addison-Wesley, 1986.

Hagberg, Janet, and Guelich, Robert. *The Critical Journey: Stages in the Life of Faith*. Dallas: Word, 1989.

Heilbrun, Carolyn. *Toward a Recognition of Androgyny*. New York: Harper & Row, 1973.

————. *Reinventing Womanhood*. New York: W. W. Norton Co., 1979.

Janeway, Elizabeth. *Powers of the Weak*. New York: Morrow Quill, 1980.

Josefowitz, Natasha. *Paths to Power*. Reading, MA: Addison-Wesley, 1980.

Jung, C. G. *Modern Man in Search of a Soul*. New York: Harcourt, Brace and Co., 1933

Jung, Emma. *Animus and Anima*. Zurich, Switzerland: Spring Publications, 1957, 1972.

Kantor, Rosabeth Moss. *Men and Women of the Corporation*. New York: Basic Books, 1976.

————. *The Change Masters*. New York: Simon and Schuster, 1983.

Kavanaugh, James. *There Are Men Too Gentle to Live Among Wolves*. Los Angeles: Nash Publishing, 1970.

Keen, Sam. *Fire In The Belly*. New York: Bantam, 1991.

Leonard, Linda. *Wounded Woman*. Boston: Shambhala Press, 1982.

Lerner, Harriet. *The Dance of Anger*. New York: HarperCollins, 1985.

————. *The Dance of Intimacy*. New York: HarperCollins, 1989.

Levinson, Daniel, et al. *Seasons of a Man's Life*. New York: Ballantine, 1979.

Lips, Hilary. *Women, Men and the Psychology of Power*. Englewood Cliffs, NJ: Prentice-Hall, 1981.

Maccoby, Michael. *The Leader*. New York: Simon & Schuster, 1981.

Maitland, David. *Against the Grain*. New York: Pilgrim Press, 1981.

Maslow, Abraham. *Religions, Values, and Peak Experiences*. New York: Viking Press, 1964, 1970.

Mason, Marilyn. *Making Our Lives Our Own*. San Francisco: HarperCollins, 1991.

May, Rollo. *Power and Innocence*. New York: Dell Publishing Co., 1972.

McCall, Morgan, and Michael Lombardo, eds. *Leadership: Where Else Can We Go?* Durham, NC: Duke University Press, 1978.

McClelland, David C. *Power: The Inner Experience*. New York: Wiley, 1975.

McConnell, Patty. *A Workbook for Healing: Adult Children of Alcoholics*. New York: HarperCollins, 1986.

Miller, William. *Your Golden Shadow*. San Francisco: HarperCollins, 1989.

Nakken, Craig. *The Addictive Personality*. Minneapolis, MN: Hazelden Foundation, 1988.

Nickles, Elizabeth. *The Coming Matriarchy*. New York: Seaview Books, 1981.

Nixon, Richard. *Leaders*. New York: Warner Books, 1982.

Nouwen, Henri. *In the Name of Jesus*: New York: The Crossroad Publishing Co., 1989.

Palmer, Parker. *The Active Life*. San Francisco: HarperCollins, 1990.

_____. *Leading From Within: Reflections on Leadership and Spirituality*. Washington, DC: Servant Leadership Press, 1992.

Pascale, Richard and Anthony Althos. *The Art of Japanese Management*. New York: Simon & Schuster, 1981.

Paulus, Trina. *Hope for the Flowers*. New York: Paulist Press, 1972.

Perera, Sylvia. *Descent to the Goddess*. Toronto: Inner City Books, 1991.

Peters, Thomas and Robert Waterman, Jr. *In Search of Excellence: Lessons from America's Best Run Companies*. New York: Harper & Row, 1982.

Progoff, Ira. *Jung, Synchronicity, and Human Destiny*. New York: Julian Press, 1973.

Rubin, Lillian. *Intimate Strangers*. New York: Harper & Row, 1983.

Russell, Bertrand. *Power*. New York: Norton & Co., 1938.

_____. *In Praise of Idleness*. New York: Simon & Schuster, 1972.

Sangiuliano, Iris. *In Her Time*. New York: Morrow Quill, 1980.

Schaef, Anne Wilson. *Women's Reality*. Minneapolis, MN: Winston Press, 1981.

Sheehy, Gail. *Passages*. New York: E. P. Dutton, 1976.

_____. *Pathfinders*. New York: William Morrow & Co., 1981.

Sinetar, Marsha. *Ordinary People as Monks and Mystics*. New York: Paulist Press, 1986.

Singer, June. *Androgyny*. Garden City, NY: Anchor Books, 1977.

Steiner, Claude. *The Other Side of Power*. New York: Grove Press, 1982.

Thompson, Helen. *Journey Toward Wholeness*. New York: Paulist Press, 1982.

Underhill, Evelyn. *The Life of the Spirit and the Life of Today*. San Francisco: HarperCollins, 1986. (originally published 1922.)

_____. *Practical Mysticism*. London: 1914.

Vaill, Peter. *Managing as a Performing Art*. San Francisco: Jossey-Bass, 1991.

Whitfield, Charles. *Healing the Child Within*. Pompano Beach, FL: Health Communication Inc., 1987.

Woodman, Marion. *Addiction to Perfection*. Toronto: Inner City Books, 1982.

_____. *The Pregnant Virgin*. Toronto: Inner City Books, 1985.

Yankelovich, Daniel. *New Rules*. New York: Random House, 1981.

Also of Interest . . .
HOW DO I LOVE ME?, 2/E
Helen M. Johnson

This excellent book on self-esteem grew out of the author's many years of successfully teaching people of all ages and walks of life how to get a high level of self-esteem *and how to keep it*. Ms. Johnson's experiences as an elementary school teacher, high school and college counselor, lecturer, consultant and workshop leader have been drawn upon to develop this readable and practical "How To" book on self-esteem.

Important features:
- Down-to-earth examples
- "Work Outs" in each chapter help facilitate application
- Can be used in classroom, group, one-on-one, or personally
- Concise and readable
- Action plan puts it all together

105 pages, paperback, ISBN 0-88133-224-0

For additional information or to order, please write or call:

Sheffield Publishing Company
P.O. Box 359
Salem, WI 53168
(414) 843-2281